SchoolCounselor.com

A Friendly and Practical Guide to the World Wide Web

Russell A. Sabella, Ph.D.

Copyright 1999, 2000

Russell A. Sabella, Ph.D.

Library of Congress Catalog Card No. 99-60710

ISBN 0-932796-94-X

Publisher—

Educational Media Corporation®
P.O. Box 21311
Minneapolis, MN 55421-0311

(612) 781-0088

Production editor—

Don L. Sorenson

Graphic design—

Earl Sorenson

Cover design—

Adquarters, Inc
Ft. Lauderdale, Florida

954-476-6060

www.adquarters.com

Preface

School counseling is a relatively young profession compared to other mental health related fields. Thanks to many pioneers and dedicated practitioners, the profession has made tremendous progress in developing a systematic approach to assisting students succeed in their personal, academic, and career endeavors. Comprehensive developmental guidance and counseling programs have become more clearly defined as are emerging school counselor roles. The arrival of the Internet and the World Wide Web can be both an opportunity and a threat to future progress.

An opportunity exists for embracing this powerful medium for training and service delivery. Professional school counselors have the opportunity to use the Internet to better inform and interact with important others. The Web can help us teach school administrators, teachers, parents, and community stake holders about the nature of school counseling. Indeed, if educators and others better understood school counseling, they could then better support the sometimes extensive challenges that school counselors face. The Web presents an opportunity to engage our students whom are quite rapidly adopting information technology. There also exists ample chances for more creatively, and perhaps more effectively, delivering guidance and counseling knowledge and skills via the Internet. However, since interactivity, by its very nature, requires both senders and receivers, the potential is only realistic when everyone is involved.

Like any powerful tool, the World Wide Web also poses potential threats to school counseling. It presents a dilemma between enhanced availability and outreach (high-tech) and facilitating the core conditions of empathy, genuineness, and unconditional positive regard (high-touch). In the absence of Internet literacy, school counselors may soon be left behind in a state of inadequacy, confusion, and incompetence. At the very least, those who avoid learning about technology will not be able to make informed decisions about how to invest their time, work, and money. Opting out of technology literacy is to opt out of a rapidly developing information culture.

Although there have been many texts written about the Web, this book is especially designed to help school counselors in a step-by-step fashion. The chapters will introduce you to the Web, help you gain access, effectively navigate, and interact with others around the world. As a starting place, I have included illustrations and examples of resources throughout including over 700 counseling Websites. This book will also help you think about and design your own guidance and counseling Web page. Finally, I have included a chapter regarding special issues, ranging from Internet addiction to WebCounseling, which I believe counselors should be aware.

You will also find helpful the supporting website for this book located at www.schoolcounselor.com. There, you may find summaries and links of chapters, an option to subscribe to a free newsletter, extra resources, a bulletin board service, and more.

Traveling the World Wide Web can sometimes be an adventure and other times a daring journey. Our competence in using the Web will in large part determine our experience with this blazing medium. Before you begin, you might imagine that you are on an exotic vacation to multiple destinations. Prepare, have fun, learn a lot, and be amazed.

Russell A. Sabella, PhD

March, 1999

Educational Media Corporation®, Box 21311, Minneapolis, MN 55421-0311

Acknowledgments

I would like to thank the thousands of people whom have freely shared their resources over the Web and contributed to its usefulness. I also want to thank my family, Betty and Joseph Sabella, for their continued support, understanding, and encouragement. And to my parents, Giuseppe and Sina Sabella, and my brothers, Sal, Jimmy, and Joseph, for instilling in me by example the values of courage, diligence, and determination.

About the Author

Russell A. Sabella, PhD is a counselor educator in the Counselor Education Program, College of Education, Florida Gulf Coast University. He specializes in comprehensive developmental guidance and counseling, counseling and technology, sexual harassment risk reduction, and peer helper programs and training. Dr. Sabella conducts Internet literacy training for counselors throughout the country. He may be reached via e-mail sabella@schoolcounselor.com.

Table of Contents

Russell A. Sabella, Ph.D.

CHAPTER ONE

Get Ready ...
School Counselors and Computers

The following transcript of a conversation between a computer user and a technical help person was circulated over the Internet not too long ago:

Q - "Computer helpdesk; may I help you?"

A - "Yes, well, I'm having trouble with my word processing program."

Q - "What sort of trouble?"

A - "Well, I was just typing along, and all of a sudden the words went away."

Q - "Went away?"

A - "They disappeared."

Q - "Hmm. So what does your screen look like now?"

A - "Nothing."

Q - "Nothing?"

A - "It's blank; it won't accept anything when I type."

Q - "Are you still inside the program or did you get out?"

A - "How do I tell?"

Q - "Can you see the C:\ prompt on the screen?"

A - "What's a C:\ prompt?"

Q - "Never mind. Can you move the cursor around on the screen?"

A - "There isn't any cursor, I told you, it won't accept anything I type."

Q - "Does your monitor have a power indicator?"

A - "What's a monitor?"

Q - "It's the thing with the screen on it that looks like a TV. Does it have a little light that tells you when it's on?"

A - "I don't know."

Q - "Well, then look on the back of the monitor and find where the power chord goes into it. Can you see that?"

A - "Yes, I think so."

Q - "Great. Follow the cord to the plug, and tell me if it's plugged into the wall."

A - "Yes, it is."

Q - "When you were behind the monitor, did you notice that there were two cables plugged into the back of it, not just one?"

A - "No."

Q - "Well, there are — I need you to look back there again and find the other cable."

A - " Okay, here it is."

Q - "Follow it for me, and tell me if it's plugged securely into the back of your computer."

A - "I can't reach."

Q - "Uh huh. Well, can you see if it is?"

A - "No."

Q - "Even if you, maybe, put your knee on something and lean way over?"

A - "Oh, it's not because I don't have the right angle — it's because it's dark."

Q - "Dark?"

A - "Yes - the office light is off, and the only light I have is coming in from the window."

Q - "Well, turn on the office light then."

A - "I can't."

Q - "No? Why not?"

A - "Because there's a power outage."

Q - "A power... A power outage?" Aha, Okay, we've got it licked now. Do you still have the boxes and manuals and packing stuff your computer came in?"

A - "Well, yes, I keep them in the closet."

Q - "Good. Go get them, and unplug your system and pack it up just like it was when you got it. Then take it back to the store you bought it from."

A - "Really?" Is it that bad?"

Q - "Yes, I'm afraid it is."

A - "Well, all right then, I suppose. What do I tell them?"

Q - "Tell them you're not ready to own a computer."

Some stories make us laugh because they make us think of an aspect of our own similar experience. The helpdesk story made me laugh out loud because it made me remember that using computers can be so frightening that we may sometimes lose our common sense. The story also reminded me that, because computers have become so pervasive, we may erroneously assume that using them only requires common sense. We need only to recall that VCRs have been around much longer and, with the exception of the play and eject buttons, many people still don't know how to use them. Just because home computer purchases now outnumber new television purchases does not mean that people are instantly becoming computer literate. For those of us whom have developed a relationship with computers since their early inception, this assumption is easy to make. To the contrary however, there are numerous people, certainly including counselors, whom are only recently wondering about "this computer thing."

In the early 1980s there was a cry heard by counselors across the nation, "The computers are coming! The computers are coming!" Computers were to open a new professional world to counselors and other educators. It was to be the dawning of a new age of technology, education, and guidance. When first introduced to counselors, computers were viewed as magnificent,

albeit mysterious, machines that promised to expedite routine clerical tasks and offer students innovative learning opportunities. Tools for information retrieval would be at the hand of the counselor, who could examine a student's record in the blink of an eye. Counselors were about to enter the twenty-first century of modern technology and computer-assisted counseling. However, it did not quite work out that way.

The pace of educational technology quickened when desktop personal computers were introduced and became more accessible. This allowed counselors to have computers on their desks and to go beyond the district mainframe. The now commonplace floppy disks and local area networks allowed them to have a storage system with numerous files that could be drawn on. Within the past few years, recent changes in technology have introduced many new computer-based tools that have enormous potential for education and, once again, counselors have taken notice. The new technology tempo picked up even more with the establishment and proliferating popularity of the Internet. The Internet, sometimes called the "Net," is a vast global network that enables computers of all kinds to share services and to correspond directly, as if they were part of one giant machine. It has the capability of changing many of the ways in which people interact and communicate (Myrick & Sabella, 1995).

Counselors whom have used computers to assist them in their work have done so in many areas such as computer-assisted live supervision (Froehle, 1984; Neukrug, 1991); discussions of counseling issues with other counselors (Rust, 1995); supervision (Myrick & Sabella, 1995); counselor training (Cairo & Kanner, 1984); as part of counselor interventions with children (D'Andrea, 1995; Glover, 1995; Shulman, Sweeney, & Gerler, 1995) and counseling simulations (Sharf & Lucas, 1993). Probably the most extensive use of computers in counseling so far has been in the area of career development (e.g., Chapman & Katz, 1983; Haring-Hidore, 1984; Harris, 1972; Katz & Shatkin, 1983; Kivlighan, Johnston, Hogan, & Mauer, 1994; Pyle, 1984). Career counselors need to amass and process a great deal of information about various careers, the career decision-making process, and a diversity of client personal and professional characteristics. Computers do a splendid job of compiling such data and helping individuals select the best fit among working environments, required aptitudes, interests, values, and other human qualities.

Many counselors, however, have avoided or only very recently began using computers in their work. One reason for relatively late entry into computing is that some see computer technology as an evil force to be circumvented at all costs. Such counselors hold computers in contempt because they see them as replacing people in jobs such as telephone operators, professional desktop publishers, and perhaps even teachers. This belief is sometimes true for people in more product oriented professions or those in human service professions that involve simple and repetitive tasks. For counselors however, no technology has ever come close to providing quality and appropriate counseling services. Computers have merely changed the shape of the work force by introducing new vocations and changing the methods for how we accomplish our work tasks.

Some counselors say they can still effectively perform their jobs "the old fashioned way" — keeping index cards instead of a database; using a typewriter rather than a word processor; using overheads in lieu of multimedia presentations; and trekking to the library rather than accessing online text resources. Their reasons for avoiding computer technology may be justified since comparative research on delivery and learning effectiveness is not yet conclusive. On the other hand, critics of this excuse say that such thinking is shortsighted because the world of technology is the world in which our children live and will be more an integral part of their society than even ours.

And, yet other counselors might acknowledge the usefulness and need for keeping up with the rapidly changing times although are frozen in the fear generated by an unknown frontier. "I feel intimidated by computers," has been a common comment by counselors, who even after training, frequently revert to more traditional procedures. The customary statements, "My kids know more about computers

than I do" and "I'm not a technical person" suggest that although counselors may be interested or even intrigued, they frequently feel awkward and uneasy with computers and their operations (Myrick & Sabella, 1995). I have witnessed such fear in the faces of some of my students, especially those returning to higher education after raising their families for many years. Ironically, it's the same fear that, when attempting to become computer literate, makes the learning curve significantly more steep. Joyce L. Winterton, Ph.D., national education advisor for USA Today couldn't have said it better during a presentation I attended when she quipped that, "Computers are like horses, if they know you're scared of them, they'll try to throw you off."

Although computers and related technologies are rapidly changing, one fact remains constant — counselors who resist the new tools of this and future centuries will find it increasingly more difficult to do so. One tool in particular that is changing the fabric of how we interact, work, and conduct business is the Internet (also known as the Net). Consider that the Internet, which connected 2,000 computers in 1985, now connects 30 million computers, and is continuing to double in size every year. By the end of 1997, it was estimated that more than 100 million people worldwide were using the Internet. The number of users could surpass one billion as early as 2005. And, in addition to growing in terms of people accessing the Internet, it is growing in regard to the types of services provided over the network. Satellite and wireless systems will soon provide users with "anytime, anywhere" communications. Directory and search services help users locate important resources on the Internet. Electronic mail servers manage and store critical information. Authentication and electronic payment services handle more and more of the Nation's commerce. Building blocks for new applications are being developed such as digital signatures, secure transactions, modeling and simulations software, shared virtual environments for collaboration, tools for discovering and retrieving information,

---

and speech recognition (President's Information Technology Advisory Committee, 1998).

The Internet provides access to a wealth of information on countless topics contributed by people throughout the world. On the Net, counselors have access to a wide variety of services: electronic mail, file transfer, vast information resources, interest group membership, interactive collaboration, multimedia displays, and more. The reality of the matter is that no aspect of society or economy can function effectively and compete without such tools (McClure, 1996). Counselors who decide to "opt out" of information technology such as the Internet will essentially be working with students whom will perceive them to live in a world that no longer exists. Whether we like it or not, information technologies are now essential tools for manipulating ideas and images and for communicating effectively with others — all central components of a counselor's job (Sabella, 1998).

If not for professional competency, then perhaps more personal reasons for becoming proficient in information technologies might make the case for counselor technology literacy. Within the next two decades, computer networks will have penetrated more deeply into our society than any previous network, including telephone, radio, television, transportation, and electric power distribution networks. Soon we will depend on the information infrastructure for delivery of routine services such as banking and financial transactions, purchases of goods and services, entertainment, communications with friends, family, and businesses, as well as for vital services, such as government and medical services. As users come to depend on the Internet each and every day, and as billions of dollars are transacted using electronic commerce, the information infrastructure becomes more critical to each counselor's and our Nation's well being. A [counseling] profession literate in information technology will be critical for ensuring that it is prepared to meet the challenges and opportunities of the Information Age (President's Information Technology Advisory Committee, 1998). Therefore, be it by necessity or interest, the time is now for explor-

ing contemporary methods for accomplishing our work using computer and networking technologies such as the Internet.

According to Sabella (1998), counselors who took an early interest and continued to gradually follow technology's progression have probably accumulated relatively high levels of technology literacy at a manageable pace. Veterans to the Net, for instance, may find themselves only having to keep pace with incremental changes, new additions, and creative ways for harnessing the Net's power to more effectively and efficiently do their jobs. For those whom have more recently taken an interest, or force themselves to be exposed to technology because of trends or new standards, becoming technologically literate may be a burdensome venture. The good news, however, is that you can effectively start today. The road to technology literacy does not necessarily have a beginning and an end, but like an intricate system of highways and sideroads, can be accessed from many on-ramps. Today's software is more user-friendly and more highly automated than ever before. Beginning a course of self-study and formal training will better assure more enjoyable travel for the road ahead. Before you know it, you will be traveling along side others whom have laid many more miles behind them on the information superhighway. And sooner, rather than later, you will be staking and claiming your property on this vast electronic terrain.

Russell A. Sabella, Ph.D.

Benefits of Counselor as Cybernaut

Some use technology because it is the "latest and greatest" without careful consideration for the technology's utility. Such people usually want to achieve new levels of power, efficiency, or perhaps to mesmerize or excite others when demonstrating their newfound capabilities. However, just because a new technology application can do more or perform a task more quickly, does not mean we should all go out and purchase it. New technologies arrive on store shelves every day, and although many are alluring, only a few will truly result in great benefits to a counselor's professional and personal productivity. Every technology must be carefully evaluated for its merit. As smart consumers of technology, counselors must ask questions such as:

❦ How much are the initial costs for purchasing the software or hardware?

❦ Will my computer run the software or will I need to upgrade (e.g., add more memory or purchase a new peripheral, therefore adding to the overall cost of the new application)?

❦ If I choose to purchase new software or hardware, what will it cost to maintain it in the form of upgrades and especially in the form of human resources, specifically paying someone for upkeep, training, or consultation?

❦ How user-friendly is the technology? How much time might it require to adequately learn and apply the new technology? Can I do this on my own or will I need to spend even more money for training?

❦ Is the company that provides the technology reputable and stable? Or, will the technology lose long-term support because of a fleeting company?

❦ How well will the new technology work with other already adopted computer applications?

❦ How compatible is the new technology to already existing technologies? That is, will others be able to share and collaborate with someone who uses the new technology?

❦ Is the new technology convenient and enjoyable to use?

Ultimately, the main question is, will this technology provide me with a significant Return of Investment (ROI)? That is, will an initial and anticipated investment of financial and human resources provide me with a long-term and desired level of benefit to my work? If the ROI for a technology is significant, then one might more easily make the decision to learn and use it. If the ROI is poor, then one might only spend the time to understand the technology to better make informed decisions about its use. For example, I avoid software for managing citations, bibliography databases, personal information managers, and electronic post-it notes. Through careful consideration, I have determined that these applications are inefficient and too time consuming for my work style and needs. For others, they are essential tools that, without them, would cause undue stress.

The Internet is one technology that has a high ROI for virtually all professionals, especially those who deal with products and increasingly for us in the human services sector. The Net has become cheaper to use now than ever before due to continually falling computer prices and competition among Internet service providers. Business and education have recognized for some time that their employees, faculty, staff, and students need Internet access to effectively function in a more global and information driven world. So for many counselors, Internet access is provided, at least somewhere in the school, as the cost of "doing business." If not, counselors can now access the Net from many public libraries or community centers until more convenient access is available. At the same time, the Net brings more returns on shrinking investments for an overall exciting picture of its benefits. What are some potential ROI factors when deciding to use the Internet? Consider that:

❖ The Internet is highly customizable. Such technology, when used with students, allows counselors to accommodate individual differences in student goals, needs, learning styles, and abilities, while providing improved convenience for both students and counselors on an "any time, any place" basis.

❖ Of all the new technologies, online communications has the strongest potential to break down the barriers and inequities encountered by students of different socioeconomic, racial, linguistic, and ability backgrounds. Networks expand the limits posed by time and space, giving students and counselors more equitable access to expertise, information, and tools. Through such tools as the Internet and the various online databases, access to enormous quantities of information is becoming quite common. As systems become increasingly sophisticated, the Internet will continue to provide a growing capacity to navigate among even greater information resources at an increasingly lower cost. Counselors and their students will progressively interact with advanced media that augment the school-to-work process and promote guidance and counseling standards for all children.

❖ Over the Net, counselors can communicate with students, teachers, administrators, parents, other counselors, and community members with continually greater convenience and efficiency. For example, one study conducted with teachers with online access showed that teachers had more positive teacher conferences, more parents visiting the classroom, and more positive communication with parents online, than did teachers without online access (Center for Applied Special Technology, 1996). While you are reading this, hundreds of school counselors enjoy the convenience of corresponding and consulting with each other through listservs such as the International Counselor Network (http://members.home.com/ruste/icn.html). Already in progress is the ability to communicate from simple text based messages to sending video messages to others across the net (e.g., see www.cvideomail.com). This will further enhance professional collaboration, consultation, and open even greater opportunities for working with our students.

❖ Schools are paid for by their communities: the taxpayers or tuition-payers. They have a stake in the school, and they want to know what is going on there. Counselors who maintain a website have taken the next step for keeping these important citizens informed and motivated to support their mission and activities. The Internet is becoming a standard feature in American homes, libraries and businesses. As it does so, this form of connection with the community becomes increasingly important to maintain community support for your guidance program. In essence, through maintaining a guidance and counseling website, you can hold an "anytime, anywhere" open house.

❖ A more sophisticated website can be home to more than a tool for information dissemination. When counselors make their sites interactive, it can become a virtual guidance center that helps various stakeholders interact with us and each other, submit data, make requests, and engage in self-guided lessons. For instance, a website can help a group of middle school children learn more about conflict resolution by watching a streaming video of pertinent skills, respond to interactive scenarios, and play a game which supports multicultural sensitivity. Parents might use the site to explain to the counselor a presenting problem and then request a meeting. Similarly, teachers can request consultation.

❖ After reviewing your online portfolio, a community member may want to recognize you (and the school) with a grant or award.

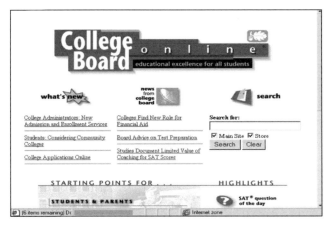

❖ Professional development opportunities are being made available all year round with the help of the Internet. Instead of attending a workshop or presentation during a specific time and place, a counselor can conveniently engage web-based modules, for continuing education credit, that assist in learning new information, discuss issues, ask questions, and submit homework. For instance, the College Board Online (http://www.collegeboard.org/) provides many services for counselors including online professional development workshops.

❖ Counselors who take part in e-mail communication and Internet interactions can stay better alerted to the many events and situations which affect the profession on a seemingly daily basis. Information about a new legislative bill, counseling resource, grant opportunity, or perhaps professional challenge can be met with appropriate response in a more timely manner. Time in the information age seems to be changing from human years to "dog" years as information can change a situation in a matter of days or even minutes. So, for example when the state of Virginia faced new legislation that would seemingly diminish the potential for children to receive guidance and counseling services (see http://www.counseling.org/ctonline/archives/ct0797/ct0797a7.htm), counselors from all over the world, who otherwise would not have known for days, where instantly informed over e-mail broadcasts. In a public comment period that ended May 17, 1997, more than 5,500 of the 7,514 comments addressing elementary school counseling expressed support for the program. As a result, both houses of the Virginia legislature voted in late February of that year to require that public elementary schools in the state provide school counseling services, restoring a mandate that was eliminated by the Virginia Board of Education in September of 1997.

❖ The Internet has become a convenient and efficient way to obtain a profusion of computer programs and other files that can make our work simpler and more manageable. For instance, a counselor can easily locate, download, and use programs such as contact managers, desktop publishing programs, computer-based career interest inventories, search utilities, graphics, sound files, and much more with a couple of clicks of the mouse. Some of these programs are free and can be used at no charge (if you are willing to accept some advertising or periodic e-mails about other related products). Many of the programs available for download are specific to counselors (e.g., http://www.mcli.dist.maricopa.edu/proj/sw/counseling/index.html). Relatedly, some organizations are providing many more member services over the Net, usually in the form of secured websites and downloadable files, such as professional development kits, already created multimedia presentations about various topics, brochures, newsletter materials, journals, forms, and entire texts.

❖ Online stores have made it quite simple and convenient for counselors to research and securely purchase counseling related materials. Instead of traveling to a store, walking the isles, and waiting in line, a counselor can literally spend 4-5 minutes to find and purchase anything from counseling related books, play counseling media (e.g., puppets, games, or music), to specialty paper, business cards, food, or extra supplies. And, because the cost of doing business over the Net is usually much less than in a storefront, companies can offer their wares over the Net at a significantly reduced price. Within a couple of days, your order is delivered to you or anyone else you choose. People in general who shop online do so because they say it is a great time saver and convenient because one can shop in multiple "stores," anywhere in the world, and at any time of the day or night.

❖ Counselors can noticeably supplement their small or non-existent budgets by finding and applying for grants which may be more easily processed on the Net.

❖ Because counselors understand the benefits of leisure, what about the vast opportunities for entertainment over the web? So that a weary counselor can rest and rejuvenate, there are sites that allow users to play games with others around the world, do a cross-word, read an online novel, play a song, or even print the pattern for your favorite cross stitch.

❖ By becoming proficient at Internet literacy, counselors can more skillfully helping their clients to become proficient. Inroads have already been made to support the use of the Net for enhanced student performance within traditional curricula (Bialo & Sivin-Kachala, 1996; Dwyer, 1994; Indiana's Fourth Grade, 1990; Kulik, 1994). One in particular, *The Role of Online Communications in Schools: A National Study* (CAST, 1996), demonstrated that students with online access perform better. The study, isolated the impact of online use and measured its effect on student learning in the classroom. The study compared the work of 500 students in fourth-grade and sixth-grade classes in 7 urban school districts (Chicago, Dayton, Detroit, Memphis, Miami, Oakland, and Washington DC) - half with online access and half without. The results showed significantly higher scores on measurements of information management, communication, and presentation of ideas for experimental groups with online access than for control groups with no online access. It offered evidence that using the Internet can help students become independent, critical thinkers, able to find information, organize and evaluate it, and then effectively express their new knowledge and ideas in compelling ways.

In what ways will counselors and students using online resources better be able to achieve the goals of guidance and counseling? At minimum, the Net provides a great deal of resources which help counselors share best practices and ideas. Additionally, others have already discovered uses of the Internet to augment various guidance and counseling goals. For instance, consider the following examples of how the Internet may enhance your school counseling mission:

❖ In late 1996, The Georgia Board of Regents Office of Information and Instructional Technology (OIIT) in collaboration with the Georgia Department of Education (DOE) Office of Technology Services announced that an electronic account will be provided to middle school and high school buildings as part of an on-going project called "Connecting Students and Services." The account is intended for use by middle school and high school counselors only and provides schools with a single point of access to various Internet resources including e-mail addresses. The goal is to enhance the guidance counselor's utilization of resources available on the Internet's World Wide Web (WWW). School counselors are able to access admission's information for institutions in the University System of Georgia through the institution's web pages, exchange information via e-mail, access the "Georgia Career Information System" and do electronic transcript transfers between high school and colleges and universities.

❖ Similar to traditional penpals that maintain a relationship via correspondence using letters sent through the mail, KeyPals send electronic mail to establish and maintain a friendly peer relationship. One such site contains the following introduction:

Mighty Media presents the KeyPals Club , a place for young people, teachers and students to locate and correspond with other youth and students around the world. The service provides an incredibly easy-to-use interface and database to quickly locate and contact a student or a class from around the world. Start a project with another class, or just create a new friendship with someone on the other side of the globe. KeyPals Club is another free educational service from Mighty Media, creators of the Youth in Action Network and Teacher Talk (Mighty Media, 1997).

Counselors might think about the following example of how KeyPals was used as a way to create, implement, and evaluate more expanded peer helper programs using the Internet: One high school teacher wanted to improve student activity, participation, and outlook toward physical education. His alternative class of special education students became "KeyPals" with university kinesiology majors. Through e-mail communication, the students established rapport with older students who value physical activity. A bond developed between the high school and college students, which helped the younger students improve their attitude about positive active participation. A research study to help determine whether this KeyPal relationship between high school alternative Physical Education (PE) students and university kinesiology majors could positively influence their participation and attitude toward gym class was conducted. Results suggested that attitudes, motivation, and relationships positively influenced the KeyPal relationships. Complaints about participating in PE class had been replaced by enthusiastic participation in basketball and volleyball games with the university KeyPals. Most of the KeyPals demonstrated a sense of belonging and connectedness, perhaps for the first time since their elementary school PE experience. And, most important, the essential ingredient of fun in gym class had reappeared (Fargen, 1996).

❖ Hewlett Packard (HP), a well-known computer and printer company, created an E-mail Mentor program. This program creates one-to-one mentor relationships between HP employees (worldwide) and 5-12th grade students and teachers throughout the United States. HP employees motivate students to excel in math and science and improve communication and problem-solving skills. In addition, students are encouraged by their mentors to pursue their unique interests and link these interests with their daily school experience. The 1996/1997 program created 1654 mentor relationships with participation from 1546 HP mentors, 1508 students, and 146 teachers (HP, 1997)

❖ D'Andrea (1995), wrote about how peer helpers can consult the WWW and provide teachers with educational resources and information related to people from diverse cultural, ethnic, and racial groups, which might be helpful when planning class discussions and activities. This might include sharing materials that describe the unique traditions, values, foods, clothing, and lifestyles associated with people from various cultures. Also, peer helpers may gather information about the ways in which children are raised in other cultures and the roles they are likely to play within their communities, families, or tribes. This sort of information may be of particular interest to elementary school students who enjoy making comparisons between their own lifestyles and other youngsters from different cultural, ethnic, or racial groups. D'Andrea also suggested methods for using telecommunications such as the Net to promote multicultural awareness among elementary school age students. Students can exchange photos, text, sound (e.g., music), and language from various cultures to gain a better appreciation of self and others.

❖ Some counselors have provided websites with links to colleges, financial aid sources, GPA calculators, planning checklists, after school homework centers, and resources for parents to name a few.

What Exactly Is the Internet?

The Internet is a series of computer networks linked to one another around the world, communicating almost instantaneously with one another. A single network of computers might be all the computers linked to one another within an office or school building. A larger network might be all the computers connected within an entire school district. The Internet is many thousands of these networks communicating with one another — University networks connected to government networks connected to business networks connected to private networks. The networks are physically linked to one another by telephone, radio, cable lines or via satellite. Networks from other continents are interconnected by the large, intercontinental telephone and fiber optic communication lines that run beneath the ocean floor (Using the Internet for Teachers, Schools, Students: An Introduction, 1997). The Net encompasses various special parts which include electronic mail (e-mail), listservs, discussion groups (Usenet), bulletin boards, chat rooms, telnet, file transfer protocol (FTP), and the World Wide Web. This text introduces counselors to the various aspects of the Net although focuses primarily on the World Wide Web, the most popular and powerful part of the Net, as a vital resource and interactive medium for facilitating our work.

Electronic Mail

E-mail is like sending a letter or message through the post office, only it is much faster. In some respects, it is like talking on the telephone, except that you type out everything that you want to say. In general, it connects the message sender to one or more receivers at other computer stations. Each person has his or her own e-mail address in which messages or files can be sent and retrieved by a recipient. When an e-mail message is sent to another user via a network, it is posted until the recipient turns on his or her computer and pushes a few keys to tap into the Net. The computer's e-mail message board shows that a message is pending. At the recipient's convenience this message is retrieved and read. If desired, the message can be forwarded to others. Or, by pushing one or two keys, a reply can be sent directly back to the sender. The message can also be printed as a hard copy or saved to a floppy disk. One e-mail advantage to school counselors is the opportunity to participate in a network that enables participants to share professional ideas and information. It offers counselors a unique and valuable opportunity for supervision and consultation.

As personal computers become available in more counselors' offices and as more schools come on-line with the Internet, there will be new opportunities for e-mail applications such as in consultation and coordination. More specifically, e-mail offers counselors the same kind of advantage that it offers those involved with distance learning education. It forms the basis of a network that conveniently connects counselors and others (e.g., supervisors, community members, parents, and students) individually and in groups (Myrick & Sabella, 1995).

Advantages of using e-mail to communicate with others includes:

❖ the convenience of doing so at any time of the day or night;

❖ being able to think through a communication before making it;

❖ not having to rely on a mutual time to communicate as one would with a phone conversation;

❖ saving money in long distance charges when having to make only brief comments;

❖ instantaneously communicating the same message to multiple people on a distribution list;

❖ diminished inhibitions that face-to-face conversation may present;

❖ that, whereas spoken words must remain in memory and are sometimes lost in a quick exchange, written e-mail messages can be reviewed;

❖ large files, especially documents, can be instantly sent to others via e-mail which can save precious time and money as compared to printing and shipping the document via traditional postal carriers.

Disadvantages of e-mail communication include:

❖ for some, typing can be slow and tedious;

❖ the absence of nonverbal communication such as gestures, facial expression, or tone of voice can sometimes lead to mistaken interpretations of an e-mail message;

❖ although relatively very secure, sending an e-mail over the Net is sometimes like sending a postcard through the mail — others whom desire to do so might intercept and read an e-mail. Therefore, issues of confidentiality and privacy are central to communicating sensitive information;

❖ if not careful, counselors can receive too many e-mail messages which may lead to time and organizational management challenges. In this sense, counselors must be smart consumers of information and determine how much one reads, digests, and to which messages one should respond.

Listservs

When you sign up for a magazine subscription, your personal information is placed into a database. When it's time for the magazine to be published and mailed, you automatically receive a copy. Listservs are kind of like that except that they are usually free and you contribute to their publication. Specifically, you decide which lists to subscribe depending on your area of interest. Once you subscribe to a list, you will receive any messages that list members send to the group. Other members receive messages you send to the group. So, listservs are a high-tech electronic discussion group. On a popular list, you can literally receive hundreds of e-mails in a single day. Some lists offer digests in which individual messages are bundled together daily or weekly and sent to the list as a single, large e-mail. These help prevent your mailbox from getting overloaded. One listserv, Peer Helping Programs

and Training (Peer Helping) was created to help those interested in peer helping share information such as ideas, techniques, and resources. Peer Helping is also a viable place for having "virtual" discussions about peer helper programs and training. Contributors may share articles or papers they have written and ask for comments. Those who are more familiar with the Internet may guide newcomers to useful World Wide Web sites, other mailing lists, and peer helper resources. The Peer Helping network may also be helpful in discussing ethical dilemmas, practical training approaches, new activities, or perhaps simply to provide some encouraging words. Peer Helping is a non-moderated discussion group open to anyone invested in peer helper programs and training. Participants may include, trainers, counselors, educators, parents, administrators, or community members. Professors, especially, might use Peer Helping to stimulate discussion in their graduate classes and encourage students to ask questions of other experts in the field.

To subscribe to Peer Helping, a person only needs to enter his or her email address in a form located on the website of the National Peer Helper Association (www.peerhelping.org). Or, you may send a blank email to peerhelping-subscribe@egroups.com to automatically place yourself on the subscription list. In a few minutes you should receive a message confirming your subscription. Once subscribed, a user can then send a message to all other Peer Helping members by sending only one message to peerhelping@egroups.com. To reply to an individual on the list, send mail directly to his/her email address (usually found in the heading of the message). Using the "reply" button of your email software in response to a Peer Helping message may send your reply to the entire group, depending on how your software is set up.

There are primarily two methods for learning about available listservs of interest. First, you might learn about a specific listserv as it is announced in professional or other publications such as journals, newsletters, or newspapers. Second, you may seek listservs of interest by querying a database of listservs maintained on

---

some Internet sites. One of the most comprehensive databases of listservs can be found at http://www.liszt.com. Once at this site, you can conduct a search using keywords or phrases and receive a "list of lists" that contain your keywords in the title of the list or in the body of the list's description. Moreover, this site makes it especially easy to then subscribe to the listserv by providing simple directions and a convenient link that automatically calls on your e-mail software and inserts the proper address for the listserv.

Another common type of Internet listserv is the post-only listserv. This kind of listserv acts more like a mailing list for those who simply want to receive reminders, newsletters, or announcements. For example, I am co-editor of my departmental newsletter. About every month, subscribers receive via e-mail news, announcements, and other information of particular interest to students, alumni, faculty, and others whom have any curiosity about our on-goings. My co-editor and I are the only users who can broadcast using this listserv. Any one else who tries is humbly and automatically rejected.

Newsgroups
(aka, Usenet or Bulletin Boards)

Newsgroups are basically electronic bulletin boards. Using a program called a news reader (you can use the one that comes with Microsoft IE or download one from www.hotfiles.com), you select a topic that interests you and then read the messages posted by others. If you choose, you can subscribe to the group and respond to the messages you read. You have the option of replying publicly to the newsgroup, so everyone can read your response, or you can reply to the original author via e-mail. You can even do both. Newsgroups are divided into hierarchies such as listed below (for a comprehensive list of newsgroup categories, you may visit http://home.magmacom.com/~leisen/master_list.html):

alt Alternative. The creation of these groups is not moderated.

biz Commercially oriented (business)

comp Computers: many groups, all subjects

gnu The GNU project of the Free Software Foundation

info Informational groups (moderated)

k12 Kindergarten through 12th grade education

misc Miscellaneous groups (small ads, etc)

news About the news system itself

rec Recreation groups

sci Science groups

soc Society groups

talk Talk - gossip and discussion about current affairs

A few tidbits about what Usenet is not (adapted from Mark Moraes e-mail at http://www.netannounce.org/news.announce.newusers/archive/usenet/what-is/part1) follow:

❖ **Usenet is not an organization.** No person or group has authority over Usenet as a whole. No one controls who gets a news feed, which articles are propagated where, who can post articles, or anything else. There is no "Usenet Incorporated," nor is there a "Usenet User's Group."

❖ **Usenet is not a democracy.** Since there is no person or group in charge of Usenet as a whole – i.e. there is no Usenet "government." Reason follows that Usenet cannot be a democracy, autocracy, or any other kind of "-acy."

❖ **Usenet is not an academic network.** It is no surprise that many Usenet sites are universities, research labs or other academic institutions. Usenet originated with a link between two universities, and the exchange of ideas and information is what such institutions are all about. But the passage of years has changed Usenet's character. Today, by plain count, most Usenet sites are commercial entities.

Russell A. Sabella, Ph.D.

❖ **Usenet is not the Internet.** The Internet is a wide-ranging network, parts of which are subsidized by various governments. It carries many kinds of traffic, of which Usenet is only one. And the Internet is only one of the various networks carrying Usenet traffic.

❖ **Usenet is not an advertising medium.** Because of Usenet's roots in academia, and because Usenet depends so heavily on cooperation (sometimes among competitors), custom dictates that advertising be kept to a minimum. It is tolerated if it is infrequent, informative, and low-hype.

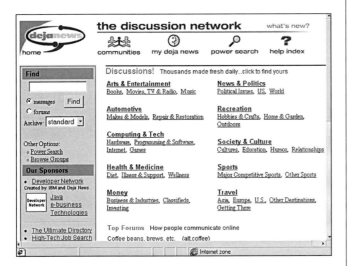

The Deja News Web (www.dejanews.com) site provides an admirable introduction to newsgroups and a way to search them. Another great resource for learning to become a productive and useful member of a newsgroup community is found at http://www.usenet.org.uk/usenet-information.html. Creating a new newsgroup can be initiated by anyone although requires quite an involved process. A document that describes the current procedure for creating a new newsgroup is entitled "How To Create A New Newsgroup." Its common name, however, is "the guidelines" and may be found at http://www.netannounce.org/news.announce.newusers/archive/usenet/creating-newsgroups/part1.

Chat Rooms

E-mail is a great way to communicate electronically although this method suffers from the lack of real-time interaction between one person and with others whom he/she would like to communicate. Historically, real-time communication has occurred either in face-to-face conversation or over the telephone. The use of chat software, especially over the Internet, makes it possible to electronically converse in real time. Following the metaphor for which this technology is named, imagine yourself entering a room in which you can converse with other users you will find there. You can see on screen what each user is typing into the conversation, and when you type something, the other users in the room can see your message as well (Hofstetter, 1998).

Chat environments have progressed from simple text-based interactions to full blown graphical user interfaces (GUIs). Today's chatrooms allow users to personalize their communications by posting their photos or a close facsimile (sometimes a computer generated likeness) next to their text communications. Other programs also allow for sending to members of the chatroom audio files that contain music, sound effects, or the users own recorded voice. One of the most popular chat clients is a program called mIRC available for download at most shareware sites. However, I will focus on the newest kid on the block, Microsoft's Comic Chat, because out of all the chat clients I have reviewed, I believe Comic Chat to be most useful to counselors, especially elementary school counselors. After reading about this program, I think you'll agree.

Microsoft's Comic Chat. Microsoft offers a number of chat areas based on a comic strip interface. You must first download some software (put the phrase comic chat in the search bar at www.hotfiles.com to most easily locate the software for download). When you then log on to the chat area, you can choose from one of several cartoon characters ranging from a beatnik to a space alien or even a simple boy or girl. By using a simple on screen tool, you can also transmit a range of facial expressions or body positions for your character including raving laughter to out-and-out screaming. When you type in something to say, your character appears on screen with a text bubble over its head. Everyone else in the chat room sees this at the same time and will have the chance to respond in the same way. Comic Chat, therefore, allows users to emphasize and enhance text based communication by accompanying it with some nonverbal communications. Further, Comic Chat makes it very simple to dispatch sound files. With a collection of personal sound bites or sound effects, together with character motion and text, a user stands a good chance of accurately and more clearly communicating with others in the chatroom. For children, Comic Chat may also be way of facilitating the communication of emotions or clarifying a situation.

IRC.MSN.COM is a free Internet chat service provided by Microsoft which is accessible to anyone with Microsoft's Comic Chat, IRC, or IRCX chat client. IRC.MSN.COM is a dynamic network, meaning that users are free to create and run their own chat rooms as well as join existing rooms created by other users on the network. In addition to public chats, users on IRC.MSN.COM are free to engage in private conversations with other users and send files to one another. While using IRC.MSN.COM, Microsoft does not monitor public or private conversations on the chat network, nor does Microsoft monitor file transfers which take place between users of IRC.MSN.COM. While the sysops on IRC.MSN.COM make regular scans of chat room names and topics on the network for profanity and unlawful implications, the content of the public and private conversations is unrestricted. In addition, you should be aware that files you receive from other users via the chat

network may contain viruses or otherwise harm your computer. When you join a chat room, engage in a private conversation with other users, or receive a file from another user, you are doing so at your own risk. There are many companies and organizations that provide chat services. Others include:

austin.tx.us.undernet.org

irc.bu.edu

irc.colorado.edu

irc.harvard.edu

irc.netcom.com

irc.texas.net

irc.uiuc.edu

manhattan.ks.us.undernet.org

nasa.ideal.net

sanjose.ca.us.undernet.org

tampa.fl.us.undernet.org

washington.dc.us.undernet.org

One of the things that you might notice upon entering a chat room and lurking for a while is that participants will use many acronyms. There are a host of common abbreviations used by members of newsgroups and chat areas whenever the full message is just too long to type out. Several include:

AFAIK As far as I know

AKA Also known as

AFK Away from the keyboard

BAK Back at the keyboard

BTW By the way

CUL See you later

DL Download

FAQ Frequently asked questions

FOTCL Falling off the chair laughing

FTF Face-to-face

FWIW For what its worth

FYA For your amusement

FYI For your information

GMTA Great minds think alike

HHOJ Ha ha, only joking

HHOK Ha ha, only kidding

HHOS Ha ha, only serious

IAC In any case

IAE In any event

IMO In my opinion

IMHO In my humble opinion

IMNSHO In my not so humble opinion

IOW In other words

LOL Laughing out loud

LTNS Long time no see

MOTD Message of the day

MOTS Member of the opposite sex

NBIF No basis in fact

NBD No big deal

OIC Oh, I see

OTOH On the other hand

PITA Pain in the a**

PMJI Pardon my jumping in

POV Point of view

ROFL Rolling on the floor laughing

RTM Read the manual

RTFM Read the f****** manual

SOS Same old stuff

SYSOP System Operator

TIA Thanks in advance

TIC Tongue in cheek

TPTB The powers that be

TTFN Ta-ta for now

WTG Way to go

WTH What the heck/h***

YMMV Your mileage may

You should know that, like anything else on the Net, some chatrooms are not for the easily offended. Not all, but many of the rooms are R to X rated because they contain highly graphical communications including text, sound, and sometimes graphics. Also, users of chatroom can easily maintain anonymity and, even worse, pose as someone they are not. Consider the following quote from a story printed across many newspapers on October 20, 1997.

A man dubbed the "Internet Romeo" warned parents to supervise their children's use of the network after he was sentenced to more than five years in prison Monday for using an on-line chat room to solicit sex with a teen-ager. Keir Fiore, 21, of Manchester, N.H., pleaded guilty to two federal counts of interstate transportation of a minor for illegal sex after using an on-line chat room to solicit sex from a 13-year-old girl in Salem, New Hampshire. U.S. District Judge Joseph DiClerico sentenced him to five years and three months in prison. Fiore, who faces sentencing in New Hampshire and Massachusetts Tuesday on state charges of sexual assault and soliciting, read a statement to the court apologizing to the teen-ager and her family. "The Internet is dangerous for young children who use it without parental supervision," the statement read in part. Prosecutors said Fiore flirted with the teen-ager in an on-line chat room last summer and convinced her to run away with him. Police eventually found the pair in New Hampshire after a national search.

Netiquette. The Net is a very busy place which, at least for now, is mostly self-regulated. Thus, there are certain commonly understood rules of "Net Etiquette" or "Netiquette" that users of the Internet and especially listserv should adhere. Following commonly established rules of discourse which will help keep the Net a mutually respectful, viable, and flexible place to connect with others whom may have different needs. Keeping peace and harmony on the Net is easier said than done, however, On one hand, a modicum of etiquette is needed to allow communication over listserv and newsgroups to function efficiently, without delving into unhampered and unbecoming discourse. On the other hand, there are issues of sheer volume that dictate frugal posting and replies. Finally, there are issues of freedom of speech and access control that many users are sensitive to and willing to uphold for themselves. Following are several well-established "rules" and/or guidelines for communicating over the Net:

❖ **Do Your Homework First**. Learn about the nature of the group before joining a listserv. It is very difficult to decipher the purpose and personality of a group simply by it's title. For example, upon first learning about one listserv named ECSTASY, you might be lead to believe that the group is sex-related or even pornographic. However, this listserv focuses on the role of spirituality in counseling. The title merely refers to the experience of higher order living. Similarly, you might join a listserv named SHEPHERD because of an interest in this type of canine. However, the group may actually be a small group of friends in Kansas who meet for lunch on Thursday and call themselves "the shepherds". It might be a softball team in Australia or perhaps a members-only group of religious crusaders. To learn more about a group, you can first visit the LISZT (www.liszt.com) database to see if a description is available. If not available, then you might write the owner of the list, usually listed, and ask for one. As a last resort, you might join and simply observe before making a decision to continue or unsubscribe from the list.

❖ **Lurking.** When you first subscribe to a list, its good netiquette to practice the fine art of lurking. That is, to spend a few days reading the messages to get a feel for the tone and the topic of the conversation (also known as threads) before jumping in with your own two cents. This is simply a "look before you leap" principle to see what kind of topics are deemed appropriate by current members of a listserv or newsgroup, to see how lenient others are of divergent opinion, and to learn about the overall culture of the group.

❖ **Study the Freqeutnly Asked Questions (FAQ) file.** The FAQ is a document (often a hypertext document) containing common questions and answers for a particular website or topic. This list is especially prepared to help novice users to more quickly adapt to new standards of practice, especially in a chat room or listserv discussion. It is important to locate the FAQ for a listserv or newsgroup and read it before beginning to post anything, especially questions, to the group for two reasons. First, it usually contains a bounty of information about the subject matter of the group. Second, many users of an electronic group are highly prejudiced of users who ask questions or post information that suggests they have not read the FAQs, and let them know quickly of their despondence in e-mail and postings to the newsgroups. It is expected that FAQ questions, having already been answered and placed in an easily accessible archive, will not be asked again within the newsgroup. Your question may have already been answered, many times over; asking it again will not get you off on the right foot in an electronic group.

❖ **Avoid Flame Wars.** A flame war consists of a barrage of personal attacks, usually targeting an individual or more than one member of the group. As do many real-life verbal exchanges, these virtual screaming matches are usually initiated due to a misunderstanding about the exact meaning of a message. What the sender may have intended as a gentle confrontation, the recipient may view as an outright attack. Much of this is due to the impersonal nature of e-mail. Without face-to-face contact, it is difficult to convey tone. Readers do not have body language to help decipher the meaning behind written words. I imagine, too, that those who flame may also get caught in the "heat of the moment" when adversely responding to a listserv message and, hidden behind the safety of distance, find it much easier to be very frank. Even worse, those who flame will often times do so by conveying contemptuous messages about an individual in front of the entire group which may stir up others to join. If you don't think this happens among compassionate, understanding, empathetic, and unconditional counselors — you're wrong. To my continual surprise and dismay, I have learned from participating in many counseling oriented listservs that counselors are not immune. Such conversation is embarrassing for individuals; puts a damper on spirited electronic discussion in the group; and for the counseling profession, runs the risk of tarnishing the reputation of a noble profession, especially among noncounselors who subscribe to counseling listservs for educational purposes.

❖ **Spamming.** Particularly reprehensible to many cybernauts is the practice of posting something to every group available, whether appropriate or not. For example, posting advertisement promoting a commercial product or service could easily be considered spam. Those judged guilty of spamming the Net may be "flamed" (i.e., a searing e-mail message in which the writer attacks another participant in overly harsh, and often personal, terms) so badly that their computer systems become frozen for a period because of the unadulterated volume of e-mail sent in protest to you and sometimes your Internet Service Provider. In some cases, an offense is unforgivable and may result in revocation of your account. Often though, material being posted is appropriate for several groups, and it is quite acceptable to post to multiple groups in that case. If you have a product such as a book or service such as consulting about a special topic that you really believe would be of benefit, you might post a sentence or two about the opportunity with instructions for requesting further details. You might also forward a message to a listserv owner to evaluate and decide whether to forward to the group which should soften the burden of responsibility for your message.

❖ **Personal vs. Private Messages.** Before responding to a listserv message, make certain that your response will be received by those whom you intended. Especially be careful that you send personal and private messages only to individuals and not to the entire group. Having a private conversation over a listserv is similar to doing the same in a room full of other people who are trying to focus on the issues – it's annoying.

Telnet

The Internet allows computers to converse with each other over networks. A telnet program allows us to log into a distant computer almost as if we were actually sitting physically at that computer. When you use a telnet client program to connect to another computer, the software sends your keystrokes to the other computer and displays the returning results on your monitor. Most telnet interfaces use only the keyboard for input and display using the monitor or printer. Most are character based, which means they only display the alphabet, numbers and punctuation. Telnet client software is available from many sources and may have come installed with your Internet connection. One popular source of such software comes from the National Center for Supercomputing Applications (http://www.ncsa.uiuc.edu/Indices/Software/).

FTP

According to the Internic (http://www.braintools.org/exhibits/internet/15min/ftp/sld01.html), FTP stands for "File Transfer Protocol," a system of rules and a software program that allow you to log on to another computer and transfer information between it and your computer. FTP works on the client/server principle. A client program enables the user to interact with a server in order to access information and services on the server computer. Files that can be transferred are stored on computers called FTP servers. To access these files, an FTP client program is used. This is an interface that allows the user to locate the file(s) to be transferred and initiate the transfer process. The basic steps to use FTP are: (a) connect to the FTP server; (b) navigate the file structure to find the file you want; and (c) transfer the file. The specifics of each step will vary, depending on the client program being used and the type of Internet connection.

Many websites have been configured to work around FTP programs by allowing you to access FTP systems using a browser to locate and transfer information. These site addresses begin with FTP:// instead of the more common http://. Many FTP servers require an appropriate user identification and password for entry. However, many other servers allow access through what is known as anonymous FTP. Anonymous FTP only requires you to enter the word "anonymous" as your userid and your e-mail address as your password. Once you have access, you will probably find many kinds of files such as shareware, freeware, upgrades and documents.

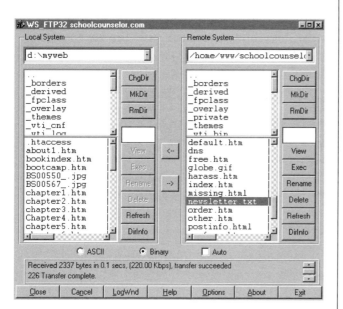

THE WORLD WIDE WEB

The World Wide Web (also known as the Web) is the multimedia part of the Internet. Once accessed, a counselor can view information in the form of text, graphics, sounds, video, and animated icons. A distinctive feature of the Web is the breadth and depth of culturally rich information that one can almost instantaneously access from anywhere around the globe. Also, rapidly changing data can be updated within minutes thus allowing counselors to retrieve information that is highly current. The Web has, until recently, mostly been found useful among academicians, scientists and businesses as a way to share and coordinate information, communicate, and conduct transactions. However, the current proliferation of Web content in the areas of human resource, psychology, counseling, and mental health (for example, see Grohol, 1997), has now rendered the Web as a valuable resource for counselors. School counselors can be better informed about knowledge and practical techniques via the repertoire of materials in the form of scholarly journals, resource information, program descriptions, and articles to name a few. And, as the cost of getting on-line becomes more affordable, counselors may find that gaining Web access is steadily more realistic.

Web sites are dynamic documents which usually contain links to other related documents in the form of selected words or symbols (called hypertext links). For example, when a new word or concept is introduced in a document, hypertext makes it possible for a user to point to that word or symbol and retrieve another related document which gives more details about the original reference. The second document may also contain links to other documents providing further details, and so on. The user need not know where the referenced document is, and there is no need to type a command to display it, browse it, or to find the right paragraph. Hypertext links may also lead a user to graphics, photos, data, maps, movie clips, sound clips, or any kind of information that can be digitized. Viewing this rich array of information can occur from any computer in the world that has the requisite hardware, software, and Internet connection (Sabella, 1998)

How did the Web Begin?

The following time line, adopted partly from Dave Kristula's *The History of the Internet* (http://www.davesite.com/webstation/net-history.shtml), Robert H'obbes' *Hobbes' Internet Time line v1.3a* (www.hobbes.mitre.org), and Henry Hardy's Master's Thesis, *The History of the Net* (http://www.ocean.ic.net/ftp/doc/nethist.html) should help you to appreciate the rapid development of the Web:

➤ **1957**

The USSR launches Sputnik, the first artificial earth satellite. In response, the United States forms the Advanced Research Projects Agency (ARPA) within the Department of Defense (DoD) to establish America's lead in science and technology applicable to the military.

➤ **1962**

Paul Baran, of the RAND Corporation (a government agency), was commissioned by the U.S. Air Force to do a study on how it could maintain its command and control over its missiles and bombers, after a nuclear attack. This was to be a military research network that could survive a nuclear strike, decentralized so that if any locations (cities) in the U.S. were attacked, the military could still have control of nuclear arms for a counter-attack. Baran's finished document described several ways to accomplish this. His final proposal was a packet switched network. Packet switching is the breaking down of data into packets that are labeled to indicate the origin and the destination of the information and the forwarding of these packets from one computer to another computer until the information arrives at its final destination computer. This was crucial to the realization of a computer network. If packets are lost at any given point, the message can be resent by the originator.

➤ **1969**

A Honeywell minicomputer was chosen as the base on which they would build the switch and would link four nodes or sites: University of California at Los Angeles, Stanford University, University of California at Santa Barbara, and the University of Utah. The network was wired together via 50 Kbps circuits.

➤ **1972**

The first e-mail program was created by Ray Tomlinson.

➤ **1973**

Development began on the protocol later to be called TCP/IP, it was developed by a group headed by Vinton Cerf from Stanford and Bob Kahn. This new protocol was to allow diverse computer networks to interconnect and communicate with each other.

➤ **1974**

The term Internet was coined by Vint Cerf and Bob Kahn in a paper they wrote about transmission control protocol.

➤ **1976**

Dr. Robert M. Metcalfe develops Ethernet, which allowed coaxial cable to move data extremely fast. This was a crucial component to the development of local area networks (LANs). Also, SATNET, Atlantic packet Satellite network, was born. This network linked the United States with Europe.

➤ **1979**

USENET (the decentralized news group network) was created by Steve Bellovin, a graduate student at University of North Carolina, and programmers Tom Truscott and Jim Ellis. The creation of BITNET (Because its Time Network), by IBM, introduced the "store and forward" network. It was used for e-mail and listservs.

➤ **1983**

The University of Wisconsin created the Domain Name System (DNS). This allowed packets to be directed to a domain name, which would be translated by the server database into the corresponding Internet Protocol (IP) number. This made it much easier for people to access other servers, because they no longer had to remember numbers.

➤ **1984**

The ARPANET was divided into two networks: MILNET and ARPANET. MILNET was to serve the needs of the military and ARPANET to support the advanced research component. The Department of Defense continued to support both networks. Upgrade to CSNET was contracted to MCI. New circuits would be T1 lines, 1.5 Mbps which is twenty-five times faster than the old 56 Kbps lines. IBM would provide advanced routers and Merit would manage the network. The new network was to be called NSFNET (National Science Foundation Network), and old lines were to remain called CSNET.

➤ **1985**

The National Science Foundation began deploying its new T1 lines, which would be finished by 1988.

➤ **1986**

The Internet Engineering Task Force or IETF was created to serve as a forum for technical coordination.

➤ **1988**

Soon after the completion of the T1 NSFNET backbone, traffic increased so quickly that plans immediately began on upgrading the network again. Research into high speed networking began and would soon result in the concept of the T3, a 45 Mbps line.

➤ **1990**

Tim Berners-Lee (considered by many as the father of the Web), with CERN in Geneva, implements a hypertext system to provide efficient information access to the members of the international high-energy physics community. Also, the Electronic Frontier Foundation is founded by Mitch Kapor.

➤ **1992**

The Internet Society is chartered and the World Wide Web was released by CERN.

➤ **1993**

Network Solutions (InterNIC) was created by the National Science Foundation (NSF). They would provide specific Internet services such as directory and database services (by AT&T), registration services (by Network Solutions Inc.), and information services (by General Atomics/CERFnet). Marc Andreessen and NCSA and the University of Illinois develops a graphical user interface to the WWW, called "Mosaic for X". Also ...

- The United States White House comes on-line;
- Internet Talk Radio begins broadcasting;
- The United Nations and the World Bank come on-line;
- The U.S. National Information Infrastructure Act is passed;
- Businesses and media begin to take serious notice of the Internet;
- Mosaic takes the Internet by storm; and
- the WWW proliferates at a 341,634% annual growth rate of service traffic.

Russell A. Sabella, Ph.D.

➤ 1994

No major changes were made to the physical network. The most significant thing that happened was the growth. Many new networks were added to the NSF backbone. Hundreds of thousands of new hosts were added to the Internet during this time period. Significant Net events included Pizza Hut offering pizza ordering on its Web page; advent of First Virtual, the first cyberbank; and the installation of the ATM (Asynchronous Transmission Mode, 145Mbps) backbone on NSFNET. Also,

- Communities begin to connect directly to the Internet
- U.S. Senate and House provide information servers
- First flower shop took orders via the Internet
- Shopping malls arrive on the Internet
- Mass marketing finds its way to the Internet with mass e-mailings
- "A Day in the Life of the Internet" begins its publication

➤ 1995

National Science Foundation announced that as of April 30, 1995 it would no longer allow direct access to the NSF backbone. The National Science Foundation contracted with four companies that would be providers of access to the NSF backbone (Merit). These companies would then sell connections to groups, organizations, and companies. A $50 annual fee is imposed on domains, excluding .edu and .gov domains which were still funded by the National Science Foundation.

➤ 1996

Most Internet traffic is carried by back-bones of independent Internet Service Providers (ISPs), including MCI, AT&T, Sprint, UUnet, BBN planet, ANS, and others. Currently the Internet Society, the group that controls the Net, is trying to figure out new TCP/IP to be able to have billions of addresses, rather than the limited system of today. The problem that has arisen is that it is not known how both the old and the new addressing systems will be able to work at the same time during a transition period.

➤ 1997

The American Registry for Internet Numbers (ARIN) is established to handle administration and registration of IP numbers to the geographical areas currently handled by Network Solutions (InterNIC), starting March 1998. And ...

- Domain name business.com sold for US$150,000
- 71,618 mailing lists registered at Liszt, a mailing list directory
- 101,803 Name Servers in whois database

➤ 1998

Web size estimates range between 275 and 320 million pages for the first quarter. Also:

- Internet users get to be judges in a performance by 12 world champion ice skaters in March, marking the first time a television sport show's outcome is determined by its viewers.
- InterNIC registers its 2 millionth domain on May 4th
- ABCNews.com accidentally posts test U.S. election returns one day early (November 2nd). They respond by saying that they were simply testing out templates.

- Chinese government puts Lin Hai on trial for "inciting the overthrow of state power" for providing 30,000 e-mail addresses to a U.S. Internet magazine.

- Speculators agree that this is the banner year for E-commerce and E-business.

NOTE: For interesting and amusing Internet snapshots, consult Win Treese's Internet-related Facts and Figures at http://www.openmarket.com/intindex/index.cfm).

A single event that many say marked the "coming of age" of the Internet was reported on September 13th, 1998 across television, print, and electronic media. An estimated twelve percent of adult Americans, some 20 million people, used the Internet to gain access to Independent Counsel Ken Starr's investigative report about President Clinton. Twenty million people all logged on to get the same information at the same time. As important, while there was gridlock in some corners, the Internet did not melt down under the demand, as some had predicted. Information technology will continue to be one of key factors driving progress in the 21st century — it is quite literally transforming the way we live, learn, work, and play. Advances in computing and communication technology will create a new infrastructure for business, scientific research, and social interaction. That infrastructure will provide us with new tools for conducting our work at home and throughout the world. And, advances in technology will help counselors to acquire knowledge and insight from others to make more informed decisions about all aspects of their programs. Information technologies such as the Internet will assist counselors to understand the effects of guidance and counseling on all stakeholders, especially children and their academic success. It will provide a vehicle for professional development and personal growth. Information technology can make the workplace more rewarding, improve the quality of services to all, and make counselors more responsive and accessible to the needs of a progressively complicated and diverse clientele.

CHAPTER TWO

Get Set ... On-Ramp to the Web

To begin your surfing adventure on the Net, you must have at least four things: a computer with a modem; a telephone or cable connection; software; and an Internet Service Provider (ISP). Similar to purchasing a car, investing in the appropriate hardware and software will depend upon your preferences and needs. For instance, how fast do you want to travel on the information highway? Which options will you require to make your travels more comfortable and enjoyable? And, probably the most important question for most people, how much are you able to invest?

A Computer

What kind of computer must one have to effectively access the Internet? This question is more simple to answer than if the question focused on the right type of computer for other applications such as desktop publishing or, say, conducting statistical analyses. Because the Internet relies on a more global programming language (hypertext markup language or HTML), just about any computer will do. Both Macintosh and Windows compatible computers work just fine because the software needed for surfing is available for both operating systems or platforms. Some companies, however, have designed their computers with the Internet in mind. For instance, Apple's IMac is marketed as a 12 minute out-of-the-box and onto the Internet PC while a Microsoft Windows computer may take a bit longer and include a few more steps for launching into cyberspace (typically about an hour from the box onto the Net).

Getting on the Net may be a large part of your computer experience although it is usually only one application among others such as word processing, information management, desktop publishing, games, and running educational software. So, if you are considering the purchase of a new computer, which one should you choose? There is no correct answer for this question because it truly depends on personal preference. Following are several questions you should ask yourself and your computer retailer when deciding on your purchase:

1. What is the quality and availability of software for the applications I will most use? For instance, professional desktop publishers and advertisement agencies typically use Macintosh related hardware and software because publishing and photo editing applications seem to be best achieved with this kind of system. On the other hand, those who engage in mostly word processing, database management, and multimedia might find that the Windows compatible hardware would serve them best.

2. Who will I be collaborating with mostly and what do they use? Although there are methods for running both platforms on either a Macintosh or Windows compatible computer, it is usually easiest to run the same software as others with whom you work closely. When using the same or similar operating systems, transferring and sharing files does not pose a problem because compatibility is very close to 100%.

3. Although cost is always a factor, competition among computer companies has made price a virtual non-issue for entry level computing. Companies seem to be driving at the lowest price that their profit margins will allow. And because all computers share many of the same parts which cost the same for all, no one company seems to have an edge over another when it comes to cost. Fortunately for consumers, price wars have now steered the cost ceiling for a complete package (computer, monitor, multimedia peripherals,

software package, and a printer) below the $1000 dollar mark for both large and small retailers, direct warehouses, and online stores.

4. The quality of technical help and customer service that come standard with your personal computer seems to be the more important concern among consumers. That is, smart computer shoppers wonder about the average wait time when calling a company's customer service, and the average time from problem presentation to solution.

5. How much power will I need? The difference between low-end and high-end hardware is significant and can easily run into thousands of dollars. A general rule in the world of computers is to purchase as much computer as you can get as allowed by your budget. The reason for this is that this year's most revered computer will be shadowed by next year's innovations. The speed at which hardware is developing is indeed amazing.

6. How expandable is the computer? That is, how much room is there to add extra hardware or peripherals such as scanners, digital cameras, extra memory, new cards (e.g., video editor), zip drive, CD-ROM writer, or a second printer?

7. Will the company customize a computer for my exact needs and charge me only for what I want? Relatedly, if I ask the company to remove a standard option, either hardware or software, will they give me a price rebate?

A Connection

The transmission rate with which you connect to your Internet service provider will determine how fast you will receive information from the sites you access. At slow rates, modems are measured in terms of baud rates. The slowest rate is 300 baud (about 25 characters/second). At higher speeds, modems are measured in terms of bits per second (bps). The fastest modems run at 57,600 bps, although they can achieve even higher data transfer rates by compressing the data. Obviously, the faster the transmission rate, the faster you can send and receive data. Note, however, that you cannot receive data any faster than it is being sent. If, for example, the device sending data to your computer is sending it at 2,400 bps, you must receive it at 2,400 bps. It does not always pay, therefore, to have a very fast modem. In addition, some telephone lines are unable to transmit data reliably at very high rates (Webopedia, 1999).

When accessing a site, what you are essentially doing is requesting that the site send to your computer all relevant elements that the site contains: text, graphics, video, audio, etc. With all else being equal (such as level of Internet traffic and computer processor speed), the faster the connection, the more quickly you are able to view the site's contents. When added together, the time required to access and view many sites during an online session can have a grave impact on your productivity and viewing pleasure. Additionally, the time required for downloading files such as software from an Internet site to your computer is vastly different depending upon the speed of your connection. The following table represents average download times for a webpage and a relatively small (100 kilobyte) picture at various connection speeds:

Russell A. Sabella, Ph.D.

Connection Method	Average Time to Donwload a Webpage	Average Time to Download a File
14.4K	33.8 sec	55 sec
28.8K	18.6 sec	28 sec
56.6K	12.7 sec	14 sec
ISDN	4.5 sec	6 sec
TI (Ethernet)	1.4 sec	0.27 sec

Cable modems. The fastest growing technology in computer connection involves using a cable modem. Basically, companies that provide you with cable television access use the same connections and a special piece of hardware called a cable modem to provide you with Net access. The speed that a cable modem provides is much greater than that of a telephone modem. The reason for this is that cable modem connections transmit data via fiber optic cable with much greater capacity (or bandwidth). The result is a transmission rate that reaches 2 million BPS. This, combined with the fact that millions of homes are already wired for cable TV, has made the cable modem something of a holy grail for Internet and cable TV companies. However, this relatively new technology is still a luxury for most people since cable companies are slowly upgrading their equipment to provide such a service which may not yet reach those that receive television services from the same companies. For those that do have cable modem access, the cost of a cable modem and the monthly fee for this kind of access significantly exceeds telephone modem access, $250 and $30, respectively.

Companies that provide digital satellite systems that beam hundreds of television channels into your home are also getting in to the Internet Service Provider business. In this case, they use satellite connections to beam Internet data to your computer. Similar to cable modem access, digital satellite access is still in its infancy and much less pervasive as compared to telephone connections.

One of the more promising communication technology hopefuls is that of ADSL. Short for asymmetric digital subscriber line, ADSL is a new technology that transforms ordinary phone lines (also known as "twisted copper pairs") into high-speed digital lines for ultra-fast Internet access. ADSL also enables access to corporate networks for telecommuters, as well as exciting new interactive multimedia applications such as multiplayer gaming, video on demand and video catalogs. It is not currently available to the general public except in trial areas, but many believe that it will be one of the more popular choices for Internet access over the next few years (Webopedia, 1999). To learn more about ADSL, visit www.adsl.com.

An Internet Service Provider (ISP)

If your school has full-time access through a network connection to the Internet, you have the shortest path of all. All you need to do is sit down at a terminal or workstation and, using the instructions and Internet applications supplied by your in-house computer experts, log on and get going. Most Internet connections have been made just like that—as connections between two networks, rather than between two computers. For example, a school's local-area network (LAN) might get access to the Internet by making a connection through a leased phone line to a regional network. Once that connection is made, in most cases, every computer on the local-area network has "full-time" access—meaning, the Internet is available all the time, day and night. More and more schools and public facilities are getting connections, and most universities provide access. Moreover, some schools allow their employees to log on to their system from home or other remote locations (LaQuey, 1994).

If your school does not have access, you will need an Internet Service Provider (ISP). ISP's equip you with a gateway to the Internet by giving you the access, software you need to connect, and some technical help. Most ISPs also include at least one e-mail account, web page services, and additional services to companies and organizations that conduct business on the Internet. You may choose from local or national ISPs. To identify ISPs and online service providers in your area, look under "Internet products and services" or a similar topic in your local yellow pages, or search for them online through The List (http://thelist.internet.com/). Then call their customer service number and interview the representative about various aspects of their service. In addition, instead of relying on published statistics, advertised claims, or the testimony of a customer service representative for this information, you might also want to take advantage of a 30 day free trial. If the ISP does not offer a free trial period, it wouldn't hurt to ask for one. During your trial, pay attention to the nature of your service, especially connection speeds at different times of the day before making your decision. Be aware, however, that some ISP's will have you provide your credit card number before issuing your free trial and automatically begin to charge your account after the 30 days expire unless you take it upon yourself to cancel your subscription in writing. Smart ISP consumers pay special attention to features such as:

1. **Dialing in.** Does the ISP or online service provider offer service through a telephone number in your area? Does it offer a local telephone number or toll-free number in areas in which you expect to travel?

2. **Access.** How often will you actually get through, rather than get a busy signal, when you dial in?

3. **Transmission rates.** To appropriately transfer information and files over the Net, the transmission rate with which you connect must match the rate of the ISP. Therefore, even if you have a top-of-the-line 56K modem, if your ISP's fastest connection is 28.8K, your connection will typically drop down to 28.8K. It is important, then, to make certain that the ISP you choose offers a connection rate that can accommodate the fastest possible connection for which your computer is capable.

4. **Technical support and customer service.** Are there knowledgeable, friendly technical support and customer service people available whenever you need them? Is the telephone call toll-free? How long will you have to wait on hold? Can you get technical support and customer service online? Is technical support included in the package or is it extra? If technical support is extra, what is the fee schedule for using the service?

5. **E-mail.** How many e-mail accounts does the ISP provide, and can you access your account through another ISP if you're outside a local ISP's area? Is their server POP3 compatible which allows for collecting your mail through various clients such as Eudora, Outlook, Pegasus, Lotus, and Netscape.

6. **Web pages.** Can you post a Web site on the ISP's server? How much space can you get for your page and at what cost? Will you be charged based on the amount of traffic your page gets? Will the server support special functions of your page such as CGI scripting (necessary if your page includes a form or is password protected) or Microsoft Frontpage extensions? Will the ISP provide webauthoring services and/or support and is this included in the monthly charges? Will the ISP help you establish your domain name? Does the ISP provide backup services in the event that their system crashes or will backing up your webpage be your responsibility?

7. **Performance.** How quickly does the service deliver your e-mail? (The industry average time is within 5 minutes 95 percent of the time.) How long does it take for Web pages to download? How often does the service experience failures and for how long?

8. **Upgrades.** What is currently the fastest connection you can make and what are the company's plans for upgrading (i.e., does the ISP plan to upgrade, for instance, to ISDN or cable modem connections)?

9. **Training.** An ISP can not only connect you to the Internet, but might also provide online technical support. For example, an ISP might maintain a webpage that offers special features and content such as Internet handbooks, manuals, useful links, and tips for enjoyable surfing.

10. **Confidentiality.** Does the ISP keep your personal profile information private or will it sell your information to interested companies? Will the company fulfill requests to identify you to others?

11. **Safety.** Does the ISP provide controls for accessing adult materials over the Net (in case you share your account with others, especially students)?

12. **Price.** Many services offer different monthly subscriptions, including unlimited access for a flat monthly fee and limited hours for a flat monthly fee with additional hours, as needed, for an extra charge. When you compare prices, consider the factors above as well as the special features and content that the online service providers offer. Thanks to some hefty ISP competition, you can now purchase unlimited access to the Net for no more than $20 per month and sometimes for as much as $14. Some companies with which you already conduct business such as telephone and newspaper may have penetrated the ISP market and will offer substantial discounts to their customers. Some ISPs also charge a set-up fee of $20-$30 dollars which should also be considered when deciding on which company that you will contract. Like anything else, this might be negotiable.

No-cost ISP

Providing Internet Service to consumers has become relatively inexpensive, especially as compared to the cost of collecting marketing and demographic data. As a result, many companies now offer free internet access at no cost in exchange for completing a survey about yourself and your interests. The other reason for providing free access is that it generates much greater traffic to the company's website which means that the company can then make a bigger profits from advertisement. When you dial in to a free ISP you will immediately notice

---

an unremovable menu bar at the top of your computer which points you to the provider's advertiser sites. So what seems to be free access is really paid access except that other companies foot the bill instead of you. The advantage of signing up for free internet service obviously includes the lack of cost although can also include extra flexibility or freedom. For instance, for travelers, your no-cost ISP may include local dial in numbers in the areas in which you most journey so that you may access the web and email from outside your locale. Even for those that already have free Internet access as a benefit of employment, you may want to consider signing up for a no-cost ISP to do non-work related Internet activities. Five well known sites which offer free internet access include www.netzero.com, http://www.yahoo.com http://www.freeinternet.com,www.freeinternet.com, www.bluelight.com, www.av.com, and www.excite.com. To select the ISP best for you, pay attention to the features mentioned above for fee based ISP's.

Freenets

A freenet is a network of computers with Internet access which is created for the purpose of allowing Net access to a certain community. This is made possible by the creation of a not-for-profit organization that receives funding, mostly through corporate and institutional donations, for hardware and software. For instance, the Alachua Freenet (AFN) is a community supported and sponsored system in Gainesville, FL which gives access to the Internet and community resources to over 10,000 people. Alachua Freenet accounts are free for those living within the boundaries of the state of Florida in the USA. Those living outside of Florida are required to pay a $20 per year access fee to use an AFN account. The organization does not provide any local dial-up access for people outside of the Gainesville, FL calling area. If you live outside of that calling area and dial-up the Alachua Freenet computer system, your phone company will charge you accordingly. A listing of international free and community networks is available at http://www.lights.com/freenet/.

The Software

The first piece of software that you need to access the net is one that establishes the connection with your ISP. Such software is usually a part of your operating system and only needs to be initially configured with appropriate information such as phone numbers, your modem type, and the kind of account you have (e.g., PPP, TCP/IP, Network). Most ISPs will include tailored software when you subscribe which is already configured and may only require minimal customization. Schools and businesses usually connect their computers to the Internet using an Ethernet connection which is always "on." Ethernet connections are hardline connections, similar to your cable television connection, and only require that you launch your browser for instant Net access (similar to simply turning on your television to begin viewing the provided channels).

One your connection is established, you will require a second piece of software to appropriately view the material you access from the Net called a browser. A browser interprets the rich content which you download, usually written in a code called hypertext markup language (HTML), and translates it into what you see on the screen. Moreover, a browser contains the basic software you need to download files, complete and transmit forms, view streaming audio and video, access bulletin boards, and send/receive messages across the Net.

The two most popular browsers, both free to anyone that will have them, are Microsoft's Internet Explorer (IE) and Netscape's Navigator (Netscape). All new computers will usually come with one or the other, and sometimes both, already installed on the hard drive. Many software packages also provide one or the other browser which can be easily installed on your computer. If all else fails, you can purchase either IE or Netscape at your local computer software retailer. Once you have access with one, you can go to the other's site and download it at your convenience.

Russell A. Sabella, Ph.D.

A Note About Browsers

Early in the development of web browsing, users could choose from various browsers including Cello, Mosaic, Navigator and others. Today, however, IE and Netscape are basically the only two viable contenders. The battle between the two is fervent, reminiscent of the battle between VHS and Beta video formats. The browser, or company that is, that endures will set the standards for how users browse the web, how developers will create content for it, and which programming languages will be used to build Internet applications. One benefit of the browser wars is that consumers are witnessing phenomenal advancements in both programs to make browsing a more heightened and productive endeavor.

So, which browser is better? Which browser should I use? Well, the answer to the first question is that neither browser has proven itself more useful or outperforms the other. Right now, the choice is a matter of preference, style, and industrial loyalty. Both browsers do the job, and do the job well. Choosing one over the other may be analogous to choosing a car in the same class, perhaps a Sedan, with a console that looks and feels different to the touch. Also, like some who buy only certain brands of automobile, some users whom have had good experiences with one or the other may desire to remain loyal to the company's product.

You can't go wrong with either Internet Explorer or Navigator. Not too long ago, websites had a message planted somewhere that informed users which browser a user should be using to best view the site. That was true a couple of years ago, but not today. Both browsers are capable of displaying all the standard HTML tags and will display a site's information on your screen regardless of which browser you are using. At worst, you will notice some minor nuances between the two because each browser formats the information slightly differently. When it comes to some of the fancier sites that show off the latest technology using HTML extensions developed by one company, but not supported by the other's browser, the HTML tags will be ignored. The text will still be displayed, but it will not be formatted as originally intended. For instance, when Navigator encounters one Microsoft extension called a marquee (fancy text that scrolls across the screen), it displays it as centered text, whereas IE users view it in all its glory.

With today's humongous hard drives, it may be typical for a user to have both IE and Netscape on their computers. You might download both IE (www.microsoft.com) and Navigator (www.netscape.com) and take each browser for a test drive. Call up your favorite site and view it with one browser. Then view the same site with the other browser. Was the data displayed differently? How do you like the toolbar? What options do you get when you right click the mouse? Can you customize the interface? Some people care a lot about these features. Others couldn't care less. It's up to you to decide which browser is right for you. You may take some comfort in knowing that, unlike purchasing a car, "trading in" one browser for the other costs nothing. And, because both browsers operate essentially the same, you can easily switch without having to overcome any learning curve. The examples in this text will rely heavily on IE although are easily applied to Netscape. Only the location of some buttons and some of their names change. For a few procedures that are conducted significantly differently, I provide examples using each browser.

Plug-Ins

Plug-ins are utilities which can be downloaded from a company's site and installed to work seamlessly with your browser. They are designed to further the usefulness of the Net and take advantage of some advanced features. Microsoft has made it very simple to install IE plug-ins. Simply access the site (www.microsoft.com), follow the links which lead to a site designed for product updates (this changes now and then or else I would just let you know where it is), and the site will then interface with your computer to determine which version of IE you currently use and which plug-ins are installed. Then, the site will report the results and allow you to choose available plug-ins or updates that you don't have. After checking the desired downloads, Microsoft will then automatically download and install them to your computer.

The following plug-ins and a short description of each are available at the site:

- *NetShow Server* allows you to experience live and recorded broadcasts such as news (e.g. CNN, FOX News, NBC Today to name a very few), concerts, music samples, multimedia reports, and anything else that is video/audio taped, digitized, and saved in a special streaming format. One powerful feature of streaming technology is that it allows you to view information as it arrives instead of having to wait for the entire file to download. Future improvement in this technology focus on making streaming video look more like television instead of a transmission from today's space shuttle while in orbit.

- *NetMeeting Conferencing* software allows users with a multimedia computer to talk to others from anywhere in the world. If you also have a Windows-compatible video capture card and/or camera, you can also exchange photos, draw diagrams on an electronic whiteboard, communicate with text-based chat, transfer files, and share computer applications.

- *ActiveX Controls* allows web authors to develop innovative, highly interactive Web sites. ActiveX Controls are the software components that run behind the scenes in Internet Explorer so that these sites come alive for you.

- The *Chat* plug-in allows users to have virtual discussions in real time with one or more people. Messages can be seen as simple text or via a more graphical user interface (GUI) such as in a comic strip environment. With Chat, you can send and receive to a group of others just about anything and including sounds, files, Web page addresses, e-mail addresses, Web pages, and newsgroups. Conversations can be public or sent in a "whisper" mode, in private, to an individual in the chat group.

- *ActiveMovie* allows you to experience relatively high quality video and audio, while minimizing file size and download time as compared to other video and audio formats. By using what is called "progressive downloading," Similar to NetShow Server, ActiveMovie lets you start playing an audio or video clip while it's still downloading.

- *Active Channel* webcasts enables rich information to be regularly sent to your computer just like a "ticker" at the bottom of a television newscast such as CNN. Content can be customized to fit your personal preferences and interests—everything from Disney entertainment to stock quotes.

- The *Subscriptions* feature is similar to a pager or notification service. It delivers pre-chosen information to your desktop, when and how you want it. To subscribe to a Web site, select the site and specify when you want the information updated and how you want to be notified, such as through an e-mail message. Internet Explorer does the rest.

Russell A. Sabella, Ph.D.

- IE 5.0 supports the *Dynamic HTML* programming language, which makes enticing, unique, fun, and fast-downloading Web pages possible. The pages download quickly because they are created using lightweight HTML instead of heavy-duty graphics. Round trips to the server are minimized, which means faster browser performance on your desktop computer.

- *Shockwave* technology, from Macromedia, is one technology that allows users to deliver and experience interactive multimedia, graphics, and streaming audio on the World Wide Web. Shockwave elements are created and played back with Shockwave Director, Shockwave Flash, Shockwave Authorware, and their players, which are plug-ins for Web browsers including Microsoft Internet Explorer browser version 5.0. Internet Explorer 5.0 includes the Shockwave Director and Flash players. For a demonstration of a "shocked" website, go to www.eye4u.com.

- Like NetShow, *RealPlayer,* co-developed by RealNetworks and Macromedia, is a client that allows you to listen to RealAudio clips, watch RealVideo clips, and view RealFlash animations live and on demand in real time. (They start playing right away rather than making you wait until the entire file downloads.

- The *Microsoft Liquid Motion Web* multimedia and animation tool makes it easy for novices and experts alike to create and publish animation on the World Wide Web. You don't need to know any programming to create Liquid Motion animations. The program gives you basic building blocks that you can use to create simple, albeit advanced, animations depending on your experience level. Liquid Motion works on any browser that supports Java on any platform.

- *QuickTime,* from Apple Computer, Inc., is one technology that makes it possible for World Wide Web sites to feature audio and video clips. It allows site builders to author digital audio and video files for their site, and it allows users to get the intended multimedia experience. With QuickTime 3 and other streaming media tools, you can listen to and watch clips as soon as they start to download from a site, rather than having to wait until download is complete. QuickTime 3 can play more than 30 video and audio file formats. QuickTime runs on the Microsoft Windows 95, Microsoft Windows NT, and Macintosh operating systems.

- *Infoseek Express* is a free desktop search product which brings multiple search and information sources together in one place. With Express you can find, explore, and do anything on the Internet faster and easier than before. Express is different from other search engines because it runs within your Web browser, searches multiple search engines simultaneously, and provides an easier to use, faster interface. In addition, Express has an open architecture that allows for mass distribution, easy updates, and extensive personal customization (download from http://express.infoseek.com/subdocuments/expressdetails.html).

To read more in detail about these software, and to learn about links for each component, visit Microsoft's website at www.microsoft.com. If you already have IE 5.0, simply click on the [Help] button and choose from the menu.

An Overview of the IE Toolbar

The Internet Explorer toolbar consists of buttons that are shortcuts for menu commands. They make browsing faster and easier. Here's a brief description of what each of these buttons do (for extra help, visit Microsoft's Online Help feature at http://support.microsoft.com/support/c.asp?PR=IE&FR=0)

 Back. Lets you return to pages you've viewed, beginning with the most recent.

Forward. Lets you move forward through pages you've viewed after using the Back button.

Stop. Halts the process of downloading a Web page. Click this if you want to stop downloading a page for any reason such as if you're having trouble downloading a site, for example. Or, if the site is taking unusually long to download and you don't want to wait, you may want to press Stop and try again later

 Refresh. Remember that when you access a site, you are actually requesting to download the information to your computer. When you return to that site, your browser, depending on how it is set up, will first check to see whether the site content resides on your computer. If it does, you will view the content on your computer which may happen to be outdated, even in a matter of days or minutes. The advantage of this set-up is that it is much quicker to access content from your computer than from a remote Internet site. The disadvantage of course is that you do not have any up-to-the-minute updates or changes to the site. To be certain that you are viewing the latest, click on [Refresh] which will update any Web page stored on your computer with the latest content. You

can configure your browser to update or [Refresh] every time you visit a site even if you accessed it seconds ago. Most sites are not updated that quickly unless you are requesting stock market data. Therefore, it is probably best to only [Refresh] manually when needed.

 Home. Your homepage is the page you will view when initially launching your browser or can simply be a blank page. You will probably want to set up your home page as one that you most frequently visit such as a search engine or your school's website. No matter where you are on the Net, you can quickly return to your homepage by pressing this button (If you can't see the [Home] button, click the [View] menu, point to [Toolbar], and then click [Standard] buttons). To set up your home page, go to the page you want to appear when you first start Internet Explorer. On the [View] menu, click [Internet Options] and then click the [General] tab. In the [Home page] area, click [Use Current]. To restore your original home page, click [Use Default]. Technically, you really have two [Home] buttons in either IE or Netscape. Both programs have made their logos, located in the right corner, a pre-configured button that takes you to the company's homepage. This is especially convenient for obtaining new and updated software, help, or other free resources that add to your Internet experience.

 Search. This button displays a choice of popular Internet search engines in the left pane. Your search results appear in the left pane, too. When you click a link, the page appears in the right pane, so you don't lose sight of your search results.

Favorites. This button displays a list of the sites (and, with Internet Explorer 5.0, the folders, files, and servers) that you've saved as Favorites. Click on any item in the list to jump to it. You can add to your list of favorite sites by clicking on this button and then choosing [Add to Favorites]. The advantage of including a site in your Favorites list is that you

Russell A. Sabella, Ph.D.

will thereafter never have to remember the site's address, only choose the site's title from your list of favorites. This is similar to the speed dial feature on your telephone. Once you enter Aunt Cathy's long phone number in once and name the button that dials the number, future calls to her only requires the press of a button. You can also organize your favorites under different folders. Before adding a favorite, choose [Create in >>] from the menu and click on the folder under which the site should be stored. If there isn't an appropriate folder available, you can first create one by choosing [New Folder].

Subscriptions. You can have IE automatically check your favorite Web sites for new content, according to the schedule you specify. Then you can choose to either be notified that there is new content available or have the updated content automatically downloaded to your hard disk (for example, at night or when your computer is idle) so you can view the pages at your convenience. This is known as "subscribing" to a Web site. Subscribing to a site does not require paying fees to the site. You can schedule daily, weekly, or monthly updates for all of the Web sites you subscribe to or for individual sites. After you've set up your subscriptions, you can view your favorite Web sites offline at your leisure. Another form of subscribing is "channels." Channels are Web sites that are automatically updated on your computer according to a schedule specified by the content provider. Channels can be displayed in the browser like other Web pages, as a full-screen window, or on your desktop. Some channels are also designed to be used as a screen saver. To subscribe to a Web site, open the Web page you want to subscribe to. On the [Favorites] menu, click [Add to Favorites]. Click [Partial subscription: tell me when updates occur] or [Full subscription: download for offline reading]. If you want to specify your schedule, delivery, and notification options, click [Customize] to use the Web Site Subscription wizard. Remember, subscribing to a Web site enables you to automatically get updated information from the site on a scheduled basis, without having to visit the site and refresh the content manually at no cost (Help, 1998).

 Print. Prints the page you're viewing which also includes page numbers and the site's address. IE will also give you the option to print at the end of the document a table summary of all the links included on the page. And, you can even fully print all the documents that are linked to the original document (although be careful with this feature unless you plan to plant several trees in your spare time).

 Font. This button lets you display text in a larger or smaller font. This feature, I find, comes in handy when a website's content doesn't quite fit on the screen. I can reduce the font size a bit to contain the entire width of the page and save time by not having to scroll back and forth. Also, I might reduce the font to save paper before printing a webpage.

 Mail. Connects you to Microsoft Outlook Express messaging and collaboration client so you can read e-mail and newsgroup messages. Or, if you desire, IE will launch your default mail program such as Qualcomm's Eudora Lite or Pro. After this option is selected, you can choose to send the a website's address, its entire contents, or read your messages.

 Edit. Opens a file in the Microsoft Word processor that contains the HTML code for the page you're viewing so you can see and even edit it. Or, if your computer contains a web authoring program such as Microsoft's FrontPage or Adobe's Pagemill, IE will launch this program instead.

 History. By pressing this button, you can view the home pages of the sites you have previously visited. The number of sites logged into your History folder is determined by the number of days you indicate to include in your historical record of sites traveled. To specify how many pages are saved in the History list, click on [View] in the browser, click [Internet Options], click the [General] tab. Then in the [History] area, change the number of days that Internet Explorer keeps track of your pages. To empty the History folder, click [Clear

History]. This will free up disk space on your computer and prevent others from knowing where you have been.

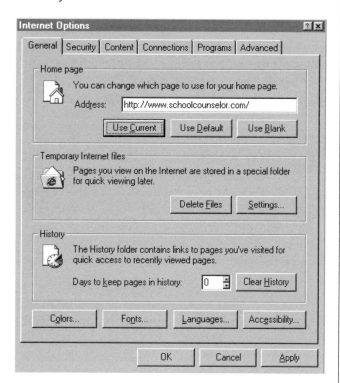

Full Screen. Toggles between displaying your web page on a full screen with a limited view of buttons or a more limited view of the webpage with a larger display of buttons.

The Address Bar. This is the white area that displays the current URL or web address. To change the address and go to another page, click inside the [Address] bar until the currently displayed address is highlighted. Then, start typing the address you want to go to. If you've visited the Web site before, the AutoComplete feature suggests a match as you type. The suggested match is highlighted in the [Address] bar. After you finish typing the Web address, or when AutoComplete finds a match, press [ENTER] on your keyboard. To view other matches, press the [DOWN ARROW] key.

For more detailed help with IE, you may also check out http://www.cnet.com/Content/Features/Howto/IE4tips/ss04.html

CHAPTER THREE

Go! ... Seeking Web Nuggets

The number of pages available on the Web is estimated to be between 30 and 80 million. So, how then, might school counselors find sites which are relevant and useful for a specific topic in a reasonable amount of time? There are typically three ways to find useful information on the Web, each having advantages and disadvantages. Counselors can (1) know the address for a Web page location, (2) navigate the Web using related hypertext links, or (3) conduct a more systematic electronic search using search engines.

Know the Web Location

Each site on the Web has it's own unique, case sensitive, electronic address called a universal resource locator (URL) that points a computer to the Web page's location. Users who discover a useful site might communicate to others, probably via electronic mail, the page's URL. A URL, usually consists of three parts: protocol, server (or domain), and file name. Sometimes, however, there's no path or file name. Here's an example of the anatomy of the "What's New" section of the American School Counselor Association's website: http://www.schoolcounselor.org/newsfor.htm

http is the protocol.

www.schoolcounselor.org is the server or domain.

whatsnew.html is the file name

Domains divide World Wide Web sites into categories based on the nature of their owner, and they form part of a site's address, or uniform resource locator (URL). Common top-level domains are:

.com	commercial enterprises.
.org	nonprofit organizations.
.net	networks.
.edu	educational institutions.
.gov	government organizations.
.mil	military services.
.int	organizations established by international treaty

Additional three-letter and four-letter top-level domains have been proposed, and some are likely to be implemented. Each country linked to the Web has a two-letter top-level domain.

Once a URL is known, a user can simply type it into his or her Web browser and go directly to the intended site. For Netscape users, enter it directly into the [Location] or [Go] box located just under the toolbar. Typically, you don't even need to enter the full URL to go to a site. For example, the full URL for the Barnes and Noble online bookstore is http://www.barnesandnoble.com. However, you can also get there simply by typing barnesandnoble. Navigator assumes the http://www. prefix and the .com suffix. This procedure is different for IE. Enter the full URL into the [Address] box to jump directly to that site. IE assumes just the http:// part of the URL, so to go to the Barnes and Noble site, you could enter just www.barnesandnoble.com. If you want to type in just barnesandnoble, you need to hold the CTRL key down before pressing ENTER key on your keyboard. Once at the site, a counselor can then place an electronic "bookmark" or favorite that will allow him or her to point and click on the site's title without ever again having to recall the URL. This form of finding information on the Web is quickest and most desirable.

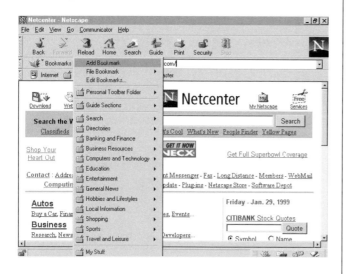

Bookmarking in Netscape

When you are at a site you would like to bookmark, go to the [Bookmarks] menu and select the [Add Bookmark] option. Click on the [Bookmarks] menu again, and you will notice the title of the current page has been added to the bottom of the menu. When you are at another site and want to jump back to the bookmarked

page, simply select it from the [Bookmarks] menu. If you spend much time browsing the Web, you will quickly accumulate a long list of bookmarks. You will probably want to organize them in some manner to make returning to those sites easier. From the [Bookmarks] menu, select the [Go to Bookmarks] menu. All your bookmarks will be displayed. One method of organization is to group sites by topic, like Guidance Departments, Grants, Fun Stuff, or Career Development. Click on the top item in the list (it will say something like Jane Counselor's Bookmarks), then, from the [Item] menu, select [Insert Folder]. In the [Name] box, enter a topic name for this new folder. Then click and drag your bookmarks into this folder. Repeat for all topics and bookmarks. If the names for your bookmarks aren't very clear, you can easily change them. Select a bookmark, then choose [Properties] from the [Item] menu. Here you can enter a new name for the bookmark. When you are finished organizing, close this window to return to your browser, and select the [Book-marks] menu again. You should see the topic names with arrows next to them. Hold the cursor over one topic, and a pop-up list will appear showing all the bookmarks you have assigned to that topic.

Add a Favorite in Internet Explorer

Favorites can be added in one of two ways: by right clicking anywhere on the site (except a link) and selecting [Add to Favorites] or by selecting [Add to Favorites] from the [Favorites] menu. By default, the name assigned to the favorite is the title of the Web page, but you can change it to something more easily remem-bered. The "favorite" will automatically be added to the [Favorites] menu, or you can place it in a specific folder. To select a folder, click the [Create In] button and select one of the available folders, or to create a new folder, click [New

Folder]. To return to a favorite, simply open the Favorites menu and select it.

Some organizations have dedicated time and work towards compiling short descriptions of Web pages, with accompanying URLs, for a specific topic. Users can send an electronic message to the organization requesting to receive these compilations (this is known as subscribing to a listserv). For instance, the Scout Report (http://scout.cs.wisc.edu/scout/report/) is a weekly publication of the InterNIC Net Scout project at the University of Wisconsin-Madison. It is provided as a fast, convenient way to stay informed about valuable resources on the Internet. Its purpose is to combine in one place new and newly discovered Internet resources and network tools, especially those of interest to researchers and educators. Hundreds, or perhaps thousands of such lists exist on the Internet for a sundry of topics. To learn about such specialized lists, counselors can conduct an electronic search of available lists at http://www.liszt.com.

Although this method for learning about available information does not require much time or work, it is sometimes not very practical. Waiting for others to present URLs forces a counselor to wait until those are available which may not be very timely. Also, this method leaves to others' judgement the value and usefulness of the information. Counselors need to supplement this information with more immediate and personalized Web sources.

Navigate the Web

A second method for finding information is to rely on the hypertext feature of the Web and "jump" from one page to another using related links. This is affectionately known as "surfing the Web." You can tell whether an item on a page is a link by moving the mouse pointer over the item. If the pointer changes to a hand, the item is a link. A link can be a picture, a three-dimensional image, or colored text (usually blue and underlined). Click any link on a Web page to go to another page within that site or another site. As you surf the Web, you might bookmark and essentially create your own compilation of valuable Web sites. The advantage of surfing the Web is that it gives the user more control over what sites are deemed valuable. The disadvantage is that such a search is less than systematic and can be very time consuming and costly in the form of on-line charges.

At this point you might ask, "What would be a good starting point for my web travels?" An increasing number of universities, libraries, companies, organizations, and even volunteers are creating directories to catalog portions of the Internet. These directories are organized by subject and consist of links to Internet resources relating to these subjects. The major subject directories available on the Web tend to have overlapping but different databases. Most directories provide a search capability that allows you  to query the database on your topic of interest. Subject directories differ significantly in selectivity. For example, the famous Yahoo! (www.yahoo.com) site does not consider content when adding Web pages to its database. In contrast, the Argus Clearinghouse (http://www.clearinghouse.net) collects and rates subject guides often compiled by experts. Consider the policies of any directory that you visit. One challenge to this is the fact that not all directory services are willing to disclose either their policies or the names and qualifications of site reviewers. A number of subject directories consist of links accompanied by annotations that describe or evaluate site content (Cohen, 1998). Some directories have evolved into what is now known as web portals. A web portal is a site or service that offers a broad array of resources and services, such as e-mail, forums, search engines, and on-line shopping malls. The first Web portals were online services, such as America Online, that provided access to the Web, but by now most of the traditional search engines have transformed themselves into Web portals to attract and keep a larger audience (for a cogent article about the future of web portals, see http://www.pcworld.com/current_issue/article/0,1212,7202+12+0,00.html).

As you continue to surf, you may want to return to a previously visited site. Of course, there are several ways to do this. You can try any one of the following:

1. To return to the last page you viewed, you can click the [Back] button on the toolbar, or press the BACKSPACE key on your keyboard.

2. To see a list of the last few pages you visited, click the small down arrow beside the [Back] or [Forward] button. Then click the page you want.

3. If you want to view one of the last five pages you visited in this session, click the [File] menu, and then on the list, click the page that you want to go to. This list is started fresh every time you start Internet Explorer.

4. IE offers a History Folder with shortcuts to all sites visited during the last 20 days (you can change this value by selecting [Options] from the [View] menu, clicking the [Navigation] tab, and setting the number of days of retained history). Select [Open History Folder] from the [Go] menu to jump to any of the sites recently visited.

Use a Search Engine

One tool that has evolved for conducting research over the Web is the search engine (McMurdo, 1995; Sabella, 1998; Symons, 1996). A search engine is a computer program that searches documents for specified keywords and returns a list of the documents, with accompanying URLs, where the keywords were found. Realize, however, that no one search engine can index every web page available. So, if a specific site is not included in the results of a search, it does not necessarily mean that the page does not exist—only that the search engine has not included it in its index. Also, just because a site is indexed, does not necessarily mean that the site is still active. The Web is quite a dynamic place with sites being introduced and deleted all the time. It is wise, then, that serious web researchers conduct searches with more than one search engine. Better yet, you might conduct a metasearch with an appropriate search engine (e.g., http://www.dogpile.com or http://www.albany.net/allinone/), one that enters your search terms in more than one engine and presents the results from each of the various engines it queries.

How do these search engines work? According to Sullivan (1998), search engines have three major elements. First is the spider, also called the crawler. The spider visits a web page, reads it, and then follows links to other pages within the site. This is what it means when someone refers to a site being "spidered" or "crawled." The spider returns to the site on a regular basis, such as every month or two, to look for changes. Everything the spider finds goes into the second part of a search engine, the index. The index,

Russell A. Sabella, Ph.D.

sometimes called the catalog, is like a giant book containing a copy of every web page that the spider finds. If a web page changes, then this book is updated with new information. Sometimes it can take a while for new pages or changes that the spider finds to be added to the index. Thus, a web page may have been "spidered" but not yet "indexed." Until it is indexed, It Is not available to those searching with the search engine. Search engine software is the third part of a search engine. This is the program that sifts through the millions of pages recorded in the index to find matches to a search and rank them in order of predetermined criteria.

Which of the many search engines really matter? Sullivan (1998) writes, "...it's the search engines that are well-known and well-used. This is true whether you are a webmaster or a researcher. A well-known, commercially-backed search engine generally means more dependable results. These search engines are more likely to be well-maintained and upgraded when necessary, to keep pace with the growing web." Check out the search engine section of Chapter 7 for a list of notable search engines to use.

Search Engine Results

If you were to receive a list of results including 200 websites or more, how would you know the best way to attack it? Fortunately, search engines usually report search results in ranked and arranged according specific criteria. My experience is that the first 30-50% of a search result list is applicable and useful. After that, the results seem to be repetitive or irrelevant. Following are the criteria that are typically used to rank and arrange search results:

Location. Word matches found in certain key document fields of a webpage (e.g., <title>, <header>, and <meta> tags for descriptions and keywords; headings tags;) and matches found on words located early on in the document.

Frequency. In general, the more frequently a search term is found in a web document, the higher its relevancy ranking. The practice of

"spamming" or gratuitously duplicating certain keywords in web documents is sometimes used by web authors to try to manipulate this criterion. Some search engines have started applying a "spam penalty"—which decreases a document's ranking—to web documents that use this tactic.

Proximity. In general, the closer together your search terms are in a web document, the higher the relevancy ranking.

Link frequency. Some search engines add up the number of links that have been made to a particular web page and use that as a measure of its "popularity". The more links to a web document made by other web pages, the higher the relevancy ranking for that web document.

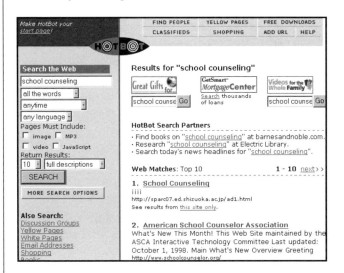

Conducting Searches

I consider conducting effective searches similar to playing golf: part skill and part luck. The integrity of your results will depend on the search engine you use and the skill with which you perform your search. The Internet is a vast computer database. As such, its contents must be searched according to the rules of computer database searching. Much database searching is based on the principles of Boolean logic. Boolean logic refers to the logical relationship among search terms, and is named for the British mathematician George Boole (Cohen, 1998).

In general, the key Boolean operators are AND, NOT, OR and NEAR although can vary slightly depending on which search engine one uses. For instance, a search for counseling jobs involving schools and families, but not financial counseling jobs, might look like this:

counseling NEAR jobs AND (school or family) NOT financial

The keyword NEAR instructs the search engine to return sites where the word "jobs" is found within ten words of counseling. The use of parentheses tells the computer to find sites with either school or family in them. The operator NOT excludes sites which discuss financial counseling. Another example would be a search about peer pressure which should be entered as a phrase in quotes ("peer pressure") or with the Boolean operator AND (peer AND pressure) so that you do not retrieve every registered page with either the word peer or pressure. Although not an operator, you can sometimes use the asterisk (*) as a wildcard to take the place of one or more characters so that a search for couns* should return sites on both counseling and counselor. Notice that Boolean operators must be in all caps and they must be separated on either side by a space. Also, the operators I describe are somewhat standard although may vary slightly. So, you should always consult the search engine site section on advanced searching.

One particular search engine, HotBot (www.hotbot.com), is consistently popular because it can easily restrict one's search to make it highly specific. For instance, HotBot contains a simple form that you plainly complete which allows you to limit your search to the following classifications:

1. search term(s)

2. specific languages

3. pages containing or not containing any words specified

4. pages published within a specified period of time

5. specified media types or technologies such as photos, sound, films, PDF files, and more.

6. pages in specific domains (wired.com, doj.gov), top-level domains (.edu, .com), and/or specific continents or countries

7. pages within only certain web sites

8. grammatic variations of your search term (e.g., searches for "thought" will also find "think" and "thinking")

9. the number of results to be displayed and the length of each description

Before conducting any serious searches of web content, you might want to consider the following guidelines:

1. Pick one acclaimed search engine and read the directions provided for you at the site. Become expert for using the site by studying how the search engine works and practicing with small variations of a search term.

2. Supplement your search by using other search engines. No search engine indexes all web sites and web pages. So if your primary search doesn't produce the results you wanted, try searching with at least one other search engine.

3. If you have a multi-term search, be sure to determine which type of Boolean logic you should use.

4. Include alternate variations of your search terms and connect these terms with the OR operator.

5. Make certain that your spelling is correct because errors of one letter, space, or wrong punctuation mark may not be forgiven by a search engine.

6. Realize that most search engines are case sensitive. If your results are not satisfactory, repeat the search using alternative terms or perhaps a different search engine.

7. If you have too many results, or results that are not relevant: Increase the number of key words that are specific to your topic linked by the AND operator. If available, you can conduct a search within a given set of results. Also, use the Boolean operator NOT to eliminate results that might show up. For instance, when conducting a broad search

Russell A. Sabella, Ph.D.

using the term counselor, you might key in *counselor NOT camp*.

8. If you have too few results: reduce the number of keywords you used to broaden your subject. Add alternate terms or spellings for individual concepts and connect with the Boolean operator OR.

9. You may want to try Web sites which allow you to search multiple search engines simultaneously (metasearch engines) such as www.dogpile.com.

10. If you are having problems connecting to a site with a long URL, try deleting the information after the last slash mark. Repeat this process until you find a valid site (possibly the site's home page). From there you can navigate the site via its on-page links.

11. If you are a power user of WWW resources, you might invest in a commercial program that conducts a metasearch of most known search engines and returns a set of processed results. Before displaying results, the typical Web search software will eliminate duplicates, prioritize by the frequency of your search terms at the site, highlight in a different color your search term(s) in the document, and even help you create your terms. These programs further assist by allowing you to save your results in your own database, print, or publish them to your website. You can learn about such software from various software review sites such as www.pccomputing.com, www.familypc.com, or www.zdnet.com. On a more frugal note, you might also check out the hottest shareware program in this area at www.shareware.com or www.hotfiles.com. Two of my favorites, both free, are called WebFerret and Copernic.

For further reading about conducting effective searches, consult one or more of the following websites:

1. The Webmaster's Guide to Search Engines and Directories by Danny Sullivan. http://calafia.com/

2. Beyond Surfing: Tools and Techniques for Searching the Web: by Kathleen Webster and Kathryn Paul. http://magi.com/mmelick/it96jan.htm

3. Understanding and Comparing Web Search Tools: http://www.hamline.edu/library/bush/handouts/comparisons.html

4. Search Engine Watch: http://www.searchenginewatch.com/

Navigational Errors

Now and then, you will unsuccessfully try to access a site and receive an error message. This happens most often due to human error, especially incorrectly typing in a URL. The Net can be cruel when it comes to mistyped URL's and will issue you an error message even when you are off by a punctuation mark or letter. The following list of error messages and suggestions for pursuing should help:

400—Bad Request

This error message indicates that the server cannot identify the URL or address you are requesting. The error is often the result of incorrect URL syntax. Check for incorrect spelling, punctuation, and the presence of spaces. Try retyping the URL while experimenting with different likely variations.

401—Unauthorized

As you may have guessed, this error occurs when the site you requested to access is protected and the server did not receive the correct password or other identification necessary for access. Retype your user identification and/or password making sure that it is correct in spelling and syntax, especially since some servers are sensitive to case sensitive passwords. Also know that you may receive this error from servers that deny access from certain domain types. For example, some universities pay for and allow access to special databases for conducting research among students and faculty. Access to such databases are granted only from connections from the university's computers or server domain. If you believe you should have access to the site, try sending an e-mail to whomever maintains the Web site. His or her e-mail address is often on the main page of the Web site, or you can try sending e-mail to the "Webmaster" of the site. If the Web address looks like http://www.xyz.com/, then the Webmaster's address will probably be "webmaster@xyz.com."

403—Forbidden or Connection Refused by Host

Quite similar to the 401 error, the 403 error message usually occurs when a server denies access because of your domain, some sort of security restrictions, or because you must first register for the site. Sometimes, this error message is generated by Web servers when you try to access a file that has not been correctly configured by whomever maintains it. (The file needs to be set with "read permissions" for all users.) In other words, you can't view the page because whomever maintains the site set it up incorrectly. The latter occurrence is most often the cause when you have had consistent access which is suddenly refused. In all likelihood, the webauthor updated the site and mistakenly configured the access settings.

404—Not Found or File Not Found

A 404 error means that there was no web page with the name you specified for the web site. This could happen for a variety of reasons. Make certain that the web address (URL) you entered exactly matches the address you intended to use. Check that the capitalization is the same, that all words are correctly spelled, and that all punctuation are correctly placed (especially using the forward slash "/" and not the backward slash "\"). Remember that there are no spaces allowed in web addresses. This error may also be the result of a renamed, moved, or deleted website. The person maintaining the Web page may no longer have an account at the location in question. Also, you may not be logged on so make sure that you are properly connected. The good news about a 404 error is that it is telling you that there exists a Web site at the address, just not the particular page you were looking for. You might try backtracking by deleting the portion of the URL that follows the last slash.

500—Server Error

Web pages are stored on servers, machines that contain files and allow other servers (computers) to download files from them. If the server has been incorrectly set up or is experiencing mechanical problems, it will return this error. If you entered the URL manually, make sure it matches the URL exactly. Spelling, punctuation, and capitalization errors can prevent you from seeing the page you re seeking. If you continually receive this error message, you should wait and try again later until the problem has been resolved by the server's administrators.

502—Services Temporarily Overloaded

This error indicates that the server is experiencing high traffic load and cannot process your request within the time limit specified. You can sometimes access the site by reloading or refreshing it with the appropriate browser button. If the error persists, you may want to try again later.

Service Unavailable

There are a variety of possibilities for reasons this error avails: your access provider's server may be down, your school's gateway (the connection between the LAN and the Internet) may be broken, or your own system isn't working. You might try to wait a minute or two and try again. If the error persists, identify the culprit (access provider, gateway, or your system) by process of elimination.

Bad File Request

This error indicates a problem with HTML coding at the site. Your browser supports forms complete with data-entry fields and drop-down lists, but not the form you're trying to access. Perhaps there's an error or unsupported feature in the form. In this case, you might send an e-mail to the webmaster and try the form again some other day.

Cannot Add Form Submission Result to Bookmark List

This error happens when you enter a search request (e.g. with a search engine such as Yahoo!) and try to save the results as a bookmark. Though it may appear as a discrete address, the result isn't a legitimate URL, so you can't add it to your bookmark list. Instead, you might try saving the result page as an HTML page on your hard disk. Use the Save As command then add the saved page to your bookmark list. You may or may not be successful although it's worth a try.

Connection Refused by Host

Quite similar to 403—Forbidden, this code indicates that you may not be allowed to access this document, probably because it's either blocked to your domain or it's password-protected. If you know the password, carefully try again. If you don't know the password but think you're eligible for one, contact the site's Webmaster and ask for it.

Failed DNS Lookup

The domain name system or DNS (the conventions for naming hosts and the way the names are handled across the Internet) can't translate the URL to a valid Internet address. This is either a harmless anomaly or the result of a mistyped URL (specifically the host name). Anomalies in DNS lookup are common, and often you can rectify this by clicking the Reload button. If that doesn't work, check your typing of the URL carefully. If the problem persists, try again after an hour or so. If you are connected via a modem and you continue to get this error for every page you try to access, chances are good that there is a problem with your connection. Try to reconnect and re-launch your browser.

File Contains No Data

This error intimates that the site you have accessed is correct although there are no web page documents on it. You may have stumbled upon this site just as updated versions are being uploaded. Try the URL again, carefully. If that doesn't help, try again later.

Helper Application Not Found

These type of errors occur when you browser does not recognize a file at the website you are visiting. This often happens when you are attempting to view a file that needs a specialized viewer such as a PowerPoint presentation or RealAudio file. The dialog box that carries this message will usually give a clue about the file type that's missing. Look at CNET's Survival Kits for your computing platform (e.g., for the PC, go to http://www.cnet.com/Help/Chest/windows.html) for viewers for the most common file types. Then follow your browser's instructions for assigning a viewer for each file format you wish to view online.

Host Unavailable or Host Unknown

Encountering this error usually means that the machine that hosts this site is probably down for maintenance. Wait a while and then try to reload.

Network Connection Was Refused by the Server or

Too Many Connections—Try Again Later

This error means that the server is probably too busy to handle one more user, but it's not configured to generate its own message, so this generic message shows up instead. As always, keep trying by reloading or refreshing the document.

NNTP Server Error

An NNTP (Network News Transfer Protocol) server error appears when you try to log on to a Usenet newsgroup, but you can't get to it. The Usenet server is something that's made available by your Internet service provider, so it may be that this newsgroup isn't available at all. However, the more innocent problem of a mistyped address or unavailable system could be the culprit. If you believe the cause of this error to be the former, you may want to contact your school's technology help person or ISP and request that they add the newsgroup in question.

Permission Denied

Several reasons for this error occurring are plausible: you are trying to upload a file to an FTP (File Transfer Protocol) site against the wishes of the site's administrator. Alternatively, you're using the wrong syntax when trying to get a file. Or, maybe the site is currently too busy to handle your upload. First check that you used the correct syntax. Then try again later. If the problem persists, send e-mail to the webmaster and ask how you can upload a file to that site.

Too Many Connections —Try Again Later

Heed the warning and try again later, or keep hitting the Refresh button until you succeed.

Unable to Locate Host

The server may be down for maintenance, or you may have lost the connection (your modem disconnected or your school's T1 line is congested). Press the [Reload] button first. If this does not work, check the URL for accuracy, then make sure you're connected by hitting [Reload], which will re-establish connections in many cases.

Unable to Locate the Server

You have either mistyped the URL, or the server doesn't exist (you may have outdated information). Check with your source to verify that the URL is correct. Or, you may have to conduct a relevant Internet search using one of the search engines.

You Can't Log on as an Anonymous User

Some FTP sites allow people who are not members and some do not. Others may allow nonmembers, but limit the number of visitors. Another possibility is that your browser doesn't support anonymous FTP access. The way most browsers handle this is to submit "anonymous" as the user ID and your e-mail address as the password. To correct for this error, either try again later during a less busy time or enter your user ID and password manually by using FTP software (e.g., WS-FTP).

Saving to Disk

When you see text or graphics on a Web page that you like or want to refer to later, you can save them on your computer's hard disk. Later, you can open the saved file and review and use it offline.

To save a text or source file:

1. On the toolbar, click [File,] and then click [Save As]

2. Choose the default file name or retype one that better suits you

3. Choose the location for where you want the file to reside on your hard drive

4. Select the format, text or HTML, for the file. Saving in text format will strip away most HTML coding and leave you with simple text. HTML format will retain all coding which can be a plus if you want to get an inside look at how web pages do what they do.

5. Finally, click [Save] to save the file.

To save an inline graphic (a graphic presented to you on a webpage):

1. Right-click the graphic. On the shortcut menu that appears, click [Save Picture As]

2. [Browse] to the folder where you would like to save the file.

3. Click [Save] to save the file.

To open a saved file in HTML, double-click it from the folder where you've saved it and you browser should start automatically and your saved file will appear in the browser window. Files saved as text can be opened by any basic word processing program and are easily read by both Windows and MacIntosh compatible computers. You can open graphics with any program that can handle the graphic's format, typically GIF or JPEG, such as the latest word processors or graphic suite programs.

Saving Data Files

There are two methods by which you can download a data file off the Internet: via your web browser or via an FTP (File Transfer Protocol) program. Generally speaking, using your Web browser is by far the easiest and most popular. So, to download a file from the web using your browser:

1. Click on the [Download] link or button on the 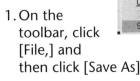 webpage and your browser will automatically ask you what you want to do with the file: open it from the current location or save it to disk. Tell your browser to save the file to disk by selecting the appropriate option. You'll then be asked where to save your file. I have created a directory on my hard drive called c:\downloads where I store all my downloaded software. If you don't have such a folder you can create one.

2. Once downloading is complete, determine what kind of file it is. If it ends in .exe, this is an executable file and you may click twice on it to run it. Once you launch the file, you will

book_wp.zip

notice that it is either one of two things, either software that will start an installation program automatically, or it's a self-extracting archive. The latter is a compressed set of files that will decompress once you double click on it. After running the self-extracting archive, you should see a file called setup.exe or install.exe in your download directory. Run this file by double clicking on it to start the installation process. The other type of file you may download is a .zip file. This is also a compressed set of files although it is not self-extracting which means that you have to decompress the files yourself. One of the best programs for decompressing and managing zip files is WinZip for Windows/Windows95, itself a shareware program, available at www.winzip.com. Once you have used a program such as WinZip and extracted the compressed files, look for the appropriate installation files and install the program.

Shareware

On the Internet you will find literally hundreds of thousands of great programs, utilities, games, screen savers, etc. that you can download for free (freeware). In the case of shareware, you are allowed to try out the software for some period of time (typically 30 days). If you find the shareware useful, the author expects you to send in a registration fee, usually between $5 and $40, with some fancier programs costing up to $99. In return, you receive something more, like a password that unlocks additional program functionality, or a printed manual. If you realize that the software isn't right for you, just delete it from your hard drive and consider it a free test drive (The Four Corners of the Internet, 1997).

Shareware was a concept born out of the need for software programmers and small companies to more effectively compete with conglomerates. A software author can distribute his or her programs essentially for free by uploading them to online services, Bulletin Board Services (BBS), and the Web. This effectively eliminates the need to go through traditional distribution procedures. Users in turn get to download the software for free and try it out before making a decision to purchase. Several of my favorite shareware sites include www.shareware.com, www.hotfiles.com, www.jumbo.com, and www.pccomputing.com. Once you have found the shareware you want, it's time to download it as described in the section on saving files to disk. It may take a while depending on the size of the file and your connection speed.

Portable Document Files (PDF)

PDF files, short for Portable Document Format, is a file format developed by Adobe Systems which captures formatting information from a variety of desktop publishing applications. This software makes it possible to send formatted documents and have them appear on the recipient's monitor or printer as they were intended. In other words, people viewing a PDF file (or document) with the free reader (download the Adobe Acrobat Reader from www.adobe.com) see the document with the exact layout intended by the author. This is its main advantage over other electronic formats such as HTML, where the layout can vary depending on the software being used to view it. If your document contains particularities such as graphics, columns, tables, charts, and multiple colors, the PDF format is highly desirable. If so intended, PDF files can also contain hyperlinks which take you to specific locations on the web or another place in the document. Advanced forms of PDF files may also contain forms which allow readers to enter customized information which is then integrated into a printable document. For example, I might send to you an award or certificate template with fancy graphics and text in PDF format. Once you receive the file, you can then enter an awardees name which is automatically formatted for type size and color and then prepared for printing.

There are two ways to view a PDF file: directly from your computer or within your browser. If the PDF file is relatively small, I will typically download it to my computer and then open the file with the Acrobat Reader software. The reason for this is that viewing is much faster and I can more easily take advantage of the reader's many capabilities. Also, I can then much more easily share the file with others with whom I work or around the world by sending it via e-mail. Once you locate a PDF file online, you simply need to download it to your computer as previously described as any other file. Once on your computer, locate the PDF file and click twice on it to open it in the reader. From here you may search for text within the document, place bookmarks or print it in part of whole. What you may not do is edit the document or save any part of it in memory. Sometimes you may not want to download the file and simply view it online. To do this, you must make certain that your browser is updated with the Adobe Acrobat reader plug-in from www.adobe.com. To see if your browser is capable of viewing PDF documents online, simply locate a PDF document and attempt to view it. If your browser is not capable, you will get a pop-up window which will ask you if you want to download the proper software. Follow the directions for download and installation and you are ready to go.

Evaluating Internet Information

The Internet is a huge and very dynamic resource. There are so many different types of information available, that identifying quality resources can sometimes be difficult at best. Some Internet resources are poorly indexed, or not indexed at all. A search in any engine or other Internet index may provide a list of hundreds or thousands of items. To make it more confusing, Web page titles are often non-descriptive. Be aware you may come across useless and even illegal information because anyone can put anything on the Internet at anytime. Some information may appear authoritative or scholarly, but after critical evaluation it may be seen as biased, or intended to sell or persuade (Evaluating Internet Information, 1998).

For example, radio, print, and television media all over the world reported on July 14, 1998 that two 18-year-olds would lose their virginity on the Internet, in the full glare of the public. The couple would have their first sexual encounter while a camera would broadcast the event over the Internet for all the world to see. The Internet's alleged first-sex event was supposedly inspired by the girl's beliefs in freedom of speech and by seeing a birth on-line (which actually happened when, only a month before, a 40-year-old Florida woman gave birth to a baby boy in the first-ever live on-line birth before an estimated audience of two million people). One justification as noted by the teenagers on their website was that they "wanted to show that the act of making love, which is the first step that brought that live birth about, is just as beautiful—and nothing to be ashamed about.'' Further, the event's sponsors billed the purpose of the episode to change repressive sexual attitudes among some people and to make a statement about safe sex and freedom of choice. Only a week later, after much discussion over the Internet and around the workplace was the story discovered as a publicity stunt for a new pornography site. Even more spectacular than the actual hoax was that many millions of people immediately believed and responded to it. Other Internet hoaxes and urban legends are documented and may be found at [http://www.urbanlegends.com/].

Being able to quickly and critically evaluate a long list of links or titles is a very useful skill. According to Schrock (1998), knowing what type of information is appropriate for particular purposes, knowing how to find such information easily, and evaluating information, is called information literacy, digital literacy, media literacy, or technoliteracy. Gilster (1997) defined the concept in his book, Digital Literacy: "Digital literacy is the ability to understand and use information in multiple formats from a wide range of sources when it is presented via computers... (Not) only must you acquire the skill of finding things, you must also acquire the ability to use those things in your life. Acquiring digital literacy for Internet use involves mastering a set of core competencies. The most essential of these is the ability to make informed judgments about what you find on-line."

One of the best ways counselors can practice critical evaluation of Internet sources is by conducting searches on topics with which they are familiar. Using an evaluation checklist such as the one provided below, counselors should be able to evaluate sites critically, examine the technical aspects of the site, the authority of the writer, and the validity of the writer's content. At the end of the evaluation, when the entire process is completed, counselors should ask themselves whether the site provides the information they need to solve their information problem. If it did not, they should ask themselves how the process could be varied to obtain the needed results. Self-assessment at the end of the information seeking process is a higher-order thinking skill that information consumers should understand and apply. Critical evaluation of information can be applied to all information sources including World Wide Web sites (Grassian, 1998; Schrock, 1998).

Criteria for Evaluating Internet Information

The following is a checklist of questions to ask yourself for effectively evaluating website content:

- **Accessibility, Availability.** How accessible is the information? How easy is it to find and use? How much time does it take to access the resource? How stable is the information resource or its provider? Will it be available again if you need it at a later date? Be aware that some Internet information can be very transitory or short lived. Also, does the site allow for reasonable download time? If a site is rated by you as excellent in all other aspects, it would remain an unusable site if it required an undue wait time just to see it. Slow access to a site may be due to a high volume of traffic to the site. In this case, it would be an option for the site server to "beef up" on their hardware to allow for more connections. Access to the site may also be slowed by too many graphics. Graphics require a great deal of time to access. Webauthors should limit the number of graphics to those that are necessary for the content. Additionally, graphics might be compressed or saved in the format which allows for desirable viewing with minimum file size. Finally, is the site accessible to those with disabilities (e.g., large print and graphics options; audio; alternative text for graphics)?

- **Are facts documented?** Does the information contained in the site confirm information from other sources? Are the other sources clearly cited and/or linked?

- **Authoritativeness, Scholarship.** Who wrote, created or published the information? How easy is it to clearly identify the authority of the authors? Is the author's perspective culturally diverse, or narrowly focused? How well has the author documented the sources of the information presented? Does the site provide contact information for the author, especially a link to his/her e-mail?

- **Balance, Objectivity, Bias, Accuracy.** What is the intended purpose of the information? Why is the information being presented, or made available? What is the perspective of the publication(s)? Is the information presented accurately and objectively? How can you tell? What clues are present to help you judge?

- **Cost.** Is the information free, or is there a fee for the information? Is the cost worth having the information and time saved? Also remember, information isn't free if it takes too much of your time to find, print, read or manage. With so much Internet information available, it is easy to suffer from information anxiety. Before clicking on a link, decide whether further investigation of the site satisfies your research needs or simply your curiosity? When in doubt, you might download the information for later perusal instead of immediately studying it.

- **Ease of navigation.** Does a site leave you buried deep somewhere without any hope of getting back to another of its pages? A site should be easy to explore and review. Navigation that changes to reflect your current location (by dimming out the navigation button for your present location, using a different color for the current link, or providing a clear header that tells where you are) helps people to orient themselves. This sort of feedback may be simple, but it's also a valuable tool for users. It's important that people know where they are, where they can go, and how they will get back to where they started (Websitejournal, 1998).

Russell A. Sabella, Ph.D.

- **Format.** Can you clearly identify what type of information it is? Is it a Web Home page? Is it a Gopher? Is it a newsgroup posting? Is it a file or downloadable software? Is it a government report? Is it an advertisement? Is the information in an appropriate or useful format for your needs? Does it have the features you need? How complete is the information? Also, is the site laid out clearly and logically with well organized subsections? Does the site include an index which includes all available information in an outline form? If the site is especially large, does it include a search engine which can point to keywords directly within the site?

- **Links.** Are links relevant and appropriate? Be sure to investigate additional sites on the topic before assuming that the linked sites are the best available. Also, are links up to date or do they point to sites which no longer exist or have moved (i.e., broken links)?

- **Originality.** Is it primary information or secondary information? Is the originality of the information important for your research?

- **Pervasiveness.** Is this a site that others have found helpful and useful? Has the site been awarded recognition by reputable organizations as evidenced by an award icon? Does a search of the site's URL produce results which indicate that other sites reference the site in question?

- **Quality.** Evaluate the content: What kind of information is it? Is it facts or opinions? Is there any documentation? Does the information support or refute your position? Are any major findings presented? How does the information compare to other related sources?

- **Security.** If you need to transmit confidential or otherwise sensitive information, does the site incorporate encryption over a secure server?

- **Timeliness.** When was the information produced? Is the information too old, or too new for the needs of your research?

- **Usefulness.** How useful is the information for your particular need? If you can't identify it's usefulness immediately, it should be considered a low priority to save, print or read online.

The web has come a long way since its humble beginnings in providing counselors with valuable information and resources. It continues to become faster, more organized, and highly interactive. New and more functional methods for locating and using information are witnessing steady progress. Also developing are methods for delivering guidance and counseling services to students and others over this medium. How exactly will this ensue is truly an exciting mystery. One thing is certain though, the future of the Web is happening every day.

Russell A. Sabella, Ph.D.

CHAPTER FOUR

Counselor as Content Provider

Great websites, like great pieces of literature, are easy to follow and enjoyable to partake. Both present ideas and stories that seem simple yet stimulate our resourcefulness and imagination. For school counselors, a website can eloquently tell a story wich informs and engages our many audiences. A website can help you to reach farther in less time by bringing your clients and their care givers to you. The technical side of a site has all but become a non-issue due to the powerful and user-friendly software now available to webauthors. Indeed, the hard part is getting the ideas right—making sure that the words and pictures on your Website represent the best of what your counseling program offers. This chapter provides some suggestions for building your website and how to get people to use it. Before constructing your website, you should definitely spend some time planning. Ask yourself the following questions:

1. **What is your school's acceptable use policy?** Your site must follow the guidelines set forth by your district. An acceptable use policy governs the responsibilities of the school administration, students, teachers and parents regarding software, the use of the Internet and adherence to copyright laws. If your district does not have an acceptable use policy, you might review such documents provided online by other schools to help you create one (see Willard, 1996).

2. **Who will help create the site?** Even the best of webmasters have an advisory group to assist in making important decisions concerning their site. For those whom are just getting started, it is highly advisable to delegate webauthoring responsibilities among an established team or committee. Members of your web development team can write content and assemble photos for the various sections of the site. Luckily, many schools have computer courses and labs where, as part of their assignment, students can help design various parts of your site. You might also include talented parents and nearby college students who would like to provide a community service. In this instance, you might take the role of editor: the person who guides others into developing appropriate and fitting material, makes any needed changes, and integrates the material with the total body of information in a way that is logical and easy to follow.

3. **How much time will I need to effectively maintain my site?** Develop a schedule for site updates. Perhaps twice per month, you might allow yourself a couple of hours to make pertinent changes. To the contrary, you can spend too much time by making minor changes more frequently. Keep a file of any edits that need to be made, make them all at once during your scheduled time, and then upload the changes all at once.

4. **What will the site's directory structure look like?** Outline the various sections of your website and what would most appropriately (i.e., content, writing style, length, etc.) be placed within those sections. Many people find it most efficient to develop this scheme in the form of a flowchart. Even if you have little or no content for a section (e.g., News and Events), it will be easier to proceed and create the section if you anticipate future content. Remember that all of the content for your site will not necessarily have to be created. You will find that current school documents and photos already include much of what you will need for your website and, with some editing, may be quite useful. For instance, a list of student homework resources, event calendar, or contact information may already exist. Also, you might create links to other important information that already exists on the Web. One suggestion for this part of the process is to consult other similar sites for ideas.

5. **What tools do I have available for maintaining my site?** To make life easy for you in your webauthoring endeavor, you will need tools to automate otherwise difficult tasks such as editing, scanning photos, uploading to a server, creating forms, and creating images. Survey your school and district for available resources such as computer software and consultants. Determine if the available resources will be sufficient. If not, what will you require and what will be the cost? How can you acquire any missing resources through purchases or donations? At the minimum, you will need a computer, webauthoring software such as Microsoft FrontPage or Adobe Pagemill, a scanner, and FTP (file transfer protocol) software.

Your Personal Webspace

Before you can post a Website to the World Wide Web, you need a unique address for the site. This address is your domain name. The American School Counselor Association's domain name, for example, is "schoolcounselor.org," and the uniform resource locator (URL) for ASCA's home page is http://www.schoolcounselor.org. Some Internet Service Providers set aside portions of their hard-disk space for subscribers' Web pages that require no domain registration. In all likelihood, you will be using your school district's web server. Most guidance websites are located directly beneath (i.e., as a subfolder) their school's website. For example, the Pottsville School District web page is located at http://apache.afsc.k12.ar.us/. The counselor at Pottsville High School, created a website at http://apache.afsc.k12.ar.us/cowel.htm, a file directly under the district's website.

If you use a different ISP, you will need to ensure each Website has an address that no other site is using. Domain names must be registered with the domain administrator. In most cases, this is InterNIC (www.internic.net). InterNIC administers domain names ending in .com (for commercial enterprises), .org (for nonprofit organizations), .net (for networks), .edu (for educational institutions), .gov (for government organizations), and .mil (for military services). You can search domain names to find out whether the name you want is taken and, for one up-front and yearly fee, can register a domain name through InterNIC (Note that the address is www.internic.net and NOT www.internic.com; the latter may cost you unnecessary money). The Registration Services section of the InterNIC site provides detailed information about how to register and what's required before you can register (www.internic.net). The site's list of frequently asked questions and answers (FAQ) is particularly helpful.

Webauthoring Tools

I began webauthoring in 1995 by studying the source code of sites that I respected and by reading about HTML codes. Then, by using my word processor, I was off and running conducting the tedious task of writing, editing, and frequently rewriting all the HTML tags to properly show some basic text with a few graphics and a table. The procedure alone made me wonder why anyone would ever want to do such a thing. I'm extremely pleased to report that such programming efforts are largely foregone and have been replaced with sophisticated software that makes creating "eye-popping" web pages a snap—without any knowledge of HTML coding.

Most top-of-the-line products come with site creation and management tools that allow you to create frames, draw tables, add rich graphics, and include support for an interactive database. Additionally, leading webauthoring programs allow you to view your site's navigational structure, directories of information, hyperlinks, hyperlink status, or all files at once. Some also include automatic hyperlink maintenance which allows you the freedom to make changes without worrying about broken links. With most programs, too, you can start your page from scratch or begin with one or more of many professionally designed, customizable templates. As if it couldn't get easier, virtually all webauthoring packages also include thousands of high-quality clip-art images, photographs, web-art graphics, fonts, animated GIF files, color schemes, and many other design elements to create publications that reflect your individual needs and personality.

Something else you should know before you go out to your nearest software store and spend between $50 and $1000 on webauthoring software: Today's leading word processing programs, especially Microsoft's Word98 and Corel's WordPerfect 8.0, will "mark up" or convert a document into HTML for uploading to your site's server. Different word processors make this happen somewhat differently, but basically, you either click on a menu item that says "send to HTML" or manually save your document in HTML format by finding this option on the [Save] menu. One word of caution however: make sure that you make a backup copy of your document in case you find that your word processor writes over your original file and vanishes it forever. One way around this is to make certain to rename the file too. My experience is that this kind of conversion is not perfect and still has a way to go. That is, the way my document is layed out as a document does not exactly look the same when converted to HTML for the web. "Cleaning up" the document while viewing it in HTML, though, is still easier than having to entirely code it by hand.

What Should Reside on My Site?

The first and most important task is to consider your website audience. Who will be accessing it? What will they be looking for? What kind of specific format might appeal to them? Many different people will access your site for many different reasons. You might want to create a general introduction, description about you and your program, and different links for parents, community members, students, faculty and people from other schools that will lead them to information of special interest to them. For instance, consider the following list of web content for each:

General Info

1. Most people know the school as a building and a place they walk into each day. There are many ways to represent the school building, and especially your office, on your Website: with a photograph; with a diagram or map; with a drawing by a student or with a written description of the architecture. On the site, show your office up-close-and-personal by using a photo and include students (with permission) in the picture so the school appears as a live space.

2. A profile of you and your background.

3. Executive summary of the School Counseling National Standards as defined by the American School Counselor Association.

4. Special features of your counseling program (e.g., photos and descriptions of peer helper projects). Use photos and frequently-updated stories to let people know what students are accomplishing and performing outside of the academic program.

5. Introduction to the members of your guidance committee.

6. This year's guidance and counseling goals and objectives.

7. Accountability data that allows others to recognize the kinds of tasks and activities that you are involved.

8. According to the American School Directory (www.asd.com) you might publish a "wish list." Do you need magazines for an upcoming small group counseling unit that calls for a collage? Could you use more computers? Are you in need of new books for your own professional development? These are just a few of the hundreds of items that might be posted on your Counselor Wish List. If you ask for a few things of reasonable value you are likely to be successful in receiving donations. Don't forget to let people know how to respond to you, update your list frequently, and include a list of thank-you's as well.

9. You might also choose to include a text based, or if you want to get fancy, a streaming video message from your principal or superintendent that supports your work and program.

10. One of the things that motivates others to return to your site is new and updated information, even in the form of a new inspirational quote of the day (or week).

11. Clear contact information that makes it simple for others, especially parents, to communicate with you and other counselors.

12. Any honors or awards that you or your program have received (don't forget to include any photos).

13. A list of important dates and events and how to prepare for them.

Parents

14. Tips for parent involvement in your school which might include a list of projects and "how to help."

15. Various educational "brochures" about parenting topics.

16. Upcoming parent opportunities for training and development, perhaps sponsored with the PTA.

17. School and district resources for parents and respective contact numbers.

18. Pertinent aspects of your schedule such as times for parent conferences.

Russell A. Sabella, Ph.D.

Community Members

19. Tips for community involvement in your school which might include a list of projects and "how to help."

20. Profiles of community members whom have participated in special guidance and counseling projects (e.g., tutoring, mentoring, or activity sponsorship).

21. How your work serves the interests of the community (e.g., school-to-work or career development activities).

22. Information about adult education services.

Students

23. Various educational "brochures" about student success topics such as homework help, time management, conflict resolution, and school adjustment to name a very few.

24. Information relevant to school success ranging from studying, making friends, choosing a college or career, to calculating your GPA.

25. Information for alumni to stay in contact.

26. Interactive guidance units.

Faculty

27. Guidance units for use within a teacher-as-advisor program.

28. Various educational "brochures" about teaching topics such as classroom management, discipline options, working effectively with ADHD children, and team building to name a few.

29. Opportunities for teacher consultation which includes the nature of school consultation and its effects. For instance, you might describe the opportunity of having you consult with a teacher for approximately four meetings to discuss ways to enhance student growth and development known to support academic achievement.

Elements of a Website

What are the essential traits of great Websites? After you visit a site and find yourself staying awhile, what makes you stay? A sense of humor helps. Flashy graphics are nice. But the fundamental traits that make a site work are more elusive. Original content is the most important trait of a great Website. Sites that provide only links to other sites are essentially meta-lists, while sites that have some information that's useful to the user stand out and will be revisited. Additionally, sites which are well organized, customized for specific audiences, and somewhat interactive, are considered highly desirable (WebReference, 1998).

After deciding what type of information and level of interactivity your website will offer, it is time to consider how exactly this will be layed out. The next level in planning is to decide how best to present your website with one or more of various elements. The following are elements which are most pervasive, although certainly not exhaustive, of all the possibilities you might include to tell your guidance and counseling "story":

Animated GIFs (Graphic Interchange Format). Animated GIFS are called so because they are actually a very special kind of graphic file. They are actually a series of single graphic files compressed into one file. When displayed by the web browser, each individual GIF is displayed in sequence to create the intended motion much like a very short film. Many of the more popular web authoring programs contain GIF animators so that you may create your own. However, just like everything else, there are available thousands of free animated GIFS throughout the Net (e.g., see http://www.cityweb.co.uk/animated.htm). Animated images are popular on the web because they can be very creative and fun to watch. They do, however, contribute to a greater overall file size of the site which can significantly increase download time. You should also be aware that some viewers find animations distracting or annoying at best. The size, purpose, and importance of an animated GIF should be considered in your decision to include them.

Background. Page backgrounds can be plain white, colored, textured or comprise a graphical image or photo. If you want your background to be a simple color, just change it from a menu of background colors offered to you by your webauthoring software. Image backgrounds are customized by creating a computer graphic using a graphics editing program or they may be one of thousands available for free throughout the Net (conduct a search with the key terms "free web graphics" or begin at http://www.clipart.com/) or included in webauthoring software . Sometimes, backgrounds appear as texture such as wood, cloth, or marble which is digitally created or sometimes scanned and altered. Background images are usually created as tiles or borders. Tiles use a small square of image that is repeated or tiled as a background. Border backgrounds are usually long skinny strips with a color or image along one side or the top, and another image or color for the body. These are also repeated to create the background. Using the method of repeating the image allows for the use of an image without increasing the file size of the page appreciably. The main advantage of this method is that it is conducive to efficient downloading.

Backgrounds provide individuality, and creativity to a site. However, care should be given that the background not become so complex it confuses the purpose of the page. Also, attention to print color in relation to background color, positioning of images, etc. is important to keeping the site easily readable to visitors.

CGI Scripts. Common Gateway Interface (CGI) scripts are mini computer programs written in any programming language (e.g., C, Perl, Java, or Visual Basic) and run via a web browser. CGI programs are the most common way for web servers to interact dynamically with users. The more popular CGI programs allow web authors, for example, to maintain a guest book, count the number of times a page is viewed, insert the current date, secure a part of the website for specific users with appropriate passwords (e.g., organization members), or automatically forward a user to a new page. Although using CGI scripts are not necessary, they may automate more complex tasks (check out http://www.cgi-resources.com/ for already available CGI programs).

Formatted Text. Text, like any other good document, should be easy to read and make sense. Similar to word processing, you may format webpage text in various sizes, shapes, fonts or typesets. The main thing to remember is to make your site look uniform and simple.

Forms. Web forms are formatted documents containing blank fields that users can fill in with data. With paper forms, it is usually necessary for someone to transfer the data from the paper to a computer database, where the results can then be analyzed. Some OCR (optical character recognition) systems can do this automatically, but they're generally limited to forms containing just check boxes. They can't handle handwritten text. Electronic forms solve this problem by entirely skipping the paper stage. Instead, the form appears on the user's display screen and the user fills it in by selecting options with a pointing device or typing in text from the computer keyboard. The data is then sent directly to a forms processing application, which enters the information into a database. Electronic forms are especially common on the World Wide Web because the HTML language has built-in codes for displaying form elements such as text fields and check boxes. Typically, the data entered into a Web-based form is processed by a CGI program (Webopedia, 1998).

Frames. Many sites are now organized with the use of frames which is essentially the presentation of two or more webpages at the same time. One frame may be used to the left side of a page to continually present a table of contents. Sometimes, authors will include a "header" frame which, as you might guess, is a frame across the top of a site which constantly shows a type of letterhead. Always included is the main frame which presents the primary web page. Although using frames tends to make navigating somewhat easier, there are serious problems with using them. Considering the following issues with frames may motivate you to abstain from using them:

Russell A. Sabella, Ph.D.

- some older versions of browsers do not support the use of frames and, when encountering a page with frames, runs into trouble. Specifically, a browser that does not support frames will simply skip over these instructions and display nothing in its place.

- as a user "clicks through" a site, there is not a way to store the state that the frameset was in. This is because framesets are not addressable. The information about the position in a frameset is not present in the framed document.

- there is no mechanism to keep track of where a user is, so the "current location" cannot be expressed using a URL.

- printing a page with frames can sometimes result in mistargeted print jobs. That is, you may end up printing the wrong frame or each frame as a separate print job.

Graphics. Including images are a way to present information more visually palatable. The two most popular image formats for the Web are GIF (Graphics Interchange Format) and JPEG (Joint Photographic Experts Group). It's not a hard-and-fast rule, but JPEG is usually a better format for photographs, while GIF is better for small line drawings, transparencies, and animations.

The use of images will necessarily slow down the loading of a page to some extent. So, they should have a valid purpose and be kept as small in file size as possible. This can be done through a number of techniques. One is to keep images physically small. Another is to "optimize" the images using graphic manipulation software, a process that reduces file size by eliminating redundant pixels and limiting the number of colors. All web images should be optimized as much as possible without losing essential quality. This improves website load time and preserves bandwidth on the Net. If larger images are important to a site, as in showing individual who won a contest, an option is to offer thumbnail images or text which link to a larger images. This

technique allows the main page to load more quickly and offers your visitors the option of waiting while a larger image loads. Check out http://uswest.gifwizard.com/ for detailed information about the efficient use of graphics, especially GIFs.

Image Map. An image map is a single graphic image containing more than one "hot spot" which can be used as a navigation tool in addition to hyperlinked buttons and text. The most lucid example is an image of the United States which takes a user to state specific information when he or she clicks on a specific state. Image maps are created by delineating a space or shape within an image and "mapping" it to a hypertext link. A counselor might have a picture of a filing cabinet with each drawer labeled for different areas of his/her website and mapped to specific sites.

Critics would tell us to avoid putting image maps on your pages unless you have a really good reason for using them. Fancy image maps can be far more confusing than a well-formatted text list or a simple set of buttons. In many cases, they say, it is difficult to tell just where to click. This is especially true if the map contains both images and words. Unlike regular text links which change color after being clicked on, image maps give no clue about what's been seen and what hasn't. This makes it more difficult for the user to navigate your site. However, used sparingly, image maps can help you to keep your site organized and they also look pretty cool.

Marquee. On web pages, this is a scrolling area of text. Starting with Version 2, Microsoft Internet Explorer supports a special tag for creating these areas. Netscape Navigator, however, does not support this tag. You can also create marquees with Java applets and Dynamic HTML (Webopedia, 1999).

Multimedia Presentations. Programs such as Microsoft PowerPoint© and Corel Presentations© allow users to create attention grabbing slides which contain sounds, graphics, animated objects, animated texts, and other elements. These programs also allow you to convert your multimedia slide shows to HTML and upload them to your site. The result is a series of highly stylized images for slide shows and reports. Multimedia slide shows can include various types of charts, graphs and text in a variety of fonts. Most systems enable you to import data from a spreadsheet application to create the charts and graphs. The conversion accuracy from multimedia to HTML varies with each version of the program although continues to get better. Check out http://www.hotwired.com/ webmonkey/multimedia/tutorials/tutorial3.html for a multimedia tutorial.

Search Engine. Many online search engines offer to place on your site a free search bar to allow users to search the contents of your site (e.g., Infoseek, http://www.infoseek.com/ Tools?pg=WebKit.html). The advantage of having a search engine for your site is that, for a site with many documents or files, users may conduct keyword searches to obtain a list of those pages of special interest to them. Another method for adding search capabilities to your site involves creating or downloading a CGI program and adding it to your site. Webauthoring programs also make it relatively simple to create search bars, try it for fun.

Short Films (AVI and MPEG). AVI stands for *Audio Video Interleave* and is the most common format for audio/video data on the PC. Inserting an AVI file is very similar to inserting a link. Once the short film is inserted, a user simply needs to click on the link which will cause the AVI file to be downloaded or viewed from the server. The browser recognizes that the AVI file is not a typical document. Then, the browser invokes a helper application that can play the AVI file, such as Media Player under Windows 3.1-98, and the movie will appear in a separate window. Sometimes, the browser may have a plug-in that provides support for AVI, in which case the video window will appear embedded in the HTML page. In both Internet Explorer and Netscape, the user can configure the browser to use helper applications or plug-ins as desired.

There are plenty of free, fun, and informative AVI files floating around the Net. These can be downloaded and inserted into your web page. To create your own AVI files, you must have the appropriate hardware and software to create a film from scratch or convert a video tape to this digital format. The limited bandwidth of the Internet is the bane of effective use of video on a Web page. So, video clips on a web page need to be small. Even then, downloading a video clip can take several minutes or hours over a 28.8 modem. The longer the wait, the better the video should be (see http://www.rahul.net/jfm/ avi.html for details about AVI and the Web).

Moving Picture Experts Group (MPEG), pronounced *m-peg*, refers to the family of digital video compression standards and file formats developed by the group. MPEG generally produces better-quality video than competing formats because it plays at a high compression rate by storing only the changes from one frame to another, instead of each entire frame. Check out http://www.mpeg.org/MPEG/ for MPEG downloads and details.

Sound. Having sound on a site can help you keep your visitors' attention and facilitate communication and interactivity. For instance, you might record your own voice and present a welcome message. You may personally narrate an event or program. Many sites contain sound effects which bring other graphics or events alive. There are several popular sound file formats which include:

• RealAudio (RA), from Progressive Networks, is a tool to stream audio-content in realtime over the Internet. You can start listening right from the moment you start downloading. This is the main difference to sound-files in conventional sound-formats, which you must download completely before playing. A RealAudio connection is interactive: you can start, stop and pause the playback, as well as adjust the volume-much as you would operate a local tape recorder. To listen to a RA file, you must download and install a free player from www.realaudio.com.

• WAV is the format for storing sound in files developed jointly by Microsoft and IBM. Support for WAV files was built into Windows 95 making it the de facto standard for sound on PCs. WAV sound files end with a .wav extension and can be played by nearly all Windows applications that support sound. WAV files can be recorded with software which comes with Microsoft Windows (sound recorder) or downloaded from the Net (e.g., check out http://www.dailywav.com/)

• Musical Instrument Digital Interface (MIDI): Pronounced *middy*, this format is the standard adopted by the electronic music industry for controlling devices, such as synthesizers and sound cards, that emit music. At minimum, a MIDI representation of a sound includes values for the note's pitch, length, and volume. It can also include additional characteristics, such as attack and delay time. The MIDI standard is supported by most synthesizers, so sounds created on one synthesizer can be played and manipulated on another synthesizer. Computers that have a MIDI interface can record sounds created by a synthesizer and then manipulate the data to produce new sounds. For example, you can change the key of a composition with a single keystroke. A number of software programs are available for composing and editing music that conforms to the MIDI standard. They offer a variety of functions: for instance, when you play a tune on a keyboard connected to a computer, a music program can translate what you play into a written score (Webopedia, 1999).

Tables. Similar to tables in word processors, website content can be displayed in various cells within rows and columns. Tables allows for exact placement of content such as with a newsletter. (For a tutor on tables see http://junior.apk.net/~jbarta/tutor/tables/index.html).

Text Art. Text art is simply text with some very fancy changes such as representing a word or phrase in three dimensions. Ultimately, it is saved into a graphic file of any format. Text art is usually created with desktop publishing, word processing, or multimedia software. Once saved, the file is then inserted into the web page.

Links. Your web page should be highly connected to the rest of the school and district. So, include links on all your pages, perhaps in the form of a frame or header, that lead users to the home pages of your school, district, and your own home page. Another set of links might be established on your home page that includes a list of other resources available both locally and around the globe. Or, if you like, you can provide a set of resourceful links in each of the above mentioned sections particular to your target audience. A list of links should be short, well organized, and truly resourceful. After reviewing the list of websites in Chapter 6, you might highlight several that are especially pertinent to you and include them as links on your website.

How do I get my site noticed?

Once your site is up, running, and presentable, you will want to make your hard work pay off. There are several things you can do to publicize your new webpage and its offerings:

• Submit your website information to Yahoo (www.yahoo.com), an impressive index of the web which expands its knowledge automatically but permits the direct submission of URLs as well.

- Submit it to a large number of different catalogs using Submit It (www.submit-it.com) and Register-It (www.register-it.com), services which allows you to register with many indexes by filling out a single form.

- Announce your new website to listservs which comprise members who should find your site of particular interest. Realize though that many listservs do not allow you to post messages unless you are a member of the group. Therefore, you will either have to temporarily subscribe or have the message forwarded by a member of the group that you know. Be aware that if your description sounds as if you are selling a product, this is considered to be "spam" and is virtually always considered inappropriate. Some users who receive spam get angry and sometimes will try to punish you by filling up your e-mail box with tons of unflattering messages and files. Some users will log official complaints with your ISP (or school) which can result in you losing your account. So, be certain to emphasize that your site provides free and relevant information.

- Post your site information on relevant news groups. You can identify relevant news groups by conducting a search of news groups using DejaNews (www.dejanews.com) using keywords relevant to your site. Then, follow the instructions for posting information to the group. Again, be careful not to accidentally spam your audience.

- You can market your website by using flyers, cards, buttons, etc. at various functions such as conferences, meetings, and in newsletters.

- Announce your site in the local newspaper and relevant community newsletters.

- Create a brochure about your site which can be handed to parents and others at the reception area.

- Include information about your site in your schools handbook and any other pertinent sources of communication.

How do I get my site used?

Although creating a website can be fun and intrinsically rewarding, most webauthors would like to know that their sites are useful to others in some way. School counselors would probably like to know that their website assists them in reaching their guidance and counseling goals and advancing the program mission. So how can counselors help others to make use of their site? Several tips follow:

- **Make your site valuable.** If the information is useful and valuable, people will stream to your site to get it. If it is information they need and want, and if it is not available elsewhere, you can be assured that your intended audience will be connecting regularly. On the other hand, if there is nothing on the site that is not already published somewhere else, or if the information is old, or if it is information that no one really needs, then you cannot expect to see many visitors.

- **Make your site timely.** One reason to use the Internet rather than the printed handbook is the ability to reflect last-minute changes. For most schools, daily or weekly updates of information will allow the Website to provide things that are available nowhere else. Regular changes will keep people coming back. Reasonably frequent updates make a site much more useful to its audience.

- **Make your site user-friendly.** If the material on the site is easy to find and easy to read, it will be used more. A clear writing style allows people to read quickly and to find the ideas they need. Accurate labels and titles and subheadings also make it easier for the user to find content for which he or she is looking. Do not be afraid to divide an article into short sections with subheadings.

Russell A. Sabella, Ph.D.

- **Help teachers to be involved.** If teachers have been involved from the beginning in the planning and development of the site, then you are on the right track. Teachers are key to utilization of the school's Website. Teachers will provide new material to keep the site updated; teachers will tell their students to connect to the site, and these students will tell their parents. The more you can involve teachers in the authoring of the various sections of the Website, the more likely you are to find your site well used. If your teachers are not familiar with the World Wide Web, then provide a short in-service training program. You can also arrange a training program of your own, perhaps calling on the school librarian or technology coordinator, who are often well-versed in using the Internet.

- **Help students to be involved.** Many schools find that students are the chief users of the school Website. Students have a big stake in their school. They are familiar with the new technologies, and they love to see their own works published on the Web. The more you call on students to develop and update different parts of your site, the more they will encourage use of the Website among their friends. You may find, as many schools have, that students are quite willing and prepared to locate and type the daily and weekly updates of information that are essential to a well-used site. Also, to get students using the site early on, consider a contest of some sort. Provide clues on your site that change each day; students who collect all the clues might win a school sweatshirt or other valuable prize. You might also conduct training sessions in the computer lab or library, to show students how to connect to the school Website, and how to find the information that is valuable for them.

- **Help parents and the community to be involved.** Use every means possible to let the parents and community know your site is up and ready. Send notices home with students. Conduct a "Guidance and Counseling Web Night" at school, with hands-on introduction to the Internet for parents and community. Put a notice in the school newspaper and in the local paper. Recruit a parent volunteer to post a notice of the site in all the large workplaces in the community. Better yet, involve parents in authoring parts of your site, perhaps a parenting support section. You might also consider an informational evening for parents, in cooperation with local Internet Service Providers. Show people how easy it is to connect to the Internet from home, give them advice on getting connected, and answer their questions on what they would need at home to become part of the "information infrastructure."

- **Help everyone remember your site.** Take every opportunity to let people know that you have a Website. Include your site's URL on your school stationery and on your business card. Include it in the school newspaper and at the bottom of all relevant announcements that go from school to home. Post it in the front hall, and on the sign in front of the school. Make a big banner of the URL, and hang it at basketball and football games. This will let everyone in the school community know that the school counselor is publishing on the Web.

A guidance and counseling website can assist you in interacting with your students and other stakeholders, post valuable and timely information, and increase your program's presence throughout the school and community. Web authoring software has made the task much easier and more fun. Like everything else, you will want to regulate your time, especially limiting yourself to those parts of web authoring which you believe truly augment your efficiency and effectiveness. The interactions with others, especially students, as part of your website development should also serve to build healthy and productive working relationships. Stay focused on your web authoring purpose and prepare to be excited by the possibilities.

Russell A. Sabella, Ph.D.

CHAPTER FIVE

Speed Bumps and Traps on the Information Superhighway

The Net's power as a medium for communication and electronic transfer lies in its ability to transcend limitations of space and time. Internet users enjoy the freedom of conducting all kinds of transactions, including counseling, over the Net. With this freedom, however, comes an important responsibility to use the Internet in a manner which is safe, secure, ethical, and contributes to the overall welfare of all involved. This chapter intends to help counselors become more aware of the dangers involved in traveling the information superhighway. With increased awareness, counselors can more effectively make decisions about their online behavior.

Internet Addiction

"One more minute," a typical Internet user often says to a spouse or parent who yearns for their attention during a long on-line session. But before they know how or why it happened, that minute invariably turns into one or more hours—at the cost of the people and activities that more and more often are ignored (Young, 1998). And so it begins ... Counselors need to be aware of and prevent the potential for developing an Internet addiction. Consider these Internet addiction quips:

1. Counterculturalist Timothy Leary was one of the first to liken computers to LSD, noting the mind-expanding, mesmerizing and ritualistic similarities between the two.

2. One of many "Netaholic" websites offers this Serenity Prayer, "Almighty webmaster, grant me the serenity to know when to log off, the courage to know when to check e-mail, and the wisdom to stay away from chat rooms."

3. A 24-year-old Ohio University graduate student, started his "Webaholics" home page in 1994 after two of his classmates ended up dropping out of school because they spent all their time on the web. "It's all tongue-in-cheek," He said. "Obviously, alcoholics don't have AA meetings in bars. But some of the people who sign into the support group definitely have problems. I've talked to some of these people; they're really looking for help." One anonymous visitor wrote: "The web has practically ruined my life. I once actually used to be popular and good at sports. . . . (Now) I have no friends, a bad attitude, and my grades dropped big time. I also get eye strain from staring at the screen for such periods of time." (Grumman, 1996).

4. In April, 1998, police in a Milwaukee suburb reported one of the first known cases of an Internet-induced spat turning to physical violence. When a woman decided she'd had enough with her husband's obsession with the Internet (and with an Australian woman he met in a chat room), she took to the phone wires outside her house with a pair of scissors, according to local police. The incident escalated into a shoving and punching match, and the couple wound up in separate jail cells for the night on charges of battery and criminal damage to property (Grumman, 1996).

5. In another case, a Maryland woman destroyed her marriage and neglected her children because she was on-line as much as 21 hours a day. She wasn't taking (her children) to the doctor, they were running out of heating oil in the winter and not having enough food because she was spending all her time on the Net (Grumman, 1996).

6. Young's Center for On-line Addiction (http://netaddiction.com/) offers training for psychologists, educators and human resource managers on how to identify and deal with individuals who spend excessive amounts of time on the Internet. Young reports that she has spoken to more than 400 self-professed Internet addicts, as well as concerned family members and friends.

7. An 18-year old from Portland, Oregon signs onto the Internet every day and spends hours telling people he has never met about his life and his dreams. He tells them things he wouldn't dare tell his high school buddies. Eventually, his grades suffered; he doesn't visit his grandparents as often as he used to; and he starts feeling restless if he goes more than a day without connecting to the World Wide Web. In an interview, he stated, "I once went two days without being on-line. I didn't like it. I was bored. Talking to real people just wasn't as exciting." (Grumman, 1996).

John Suler, PhD, a professor of psychology at Rider University and a practicing clinical psychologist writes that, "With the explosion of excitement about the Internet, some people seem to be a bit too excited. Some people spend way too much time there." He asks, "Is this yet another type of addiction that has invaded the human psyche?" Addiction specialists are not even sure yet what to call this phenomenon. Some label it an "Internet Addiction Disorder." Some cyberspace addictions are game and competition oriented, some fulfill more social needs, some simply may be an extension of workaholicism. Nevertheless, some people are definitely hurting themselves by their addiction to computers and cyberspace. When people lose their jobs, or flunk out of school, or are divorced by their spouses because they cannot resist devoting all of their time to virtual lands, they are pathologically addicted. These extreme cases are clear cut. But as in all addictions, the problem is where to draw the line between "normal" enthusiasm and "abnormal" preoccupation. "Addictions"—defined very loosely—can be healthy, unhealthy, or a mixture of both. If you are fascinated by a hobby, feel devoted to it, would like to spend as much time as possible pursuing it—this could be an outlet for learning, creativity, and self-expression. Even in some unhealthy addictions you can find these positive features embedded within (and thus maintaining) the problem. But in truly pathological addictions, the scale has tipped. The bad outweighs the good, resulting in serious disturbances in one's ability to function in the "real" world (Suler, 1998).

Psychiatrist Nathan Shapira of the University of Cincinnati College of Medicine, conducted a study that provided evidence suggesting that people who seem addicted to the Internet often show a bumper crop of psychiatric disorders like manic-depression, and treating those other conditions might help them rein in their urge to be online. He and colleagues studied 14 people who spent so much time online that they were facing problems like broken relationships, job loss and dropping out of school. One 31-year-old man was online more than 100 hours a week, ignoring family and friends and stopping only to sleep. A 21-year-old man flunked out of

Russell A. Sabella, Ph.D.

college after he stopped going to class. When he disappeared for a week, campus police found him in the university computer lab, where he'd spent seven days straight online. The study participants, whose average age was 35, were interviewed for three to five hours with standard questions to look for psychiatric disorders. Being hooked on the Internet is not a recognized disorder. Shapira writes that it is unclear whether the Internet problem should be considered a disorder or just a symptom of something else, or whether certain disorders promote excessive online use (Associated Press, 1998).

What makes the Internet addictive? According to Young (1998), the Internet itself is a term which represents different types of functions that are accessible on-line. Generally speaking, Internet addicts tend to form an emotional attachment to the on-line friends and activities they create inside their computer screens. They enjoy those aspects of the Internet which allowed them to meet, socialize, and exchange ideas with new people through highly interactive Internet applications (such as chatting, playing on-line games, or being involved with several news groups). These virtual communities create a vehicle to escape from reality and seek out a means to fulfill an unmet emotional and psychological need. On the Internet, you can conceal your real name, age, occupation, appearance, and your physical responses to anyone or anything you encounter on-line. Internet users, especially those who are lonely and insecure in real-life situations, take that freedom and quickly pour out their strongest feelings, darkest secrets, and deepest desires. This leads to the illusion of intimacy, but when reality underscores the severe limitations of relying on a faceless community for the love and caring that can only come from actual people, Internet addicts experience very real disappointment and pain. On-line personas may be created whereby they are able to alter their identities and pretend to be someone other then who they are in "real life." People who use such on-line personas help build their confidence, express repressed feelings, and cultivate a certain type of "fantasy world" inside their computer screens. Those with the highest risk for creating a secret on-line life

are those who suffer from low self-esteem, feelings of inadequacy, and fear of disapproval from others. Such negative self-concepts lead to clinical problems of depression and anxiety, which also may be intertwined with excessive Net use and manipulated self-presentations.

A special type of Net addict is the user who hurts him/herself and others by engaging in cyberporn and/or cybersex. According to Relevant Knowledge, a Washington D.C. based market researcher, 9.6 million users, or about 15% of all Web users, logged on to the 10 most popular sex sites in the month of April 1998 alone. There are an estimated 70,000 sex-related Web sites, accounting for a sizable chunk of the $4 billion U.S. adult-entertainment industry. The abundance and accessibility of such adult material makes it effortless to fall into compulsive patterns of use for sexual gratification. This creates special problems for those who suffer from sexual addiction only to use the Internet as another vehicle to fulfill their needs. For others, cybersexual addiction is a unique problem in their lives. Sexual feelings are awakened through the anonymity of private chat rooms and other eager participants.

What are the warning signs for the development of Cybersexual Addiction? According to Young (1998), several include:

1. Methodically spending significant amounts of time in chat rooms and private messaging with the sole purpose of finding cybersex.

2. Feeling preoccupied with using the Internet to find on-line sexual partners.

3. Frequently using anonymous communication to engage in sexual fantasies not typically carried out in real-life.

4. Anticipating your next on-line session with the expectation that you will find sexual arousal or gratification.

5. Finding that you frequently move from cybersex to phone sex (or even real-life meetings).

6. Hiding your on-line interactions from your significant other.

7. Feeling guilt or shame from your on-line use.

8. Accidentally being aroused by cybersex at first, and then finding that you actively seek it out when you log on-line.

9. Masturbating while on-line and engaged in erotic chat.

10. Less investment with your real-life sexual partner only to prefer cybersex as a primary form of sexual gratification.

A Behavioral Perspective

Internet addiction may also be effectively explained by behavioral principles. Specifically, Net surfing is a behavior that may be highly sustained, both in frequency and duration, due to the chaotic nature of the Net. Finding special resources is sometimes easy and can be accomplished in very few attempts. At other times though, the process is difficult and requires extensive searches and sifting through many sites. The unpredictability of results may inadvertently reinforce users for staying online with a variable interval or variable ratio schedule of reinforcement. Similar to gambling, Net surfers may find themselves continually playing until they hit the "jackpot," in this case, that perfect site (better known as the web nugget). Of course, the nature of the jackpot varies among users and depends on what is considered reinforcing. A site may be highly rewarding because it translates into high levels of sexual gratification. Others may find gratifying experiences which include power ("I know something you don't know."), prestige ("Look at what I was able to find and you couldn't."), belongingness ("I share with you this unique information."), connection ("I found you!") popularity ("Ask Mary, she knows everything about the Web."), or attention ("I wonder who may have sent me an e-mail since I checked three minutes ago?"). Behaviorists would help us manage our on-line experience by rewarding behaviors which promote self-discipline and time management.

Tips for Preventing Net Addiction

The following are tips to consider, especially for those that believe they may be susceptible to an online addiction:

1. Allow yourself a set period of time, perhaps one hour, to stay online. If you need to, set a timer with an alarm (perhaps a computer program) that reminds you to log off. When you hear the alarm, remind yourself that there is *always* another site of interest that can be discovered *later*. Also, remind yourself that there exists no website or e-mail communication that will make or break your career or professional effectiveness if you were to disregard it.

2. Install software that keeps track of the time you spend online and report it to someone else who can help you monitor your online usage.

3. Let others surf the Internet for you to find web nuggets. That is, subscribe to one or more of the many available listservs that provide annotated descriptions of websites of particular interest. After you receive the posting, visit the sites of particular interest and create a bookmark for those sites so that you can visit them during your next scheduled surf session. For instance, when I'm developing a new classroom activity, I conduct a search of my computer's hard drive for files containing relevant terms. Included in the results are the websites which I have bookmarked which contain those terms. Then, I simply focus on those specific sites with a clear purpose in mind rather than spending much time researching and re-evaluating.

Russell A. Sabella, Ph.D.

4. If appropriate, only maintain Internet access from your work rather than also obtaining access from your home. This will help to foster clear parameters for work, family, and leisure.

5. Use a debit card rather than a credit card when signing up with your Internet Service Provider so that you will not accrue any undue debt. With a debit card, if you do not have funds in your checking account to cover the expense, you will lose your Internet access.

6. When surfing for leisure, consider it an activity you might share with your significant other. This way, it will be more difficult for you to submit to adult web sites which can easily strain a relationship.

7. Prioritize your tasks. For example, if a task is pressing, postpone checking your e-mail until tomorrow.

Equitable Access

Nations are leaders because of their invention and innovation with tools and processes. Whether the topic be counseling, agriculture, medicine, the economy, the military, or influence on the masses (mass media), the status of a nation in the world community continues to be determined by the ability to invent or acquire modern tools and to master innovative processes with these tools. The tools and processes of this generation relate to information technologies, and it is on the basis of capacity for information processing that national haves and have-nots are emerging (Thomas & Knezek, 1998). As modern technology threatens to take over many tasks performed by unskilled workers, there is a danger that displaced workers who have no technology skills will see their standard of living—indeed their very ability to earn a living—nose dive amid significant technology-based economic success by the nation. In the last decade of the millenium, 5 of the 10 fastest growing careers will be computer related (Cooksey, 1994). It is vital that as the U.S. positions itself for continued world technology leadership that capacity be built among *all* its citizens for understanding, coping with and applying emerging technologies.

Schools already show significant disparities in resources, even within the same district. Internet access, especially throughout a school and district, is still quite costly to initiate and especially maintain. Could it be that more affluent schools that provide the advantages of technologies such as Internet access perpetuate the privileges already afforded to their students? Could it be that poorer schools and districts that cannot yet afford the relative luxury of Internet access face yet another hurdle that keeps students further behind? Internet literacy is known to be a desirable and even critical competency that our future workforce may not be able to do without. So, the lack of Internet access may imply that students not only learn less effectively, but may be less equipped to meet the needs of their future workplace. Consider that the expansion in computer-related industries accounted for more than one-quarter of the U.S. economy's growth for the past five years, according to statistics by the Commerce Department as of April 1998. According to the department, the industry will need 1.3 million new workers in the next 10 years. In addition, the computer-illiterate will not be able to participate in many daily functions that the World Wide Web is taking over. For example, the Commerce Department notes that consumers bought $1 billion worth of travel bookings online. In the next three years, that number is expected to jump to $8 billion (Weinraub, 1998).

On the "front burner" of the equitable access issue is how incorporating Internet advantages in learning may be systematically leaving out ethnic minorities whom may disproportionately represent poorer schools. The inequity in Internet access at school seems not to be reconciled by other forms of access either such as having a computer at home. For example, one survey completed by telephone interviews of more than 5,800 people in December 1996 and January 1997 determined that white students in high school and college are more likely than African-American students to have computers in their homes and use the World Wide Web. While 73 percent of white students had a home computer, only 33 percent of African-American students did. The gap remained even when researchers accounted for differences in income. For all ages, the computer gap was somewhat narrower, with 44 percent of whites having a home computer and 29 percent of African-American. But while 59 percent of whites surveyed reported using the Web in the past six months, only 31 percent of African-Americans reported Internet use. Researchers concluded that with the Internet becoming an increasingly important part of American education and economic progress, a significant segment of our society is in danger of being denied equal access. Consequently, there may be a generation that is completely unprepared for the economy in the new millennium (Walton, 1998).

The Federal government recognizes the importance of technologically literate Americans and has thus allocated a great deal of financial resources towards this endeavor. For instance, the Clinton Administration announced on September 22, 1998 that 20 school district partnerships in 17 states would be awarded grants totaling $30 million to help provide the additional support to meet the challenge of preparing new teachers, and supporting existing ones, to teach effectively using technology. The Technology Innovative Challenge Grant Program serves as a catalyst for positive change for schools. It supports educators, industry partners, communities, parents, and others who are using new technologies to help bring high quality education to every classroom and neighborhood.

NetDay is a grassroots volunteer effort to wire schools so they can network their computers and connect them to the Internet (for more details, visit www.netday96.com). In his weekly radio address to the country on April 19, 1996, President Clinton described NetDay and its benefits when he said:

> NetDay is a great example of how America works best when we all work together. It's like an old-fashioned barn-raising, neighbor joins with neighbor to do something for the good of the entire community. Students, teachers, parents, community groups, government, business unions—all pulling together to pull cable, hook up our schools and put the future at the fingertips of all our young people. Once we reach our goal of linking our schools to the Internet, for the first time in history, children in the most isolated rural schools, the most comfortable suburbs, the poorest inner-city schools, all of them will have the same access to the same universe of knowledge. That means a boy in Lake Charles, Louisiana can visit a museum halfway around the world, a girl in Juneau, Alaska can visit the Library of Congress on line. Since the first NetDay just over a year ago, nearly a quarter million volunteers have wired 50,000 classrooms around our country.

Today, NetDay activities are occurring in more than 40 states. .... Today I am directing every department and agency in our national government to develop educational Internet services targeted to our young people. With this action, we are one step closer to giving young people the tools they need to be the best they can be in the 21st century.

Internet access and technology literacy are of consequential concern to counselors because they facilitate our mission to, in short, assist *all* students to become successful and responsible lifelong learners. We as counselors might help seize the opportunity to obtain federal funding, coordinate professional development, and work with others to ensure rightful access and competent use of modern-age tools. Counselors can help to develop community and business partnerships which provide both equipment, access, and training to all involved. Counselors may use their skills to negotiate collaborations with local organizations and especially universitity Colleges of Education.

E-Rate

On May 7, 1997, the Federal Communications Commission (FCC) adopted a Universal Service Order outlining a plan to guarantee that all eligible schools, libraries and rural health care providers have affordable connections to the Internet. By making $2.5 billion available annually, this program provides discounts (commonly known as the E-rate) to eligible organizations on certain telecommunications services. The plan also created a $400 million fund to lower the prices rural health care providers pay for telecommunications services. The following is a list of resources containing background information, instructions, application forms, help lines and other useful information related to the E-rate (Fulton, 1998).

1. **The Schools and Libraries Corporation (SLC).** SLC is the independent not-for-profit corporation established to administer the E-rate. Schools and libraries can file their applications electronically from the SLC Web site. Those who choose to file manually are welcome to mail their applications to Schools and Libraries Corp., PO Box 4217, Iowa City, IA 52244-4217. All schools and libraries who file applications for the program will have the technology services they requested posted on the Web site in order to invite competitive bidding from vendors. The Web site operates every day from 5:00 a.m. to midnight Eastern Time and includes FAQ's, a discount matrix, and fund status. E-mail questions to: question@slcfund.org or call 888-203-8100. http://www.slcfund.org

2. **National Exchange Carrier Association (NECA).** The FCC appointed NECA as temporary administrator of the support mechanisms which will fund the Universal Service programs. This site provides information on Service Provider Identification Numbers (SPIN), consortia, eligible services, rules of priority, pre-existing contracts, disbursement of funds, instructions for completing the online forms and an overview of the E-rate program. http://www.neca.org

3. **FCC Universal Service Home Page.** For the latest official government information, FCC orders are available electronically from the http://www.fcc.gov/ccb/universal_service/

4. **Services and Functionalities Eligible for Discounts.** http://www.fcc.gov/Bureaus/Common_Carrier/Public_Notices/1997/da971374.html#2

5. **FCC LearnNet.** The FCC's Informal Education Page dealing with FCC policy and education initiatives. Contains press releases, FCC Orders, recent E-rate public notices, and FAQ's. http://www.fcc.gov/learnnet/

6. **E-Rate Forms.** In addition to the two forms (Form FCC 470 and 471), you will find instructions for completing them and an overview of the Universal Service program. The overview provides information on: kinds of schools and libraries that are eligible, consortia (which are also eligible), calculating the discount, classifying urban and rural locations, eligible services, examples of eligible and ineligible internal connections, rules of priority, pre-existing contracts, what schools and libraries must do before applying, the application process, and Web sites to go to for more information. http://www.ed.gov/Technology/erateforms/

7. **Nine Steps You Can Take Now to Prepare for the Schools and Libraries Universal Service Program.** http://www.ed.gov/Technology/ninestep.html

8. **Questions and Answers on Implementation of the Universal Service Program for Schools and Libraries.** http://www.ed.gov/Technology/qanda.html

9. **National Center for Education Statistics School (NCES) Codes.** The E-rate application forms require the district or school NCES (National Center for Educational Statistics) code. This site will help you find those codes. http://nces.ed.gov/ccdweb/school/school.htm

10. **Consortium for School Networking.** CoSN, a non-profit organization, promotes the use of telecommunications in K-12 education to improve learning. This site contains recent SLC Fact Sheets, E-Rate forms, and links to state education departments. http://www.cosn.org/

11. **The Benton Foundation's Universal Service and Universal Access Virtual Library.** The Benton Foundation is a nonprofit, nonpartisan, private foundation which seeks to promote communications in the public interest. The Universal Service and Universal Access Virtual Library includes research, history, policy briefings and bulletins. http://www.benton.org/Policy/Uniserv/

12. **EdLiNC: Education and Library Networks Coalition.** EdLiNC was formed to represent the viewpoint of schools and libraries in FCC proceedings dealing with the implementation of the Telecommunications Act. The EdLiNC Web site includes the latest updates, free publications, action kits, and links to other Universal Service Sites. One of EdLiNC's projects is the E-Rate Hotline, which includes a toll free number for questions: 1-800-733-6860 (10 a.m.-9 p.m. EST), a Web site http://www.eratehotline.org which contains a searchable knowledge base of questions, and an online form to send your questions to an e-rate expert. http://www.itc.org/edlinc/discounts/

13. **Quality Education Data Information on Universal Service Fund.** Quality Education Data (QED) is a research and database company, focused exclusively on education. This site provides information on the application process, eligibility, funding, restrictions and program implementation. http://www.qeddata.com/usfund.htm

14. **3Com.** "Everything you always wanted to know about the E-rate, but were afraid to ask." This workbook, produced in cooperation with the Consortium for School Networking, includes a disk with SLC forms, a list of state education departments, a guide to creating a technology plan, and an example of a technology plan. http://www.3com.com/erate

15. "The E-rate and Beyond," A Special Report from T.H.E. (Technological Horizons in Education) Journal. This online journal provides links to breaking news, case histories, technology ground breakers, links to technology plans, and more. http://www.thejournal.com/erate/default.asp

16. Mid-continent Regional Educational Laboratory (McREL). McREL operates several regional centers funded by the U.S. Department of Education that provide research, technical assistance, professional development, evaluation and policy studies, and information services to several state and local education agencies. This extensive site includes news, general information and resources, and state and local initiatives. http://www.mcrel.org/connect/tech/telecom.html

Pornography on the WWW

On September 2, 1998, an event made news headlines in every major newspaper in the world. About 100 people in 14 countries were arrested in what police said was the biggest ever worldwide swoop of alleged pedophiles using the Internet. Dozens of addresses were raided, including 32 in the United States alone. The raids were based on an investigation of a pedophilia ring known as the "Wonderland Club," which used sophisticated encryption codes originally developed by the KGB.

The Internet, from the very beginning, has been a tool for distributing a wide variety of information across a large number of people, and until recently, has not been a place where particularly young children would frequent. With the introduction of user-friendly online systems and the World Wide Web, and the introduction of the Internet to the classroom, more and more children are taking advantage of the power of the Internet. Its potential for education, communication, and a sense of global community is practically limitless. However, the Internet remains largely an adult forum, and so it carries with it adult subjects. This raises the question: What happens when the adult themes and a child's naive explorations meet?

Amidst the material available on the Internet that is of enormous educational potential, there is also material that even the hardiest civil libertarian would probably agree is not appropriate for small children—for example, graphical depiction of child pornography, vicious racism from bigots of various stripes, and detailed instructions on how to build bombs from some highly destructive people are all there. In some cases this material can raise questions that go beyond those of appropriateness and taste: its distribution and ownership may also be illegal, particularly within certain jurisdictions. For example, possession of child pornography is likely to be illegal as well as reprehensible. In most cases this material is also readily available from non-Internet sources (your local Adult Bookstore, for example), but its availability on the Net is a particularly sensitive issue because it is harder to monitor the age of persons accessing material on the Net than to check the age of patrons at the adult bookstore (The Web Tutorial, 1998).

Sex and pornography occur in every part of the Internet. This includes the World Wide Web, Virtual Communities like Internet Relay Chat (IRC) and Multi-User Dimensions (MUDs), and newsgroups. The presentation of sexually explicit materials differs from platform to platform, as does the degree of obscenity or indecency. While some are more visible than others, sexually explicit material can be easily found on all of them. The Web is the most visible aspect of the Internet, and the way that most people explore it. The nature of the Web itself—a multimedia carnival of pictures, movies, sounds, and colors— makes it much more popular with the general public than the other platforms. The multimedia aspect of the Web also makes it a place where all kinds of sexual material can be displayed, and many people have taken advantage of this whether for profit or for fun. One example of a type of pornography that is specific to the Web is live "video conferencing" in which the "caller" interacts with one or more individuals who perform sexual activities at the prompting of the user. These live shows vary from the tame to the lewd, and can include any number of users all typing or speaking commands simultaneously.

A simple search for any one of a number of sexually explicit words, especially slang terms for genitalia and/or sexual intercourse, on any search engine will yield a list of countless pornographic sites. Some of these are more of a soft-core nature, displaying "simple nudes"—Playboy and Penthouse are prime examples. These sites tend to make available material much like that displayed in their paper publications, which are indecent to be sure, but may not be obscene. On the opposite end of the spectrum, there are a great number of hard-core sites—far more numerous than their softer cousins. These sites display blatant indecency such as penetration of the vaginal, anal, and oral orifices of men and women by penises, hands, and various devices. They show hetero- and homosexual intercourse, bestiality, bondage, and fetishes involving various forms of human excrement, to name but a few. Since all of these sites have a common goal—profit—they tend to have a built-in security device. Namely, they only display a sampling for free, and further access is limited to credit card holders who are willing to pay a fee. This certainly helps to keep younger children from having full access to such sites, but even without ever gaining full access to any service, the amount of pornographic pictures, movies, and sounds that someone can compile for free and without ever encountering any age verification roadblocks, is enough to fill a hard drive (ACCA, 1999).

One other type of page on which pornography can be found is a personal homepage. The number of personal homepages—pages maintained for individuals, by individuals, and for no profit, is tremendous, and the content of these pages are as varied as the people who maintain them. Because of this, any level of sexual material can be found on any homepage, from soft-core to hard-core. While many sexual homepages follow the design of a shrine to a celebrity, others display their proprietors engaged in sexual activities of an obscene nature, and yet others display movies, sounds, or pictures from their favorite X-Rated movies. Finally, although most Internet Service Providers do not allow advertising on space not designated to contain it, some individuals use their homepages to advertise and sell their own homemade sex tapes, or various sundries such as sex toys, or used undergarments. These personal pages present even a tougher challenge for regulation for a couple of reasons. First, unlike commercial sites, they are not as widely recognized. Second, there are no measures taken to regulate these pages and prevent minors from accessing them, not even semi-effective measures such as credit card authorization.

Communications Decency Act

The nature of Internet pornography and the sort of person who uses it has resulted in a war that is being waged on the Internet, in children's homes, and on Capitol Hill. The debate has raised not only questions of obscenity, harassment, free speech, and censorship, but also of government control over the Internet. Whatever legislation ends up being imposed in this arena, it will set a precedent for how the government deals with the exchange of information in the future. Is the Internet a free forum for discussion, or is it a broadcasting service, and therefore subject to the same restrictions as television, print, or radio? Are communications on the Internet covered by the right to privacy? And who is accountable for what happens on it?

In February, 1996, the *Communications Decency Act* (CDA; see http://www.fcc.gov/Speeches/Chong/separate_statements/cda.txt) was passed. Many people found the CDA unconstitutional, and its passing prompted an Internet-wide protest. Since then, the CDA has been challenged and overturned, and then taken to the Supreme court where it was soundly defeated on the basis of it being unconstitutional. Whether or not Internet-specific regulations exist or not, actions which are illegal in general are still illegal on the Internet. For example, child pornography in any form is illegal. Hence, no further laws involving Internet child pornography are needed. Interestingly, though it is clearly illegal, and although there are cut-and-dry laws involving child pornography, examples of it can still be found on the Internet. Posted as often as the child pornography itself are messages from others damning the posters to Hell and warning them of imminent arrest, but, in general, no actions seem to be taken in the real world to serve to dissuade the child pornography posters, as their material invariably appear a few days later with other similar posts.

Decreasing Student Risk

There exists no guarantee that young students will not somehow access inappropriate, illegal, or obscene material over the Net. However, there are methods which schools and parents can employ to significantly decrease the danger and risk to such access among our children. Realize however, that what one person may find offensive, another might find aesthetic. Some people have proposed "tagging" all items on the Internet with a rating similar to the American motion picture ratings. This scheme is not a workable one, since even well-intentioned content authors will have difficulty rating their material in a manner that agree with your values as a counselor, parent, or educator. So what can counselors and other caring adults do to help protect children from viewing potentially abusive material on the Net? Following are several suggestions which can be implemented in schools and sometimes at home.

Supervision. "Hold hands while crossing the street" is good advice in reality and makes perfect sense on the Internet too. Adult supervision is a method for shielding our children from adult material more effective than the most advanced technology yet developed for this purpose. There exists no substitute for sitting down with your students or children and exploring the World Wide Web together. This is true when surfing for leisure, doing homework, or conducting guidance related activities. Similar to watching television together, adults and children whom surf the Web together share an experience which can prove to be beneficial to the relationship. Further, the Web provides much opportunity for discussing scores of topics and issues favorable for learning. Besides, if a student or class in your custody accesses pornographic material on the Net because you were not appropriately supervising, you may place yourself and your school at legal risk and consequently endanger your career.

Realistically however, when a group of student simultaneously access the Web, controlling which sites they enter is very difficult at best if not humanly possible. Therefore, adequately protecting students from harmful material requires both human and technological assistance. Parents and community stakeholder can help supervise and even conduct lab exercises when using the Net. Additionally, schools can incorporate hardware and software solutions for filtering and blocking (discussed later) potentially obscene materials from entering the schools walls.

Acceptable Use Policies. With Internet access becoming increasingly common within our schools, it is apparent that a clear set of guidelines for the use of the resources that this access provides are needed for the guidance of the students, teachers, administrators, parents, and board members. Using the Internet such as with classroom guidance can be somewhat risky. It is advisable to obtain consent forms from all parents at the beginning of the school year emphasizing that, while all efforts will be directed toward seeing that children access appropriate material, common sense dictates that no monitoring system is foolproof, and in the final analysis students must also assume responsibility for accessing only appropriate material. An Acceptable Use Policy is a document which establishes parameters for those who use the Internet at school. The document addressess appropriate use of the school's system, the rights of all parties involved, protocols and procedures for infractions, and liabilities such as in the case of loss or damage. For a comprehensive and downloadable template of an AUP, you may also visit http://www.erehwon.com/k12aup. Also, check out HISD's Armadillo—The Texas Studies Gopher (http://chico.rice.edu/armadillo/Rice/Resources/acceptable.html) which began collecting AUP resources a number of years ago and should prove to be helpful as a starting place.

According to Willard (1996), some school districts have established a policy of having a "sponsoring teacher" sign a student's Internet use agreement affirming that they will supervise the student's use of the account. The practical reality is that the sponsoring teacher of a secondary school student will not be in always be in a position to monitor an individual student's activities, therefore it is unclear what why such a signature is required. Sponsoring teachers will be directly in the firing line if a parent is displeased with their child's actions on the Internet. All district personnel should have general supervisory responsibility when their students are using the Internet. Counselors might be well advised to follow Willard's (1996) advice to teachers:

My advice to teachers is that they should not sign any agreement that places responsibility on them for supervising specific students in their use of the Internet. A signature indicating specific responsibility is an invitation to trouble, including the potential of being listed as a defendant in a law suit. While it is unlikely that a teacher would be held personally responsible, being a defendant in a law suit does not rank high on anyone's list of fun and games. p. 10

Provide Students with Tools. Self-defense is more than just common sense on the Internet. Of course, all the rules in the real world also hold true in cyberspace. That is, don't talk to strangers, don't give out your personal information, and watch where you're going. However, the Internet is pervaded by savvy and cunning users who can obtain information such as your system origin (e.g., visit http://www.anonymizer.com), use this to decipher your personal e-mail address, find your home address and instantly create a map to your house (e.g., see http://www.anywho.com). This information can be gathered infinitely more quickly than in real life. Thus, helping students stay on a safe and secure path of exploring the Internet by making them aware of potential hazards.

Russell A. Sabella, Ph.D.

Although children should always be supervised when online, they should also follow some "rules of the road" which should lead to having a better time in cyberspace, stay safe, and keep you and their parents worrying less. The following is an example of a "contract" that your students should read, understand, and follow (Magid, 1996).

 I will not give out personal information such as my address, telephone number, parents' work address/telephone number, or the name and location of my school without my parents' permission.

 I will tell my parents right away if I come across any information that makes me feel uncomfortable.

 I will never agree to get together with someone I "meet" online without first checking with my parents. If my parents agree to the meeting, I will be sure that it is in a public place and bring my mother or father along.

 I will never send a person my picture or anything else without first checking with my parents.

 I will not respond to any messages that are mean or in any way make me feel uncomfortable. It is not my fault if I get a message like that. If I do I will tell my parents right away so that they can contact the service provider.

 I will talk with my parents so that we can set up rules for going online. We will decide upon the time of day that I can be online, the length of time I can be online, and appropriate areas for me to visit.

 I will not access other areas or break these rules without their permission.

Blocking and Filtering Software

Software solutions to preventing access to harmful material falls into two general classes: (a) Solutions that block net access to certain addresses deemed to contain objectionable material (i.e., blocking); and (b) Solutions that block access based on the appearance of certain words or phrases in the data being downloaded (filtering).

Neither of these approaches is foolproof. One can never know all sites which might contain objectionable material, and monitoring based on the occurrence of certain words or phrases might easily screen out daily newspapers or even the Bible. For instance, typical sites mistakenly blocked by word filters may include chicken recipe sites, blocked for the word "breast," the White House Web site, blocked for the word "couple," and a county government site blocked for the phrase "Middlesex County." One the other hand, a word filter will frequently allow a picture from a pornographic site to appear in the browser before triggering a block. This is because many porn sites purposely represent all the "words" in the opening page in the form of graphics in order to defeat any word filter. And, of course, once a picture is on the computer screen it can be saved, printed, e-mailed, or posted just about anywhere else on the Net. Willard (1996) also points out that using screening software is expensive and might take resources that could better be used to provide training and support for teachers, counselors, students, and parents.

She also indicates that such software places a reliance on barriers, instead of a focus on assisting students to make appropriate choices guided by  school rules and personal values. Finally, Willard (1996) warns that a district's willingness to spend a great deal of money for such software says to the community that the district thinks the problem is bigger than it really is.

Several blocking/filtering software resources include:

1. Since children of all ages use America On Line (AOL), they have created features to help parents make sure their children have a fun and enriching experience online, while limiting access to some features of AOL and the Internet. These Parental Controls allow parents to designate different levels of access for each child. http://www.aol.com

2. Cyber Patrol is used to manage Internet access, limit the total time spent online and restrict access to Internet sites that you deem inappropriate. http://www.cyberpatrol.com

3. Cyber Sentinel allows user to block inappropriate material (web pages, e-mail, pictures, and word processing documents) no matter what format it is in, or what it is. It also allows the owner to configure the program to run in stealth mode (so the end user doesn't know it is running). The owner can the run Cyber Sentinel later and see screen shots of when the user was in inappropriate material. http://www.securitysoft.com/

4. Cyber Snoop shows you which Internet sites have been visited by your children by monitoring their on-line activity. If monitoring components are disabled without a password, the computer will shut down and reinstate the missing monitoring modules. If suspect sites are found, you can use the software to generate a link to the questionable site and visit the web site through your web browser. Full Internet Blocking is optional. http://www.pearlsw.com/

5. DiskTracy allows adults to monitor what children are doing on the Internet without filtering or restricting access. It finds and displays text and graphics files, hidden graphics and compressed files and a listing of all websites visited. http://www.disktracy.com/

6. Gulliver's Guardian is an all-in-one Internet Suite that includes a filtered Web browser (Microsoft Internet Explorer compatible), e-mail (with spell-check), news reader, and Full Armor PC Protector. Guardian provides parents, educators and businesses with a tool to control access to the Internet and their computer systems. Access to inappropriate material can be blocked by using Guardian's System Ratings or your own Customized Ratings. The Guardian Internet Suite also provides time restriction options that control the amount of hours per month, day, or time of day users can have access to the Internet. http://www.gulliver.nb.ca/

7. I-Gear is a blocking tool with many features. The software requires user authentication, gives roaming users access to bookmarks, history, and their customized access rights. It enables customizable list-based filtering with pre-filled categories such as sex, crime, gambling, and make applicable to users, groups of users. Provides ability to create "allow lists" to focus Internet access on specific sites and make applicable to users, groups of users, computers, or groups of computers. http://www.urlabs.com/public/

8. Net Nanny allows you to monitor, screen and block access to anything residing on, or running in your PC, whether you are connected to the Internet or not, and in real time. http://www.netnanny.com

9. SafeSurf is an organization dedicated to making the Internet safe for your children without censorship. They are developing and are implementing an Internet Rating Standard that is bringing together parents, providers, publishers, developers, and all the resources available on the Internet to achieve this goal. It involves marking sites with the SafeSurf Wave. http://www.safesurf.com/

10. While no filtering program is 100 percent effective, SurfWatch claims to shield users from 90-95% percent of the explicit material on the Net. SurfWatch currently tracks over 100,000 uniquely identified sites in five core categories. SurfWatch blocks access to millions of URLs, 5000 news groups, and 200 Internet Relay Chat channels that contain explicit material. SurfWatch adds over 400 new sites to the database every day. http://www1.surfwatch.com/

11. WizGuard provides features such as: customizable blocking, web access log, customizable exempt, and time management in WizGuard which allows administrators to regulate the amount of time students spent on the Internet. http://www.wizguard.com/

Child Friendly Internet Service Providers

Some Internet Service Providers have proprietary environments where content is screened as being available for the lowest common denominator of children. You, the child custodian, request that the student's account be placed into this environment. Because you are paying the service provider for the child's account, they have an incentive to do it correctly as opposed to the ratings systems previously presented. The major providers are treating this option as a customer-driven feature, fueled by requests from paying parent customers. It is a growing market and not likely to fade in the near future. Make sure to explore this option before settling on your ISP. For example, FamilyConnect (www.cleansurf.com) offers high speed Internet access, is protected by a server-side filtering system, and updates their database daily. Also, Integrity Online (http://www.integrityonline.com/) blocks searches for inappropriate words and blocks access to inappropriate sites.

Online Sexual Harassment

When Sue first met Simon, she knew that maintaining a relationship with someone from a different country would be difficult. Later, however, she realized that ending the relationship would actually be the difficult part. Immediately upon terminating the relationship Sue began receiving e-mails, almost hourly, from Simon. She then started receiving e-mails from men she did not know, soliciting her for sex. Apparently, Simon posted her phone number on the Internet, inviting men to "call for a good time." Finally, Simon posted her address and encouraged local men to stop by and see Sue (Bevilacqua, 1997).

In another incident at the University of Michigan in January, 1995, a student posted four graphically violent stories on the Internet using the name of a female student from his class. University officials removed the story from their server, but Internet users continued to post and re-post it. The student posted his fictionalized stories to the biggest pornography bulletin board on the Internet with approximately 270,000 users internationally. In his stories, the student posted the female's first, middle and last name, complete with the student's detailed physical description. Fortunately, the story was seen and reported to university officials by a University of Michigan alumnus in Moscow. Interestingly enough, the case went to court and was dismissed because the court claimed that the student's words were protected under the First Amendment. This ruling, without surprise, caused a wave of clamor across the country. The government appealed the dismissed 1995 case, but, in January 1997, the 6th U.S. District Court of Appeals in Cincinnati also dismissed charges against the student, claiming that no threat was intended to the female student (Arnold, 1998).

Both men and women who use the Web, other online services, or even internal networks report receiving invitations and messages of a sexually explicit nature in real-time "chats" or via e-mail. These messages are variously analogous to obscene phone calls or "cat calls" in the street depending on their tone. However, they take on an added annoyance factor for those who are paying to utilize the resources of the online environment. Additionally, these messages may be experienced repeatedly by women for many reasons, one of which is because there tends to be fewer women on most systems. Women looking for information online are often surprised to see that a female first name can bring a distracting and ultimately expensive volume of unsolicited contact. The problem is pervasive and annoying enough that many women choose to switch to non-gender-specific login names, for example, or to post to women-only conferences or mailing lists.

The official website of one organization dedicated to confronting online harassment, W.H.O.A. (Women Halting On-line Abuse available at http://whoa.femail.com/), endeavors to educate the Internet community about online harassment, empower victims of harassment, and formulate voluntary policies that systems can adopt in order to create harassment-free environments. W.H.O.A. fully supports the right to free speech both online and off, but asserts that free speech is not protected when it involves threats to the emotional or physical safety of anyone. In the corporate world, employers increasingly are using e-mail surveillance software to guard against sexual harassment lawsuits and the loss of trade secrets (McNamara, 1998). Evidence of the trend remains largely anecdotal, according to e-mail administrators and industry experts. However, many believe that content-filtering of workplace e-mail will become commonplace with the maturation of server-based applications.

Security

As an increasing number of people learn about the power of communicating, shopping, and basically interacting with others over the Net, protecting personal and sensitive information is sometimes a concern. Many people don't fully understand the security risks they face when using the Internet, much less what they can do about them. Some may ask questions such as, "Is it safe to give my credit card number when making online purchases?" "Can someone intercept and read my communications?," and probably most worrisome, "Can someone get into my computer and steal my files?" The good news is that businesses stand to make a great deal of money by marketing to the expansive numbers of web users who enjoy the convenience of conducting communications and transactions over the Net. Such companies, along with other entrepreneurs, are spending a great deal of money to advance technologies that assure secure transactions, whether sending a confidential e-mail about a student or conducting a stock purchase. Most everyone today agrees that they have done a good job. All in all, many parts of the web set up for sensitive transactions are quite secure places to conduct business. The major credit card companies are so sure of this that, similar to offline transactions, will absorb the cost of unauthorized or fraudulent transactions (except for the first $50 for some). One company, NextCard (www.nextcard.com) will absorb 100% of the cost in case of fraudulent transactions over the Net.

How often do you hand your credit card to a waiter in a restaurant or give out your account number over the telephone when ordering products? Such actions probably pose a greater security risk than charging items online—at least from trusted Web sites. There is a chance that a thief could intercept your credit card number as it travels from your computer to the Web site's server, but it's highly improbable. In fact, it's much more difficult to carry out such a scheme online than it is in the real world where your credit card number is printed on statements and receipts that are mailed, filed, or thrown away. Some sites may work with your browser to encrypt, or encode, your transaction information so that, if it's intercepted, it can't be read. Online banks and investment services use encryption to protect the information in your transactions. Before information leaves the Web site's server for your computer, or vice versa, it's turned into code. After it reaches the appropriate destination, it's decoded. While the information travels over the Internet—where it may be vulnerable to being intercepted by someone with malicious intentions—it's essentially gibberish (Basic Web Browsing, 1998).

Your web browser will let you know when encryption is in use by displaying an icon at the bottom that looks like a lock. Sites that are not secure show the lock open and sites that are secure show the icon as locked. Another way to determine whether a site is secure or not is by looking at the site's address. Secure sites which encrypt communications during transmission begin with https:// instead of http://. For learning about the details about the encryption type in Internet Explorer 4.0: Right-click on the page, click [Properties], and then click [Certificates]. In the [Fields] box, select [Encryption type]. In the [Details] box, information about the page's encryption will appear. Click [Close], and then click [OK].

Regardless of safe transactions, you should know that any Web site you visit can tell who and where your Internet service provider is, what site you were last at, what Web browser you're using, and what you do while you're at the site. By asking you to register, a site can collect additional information from you, such as your name, e-mail address, postal address, income level, and interests. It's up to you whether to provide this. Notwithstanding, if you're listed in the white pages of the telephone book, your name, address, and telephone number are probably in databases on the World Wide Web, available for others to search. For example, try looking yourself up in some of the more well known databases such as:

❖ www.whitepages.com

❖ Bigfoot (www.bigfoot.com)

❖ Anywho Directories (www.anywho.com). This database is one of the more impressive ones that I have encountered. For most listed persons on this database, a user can also generate a map to a listed person's house or ask for a list of others in the directory on the same street or block.

❖ Microsoft Network People Finder (http://pic2.infospace.com/info.msn/index_ppl.htm).

❖ And if you want to spend a little money, conduct a background check at www.knowx.com

Viruses

A virus is a program or piece of code that is loaded onto your computer without your knowledge and runs against your wishes. All computer viruses are created by people and most can replicate themselves. A simple virus that can make a copy of itself over and over again is relatively easy to produce. Even such a simple virus is dangerous because it will quickly use all available memory and bring your system to a halt. An even more dangerous type of virus is one capable of transmitting itself across networks and bypassing security systems (Webopedia, 1999). To protect yourself from viruses on the Internet, don't download files from sources that may not be safe. Viruses are usually hidden in programs and activated when the programs run. They also can be attached to certain other types of executable files, such as special-action Web files and video files. Generally, when you're about to download a type of file that could contain a virus, your browser will display a warning and ask whether you want to open the file or save it to disk. If you're confident that the file comes from a trustworthy source, you may want to save it. If you're not sure, you may want to cancel your download. However, rather than practicing "download abstinence", you might continue and have a protected transaction by using an antivirus program. Immediately after downloading a file to your computer and before doing *anything* with it, have the file scanned for viruses by your antivirus program. There is still a chance that the file might contain a new and undocumented virus which will not be detected by antivirus software, although this chance is very small. If you don't have antivirus software loaded on your computer, you should get it right away. You might check out the following as starters:

- http://www.drsolomon.com
- http://www.symantec.com/nav/index.html
- http://www.mcafee.com/ (this one's free)
- http://www.hitchhikers.net/av.shtml
- http://www.cheyenne.com/
- http://www.commandcom.com/

One way that you can be confident against being infected is to practice "safe downloading." That is, you should consistently and periodically upgrade your antivirus program with new updates as they are made available over the Internet, perhaps every couple of weeks. A program such as Symantec's Norton Antivirus© (www.norton.com) makes this very simple because it includes a Live Update feature. This feature allows you to click on a button which has your computer connect with the company's database of known viruses, check to see if there are available any updates since the last check, download them, and then add or install them to your computer's list of known viruses. You should also know that such antivirus software will also check for any irregularities in your computer system's configuration upon turning it on and "booting up". Your operating system will usually keep an image of your system's configuration as it legitimately changes and checks against that image, especially memory, that may change because a virus. Once detecting such a change, you are made aware of the variation and given the chance for the antivirus program to remove and innoculate against future occurrences.

A special kind of virus is one that attaches itself to documents and data files such as spreadsheets, usually in the form of a macro (a mini-program usually used for conducting repetitive tasks). Malicious users can embed destructive instructions in a document they send to you (say, as an e-mail attachment). When you open the document, the virus moves into action. Microsoft Word and Microsoft Excel are particularly susceptible to these problems—known as "macro viruses". Microsoft has provided on their website (www.microsoft.com) "patches" to their programs which ward against such viruses. Also, many virus scanners now also detect such macro viruses, but their success rate is, however, lower than that for other viruses.

Trojan Horses

According to Solid Ground (1998), a free weekly newsletter about using the Internet more effectively, a Trojan Horse program, like the legendary wooden creature after whom it is named, offers you some apparent benefit (such as a pretty screen saver), encouraging you to install it and run it. After it gains your trust, it then has access to your machine to do whatever else it likes in the background. As an example, in December, 1997, two students wrote a software product that allowed users to customize their Internet software. It appeared to work as advertised, but also secretly e-mailed the user's password to the students. This action went undetected until March of 1998, when the students themselves revealed it to the press to demonstrate the security risks faced by Internet users. Trojan horses are another good reason to invest in an effective antivirus program.

Russell A. Sabella, Ph.D.

Programming Bugs

Despite the best of intentions, many software products contain programming mistakes known as "bugs". Malicious users can exploit bugs to make the software behave in unintended ways. For example, in July 1998, researchers discovered serious bugs in some of the world's most popular e-mail software: Microsoft Outlook, Netscape Mail and Eudora Pro. The bugs allow malicious users to worm their way into your computer and perform their own actions (Solid Ground, 1998). After its detections, these e-mail software providers developed patches to correct the problem. However, the bug left many, including myself, re-evaluating their personal security during daily and routine procedures such as processing electronic mail.

Cookies

A cookie is a small amount of information stored on your computer by a Web site that you have visited. The cookie typically includes information that your Web browser sends back to the site whenever you visit it again such as your password for the site or a customized view of the site that you have chosen. The reason that cookies are designed and planted on your computer is so that your browsing experience is more personal and simplified. For instance, cookies will help you bypass a site's password logon procedures because your password is simply entered from within your cookie. Then, you might receive a hearty and personalized welcome message. More intricate cookies keep track of the type of links you follow within a site, how much time you spend there, and what you do there (e.g., download a file) so that the site owners may begin to develop a profile for you that allows them to target new information that your profile indicates would probably be of interest to you. Some less than reputable sites use cookies to determine your originating e-mail address which

they will use to send you unsolicited e-mails in the form of advertisements. Such online behavior is usually experienced as a violation and is an example of the dark side of cookie use. Consequently, cookies are the focus of debate among those who view them as a service or "the cost of doing business" and those who passionately protect their privacy and civil liberties.

In general though, cookies are common and usually harmless. They can't be used to take information about you or your computer that you have not provided (again, another reason to be very careful what you kind of information you give up at a site). But they can be used by certain services to create a profile of your interests based on the sites you visit. Then information on participating sites can be customized for you which can certainly be a time-saver.

Browsers such as Netscape or IE can help you better control cookies by alerting you whenever a server tries to give you a cookie. In Internet Explorer version 4.0, click on the [View] menu, click [Internet Options] and then click the [Advanced] tab. Scroll to [Security] and under [Cookies], select [Prompt before accepting cookies] and click [OK]. When alerted, you can refuse a cookie. Or, you can choose to prohibit all cookies by clicking on the [Disable all cookie use] option. To delete cookies from your system, simply find them on your computer, usually in a folder called "Cookies" and delete them. At least a couple of drawbacks exist to denying cookies however. One problem is that cookies are so prevalent that you may be constantly dealing with cookie alerts which will seriously inhibit you from timely and enjoyable web surfing. Also, a site may not allow you to download valuable and free utilities and updates without first accepting their cookie. For instance, if you want to download some utilities from Microsoft, and you have set up your browser to not accept cookies, the company's site will detect this and stop you from continuing. A message will appear on your screen that alerts you to this situation and instructs you to turn cookies back on if you still want to pursue your download.

ActiveX

Even if you do not intentionally download software from a Web site, elements of a site may download, run on your computer, and pose a potential security risk such as by unleashing a virus onto your system. For example, ActiveX technologies allow software to be distributed over the Internet. You'll encounter ActiveX in the form of controls, usually graphic items such as scrolling marquees, on Web sites. Think of them as small programs within the site that run on your computer. An ActiveX control is like a plug-in, but worse. It doesn't require any installation (so users will use them without thinking twice), leaves no trace afterwards, and gives the illusion of extra security. A famous example of a malicious ActiveX control occurred in early 1997 when a group of computer experts demonstrated to the German press how to use the personal financial software product Quicken to transfer money from your bank account to theirs while innocently browsing their Web site.

You can set your Web browser to enable, disable, or prompt you to decide what to do with ActiveX controls depending on whether they are labeled safe. With Microsoft Internet Explorer version 4.0, you can automatically turn off ActiveX completely: On the View menu, click Internet Options and then click the Security tab. In the Zone drop-down list, select Internet Zone. In the Internet Zone box, select [High] and then click [OK]. To be prompted before any ActiveX control is downloaded and executed, in the Internet Zone box, select [Medium]. To set individual aspects of ActiveX control security yourself: On the [View] menu, click [Internet Options] and then click the [Security] tab. In the Zone drop-down list, select [Internet Zone]. In the Internet Zone box, select [Custom] and then click [Settings]. Under ActiveX Controls and plugins, select the settings you want, click [OK], and click [OK] again. Before allowing an ActiveX control to execute, you can also check it's authenticity. An ActiveX control can be digitally signed by its creator. Then a certifying authority such as VeriSign can certify the signature. A certificate is your assurance that the control was safe when it was designed and that it hasn't been tampered with since.

Java

Java is a computer language. Java-based mini-applications, also known as applets, can be downloaded from Web sites and run by Web browsers. Generally, these applets are limited in what they can do. However, there are some Java-related bugs. For instance, suppose you're browsing the Web and an error message pops up, saying you have been disconnected and asks for your user name and password again. Would you believe this message? Many people would, and faithfully follow the instructions. But this "error message" could be a JavaScript on the Web page you're viewing that takes your user name and password and forwards it to a malicious attacker. Indeed, in August of 1998, a computer expert demonstrated how to send an innocuous-looking e-mail message to HotMail users (HotMail is a popular free e-mail provider located at www.hotmail.com) that disguises itself as a HotMail system message and ask users for their password and then reports the password secretly to the attacker. To be safe, turn off Java in your Web browser except when you're at sites that you consider trustworthy. To disable Java with Internet Explorer 4.0: On the [View] menu, click [Internet Options] and then click the [Security] tab. In the Zone drop-down list, select [Internet Zone]. In the Internet Zone box, select [Custom] and then click [Settings]. Scroll to [Java], select [Disable Java], click [OK], and click [OK] again.

Russell A. Sabella, Ph.D.

Certificates

Digital certificates, granted by certifying authorities such as VeriSign, signify that a Web site or element of a Web site has been digitally signed by its creator. A certificate lets you know who is responsible for the site or element, and verifies that it is free from malicious components (such as viruses) and has not been tampered with since it was certified. When your browser is presented with a certificate, it checks its list of certifying authorities. If it finds a match, it allows your activity to continue. If your browser warns you that something is amiss about a certificate, your safest course is to cancel your activity.

In summary, you would not be too cautioned to invest in a reputable anti-virus program, have your browser warn you of impending ActiveX and JavaScripts, and interact only with trusted sites. Your best defense, however, is probably to be somewhat distrustful of requests for sensitive information such as your password. For instance, in May, 1997, users of America OnLine (AOL) in the United States received e-mail—supposedly from AOL staff—asking them to re-enter their passwords and credit card details. Needless to say, it was a scam. In December of the same year, when Yahoo opened its free e-mail service, a similar scam surfaced, with Internet users receiving e-mail from an official-looking address at yahoo.com, informing them they had won a free modem, for which they had to pay the freight costs (by credit card, of course) to collect their prize (Solid Ground, 1998). When in doubt, don't fulfill a seemingly legitimate request if it is at all out of the ordinary. Call the company making the request to verify the authenticity of the request.

Webcounseling

To my surprise and amazement, I received the following unsolicited e-mail one day:

Hello.

I type to you tonight asking for your help. I carry a secret that I have never talked about openly to anyone before. I am a 24 year old divorced mother. Very successful and still going to college. My son and I are very active in the community we live in and to other people I am a normal person. To most I am an overachiever and extremist. God has blessed our lives, but no matter how hard I work and push myself, I'm finding that my past is always there. My over achieving has its reasons. I have never went to anyone for help. I am usually the person people come to for help. I am very understanding and my past has educated me enough in that I've been there. Tonight, for the first time on searching the net about child abuse, I see that I'm not alone and that I'm not strange. I feel the desire to talk to someone but, unfortunately, don't have a clue as to who to talk to. I suffered emotional and physical abuse from my family and sexual abuse from a nonfamily member as a child. This is my first asking for help like this. I came across your name on the web and thought maybe you would know of someone who could help. If not, I understand.

Signed,

First Name Only

Although I have kept abreast of the web-counseling (i.e., attempting counseling over the Internet) evolution, I had never quite become so directly involved. I was more an outside observer looking into this fascinating and curious development. As a result of this e-mail, the reality of webcounseling became more vivid and personal for me. Suddenly, the ethical and legal considerations applied to me. What would I do with this message? Was this message real or a hoax? How old is the writer? I decided to reply and informed the author that I was not licenced in her state and therefore would not pursue providing her with professional counseling. Next, I wrote some highly facilitative sentences with the intent of instilling hope. Finally, I suggested how she might self-refer to a therapist which could fit her needs and move her toward healing. My reply arrived at this unknown person's address although I never received further communications from her (assuming she is female as represented by her first name).

When you think of conducting counseling with your students, you probably envision you and your client(s) in your office, in the classroom, or perhaps even on a "walk and talk." However, others may also have a mental image of a counselor who sits in front of the computer and conducts counseling over the Internet. Webcounseling is the attempt to provide counseling services in an Internet environment. The environment may include e-mail, chatrooms, or Internet video conferencing. For example, one site (http://www.psychology.com/holmes.htm) allows visitors to ask psychologist Leonard Holmes for help with a personal problem, and Holmes responds with a few paragraphs of advice. Clients pay for the service only if they are satisfied with the advice (Stern, 1996). The practice of webcounseling began slowly although is rapidly finding popularity among both counselors and cyberclients. Among counseling professionals, webcounseling has created somewhat of a debate about the utility and effectiveness of this new medium. Moreover, those involved in traditional counseling ethical and legal issues are wondering how such matters relate to the Internet environment.

Sanders and Rosenfield (1998) noted that the world of social sciences in general, and counseling and psychotherapy in particular, have always had an uneasy relationship with telecommunications technology. Social scientists predicted the collapse of normal social relations after the invention of the telegraph, and even though the telephone has been with us for around 100 years, it still has difficulty being accepted into the everyday world of counseling and psychotherapy as a valid communications medium. Counseling by telephone has definitely been the poor relation compared with face-to-face counseling in terms of professional recognition. Since the advent of the Internet and the interest in computer as the new technology mediating telecommunications via e-mail, we might be forgiven for thinking that the telephone is dead.

In an attempt to determine the pervasiveness of counseling related activity on the Internet, Sampson, Kolodinsky, and Greeno, (1997) conducted an analysis in April 1996, using the WebCrawler search engine. Results of the analysis revealed that two thirds of the counseling-related home pages examined were that of groups, and fully 50% were groups advertising some type of counseling-related service. Only 15% were home pages placed by individuals. Of particular note were on-line services offered by groups or individuals for a fee, either as a reply to questions posed via e-mail or for interactive chat sessions. The credentials for practitioners involved a wide range, including M.D., Ph.D., M.A., and L.P.C. Many "counselors" identified no professional credentials at all. In fact, most home pages provided little information about the nature of qualifications of those providing services other than degree-level designation. For example, an individual with "M.A." listed after his or her name frequently did not disclose the subject area of the degree. In a separate nonrandom analysis of 401 sites from the same 3,764 home pages, 15 home pages were identified that offered direct on-line services. Offerings ranged from $15 charged for answering a question via e-mail to $65 for a 60-minute chat session. These on-line offerings ranged from single treatment interventions to an individual offering services in 35 different specialty areas.

The authors concluded that the results of their search can be used to encourage debate about counseling over the Internet. Based on the percentage of websites offering direct on-line services, there are at least 275 practitioners currently offering direct counseling services across the Internet. Given that 275 practitioners are offering services to clients, it is impossible to ignore that counseling (at some level) is being conducted on the Internet. Instead of being a "potential" future event, counseling and counseling-related activities are a "present" reality. Although these numbers are relatively small in comparison with the tens of thousands of counselors currently offering services through more traditional means, the annualized growth rate indicates that increases in Internet counseling will occur. Future enhancements in technology are likely to only accelerate the availability of counseling services through networking.

The evolution of the Internet into the information highway offers many future possibilities and potential problems in the delivery of counseling services for your students. Following is an overview of each:

Possibilities

❖ **Delivery of counseling services**: Walz (1996) noted that the information highway "allows counselors to overcome problems of distance and time to offer opportunities for networking and interacting not otherwise available" (p. 417). In addition, counseling over the Net may be a useful medium for those with physical disabilities whom may find even a short distance a significant obstacle. And yet for others whom are reticent in meeting with a counselor and/or self-disclosing, the Net may prove to be an interactive lubricant which may very well foster the counseling process.

❖ **Delivery of information resources**: The Internet is a convenient and quick way to deliver important information. In cybercounseling, information might be in the form of homework assignment between sessions or bibliocounseling.

❖ **Assessment and evaluation**: Access to a wide variety of assessment, instructional, and information resources, in formats appropriate in a wide variety of ethnic, gender, and age contexts (Sampson, 1990; Sampson & Krumboltz, 1991), could be accomplished via WWW and FTP sites.

❖ **Communications**: Especially via e-mail, counselors and clients can exchange messages throughout the counseling process. Messages may inform both counselor and client of pertinent changes or progress. E-mail can provide an excellent forum for answering simple questions, providing social support, or to schedule actual or virtual meeting times.

❖ **Marriage and family counseling**: If face-to-face interaction is not possible on a regular basis, marriage counseling might be delivered via video conferencing, in which each couple and the counselor (or counselors) are in different geographic locations. After independent use of multimedia based computer-assisted instruction on communication skills, spouses could use video conferencing to complete assigned homework (e.g., communication exercises) (Sampson, et al., 1997).

❖ **Supervision**: Some evidence has shown that e-mail is an enhancing tool in the process of counselor supervision and consultation. It provides an immediate and ongoing channel of communication between and among as many people as chosen (Myrick & Sabella, 1995). Also, electronic file transfer of client records, including intake data, case notes (Casey, Bloom, & Moan, 1994), assessment reports, and selected key audio and video recordings of client sessions, could be used as preparation for individual supervision, group supervision, case conferences, and research (Sampson, et al., 1997).

Potential Problems

❖ **Confidentiality**: Although encryption and security methods have become highly sophisticated, unauthorized access to online communications remains a possibility without attention to security measures. Counselors whom practice on the Net must ethically and legally protect their clients, their profession, and themselves by using all known and reasonable security measures.

❖ **Computer competency**: Both the counselor and client must be adequately computer literate for the computer/network environment to be a viable interactive medium. From typing skills to electronic data transfer, both the counselor and client must be able to effectively harness the power and function of both hardware and software. Similar to face-to-face counseling, counselors must not attempt to perform services outside the limitations of their competence.

❖ **Location-specific factors**: A potential lack of appreciation on the part of geographically remote counselors of location-specific conditions, events, and cultural issues that affect clients may limit counselor credibility or lead to inappropriate counseling interventions. For example, a geographically remote counselor may be unaware of traumatic recent local events that are exacerbating a client's reaction to work and family stressors. It may also be possible that differences in local or regional cultural norms between the client's and counselor's community could lead a counselor to misinterpret the thoughts, feelings, or behavior of the client. Counselors need to prepare for counseling a client in a remote location by becoming familiar with recent local events and local cultural norms. If a counselor encounters an unanticipated reaction on the part of the client, the counselor needs to proceed slowly, clarifying client perceptions of their thoughts, feelings, and behavior (Sampson, et al., 1997).

❖ **Equity**: Does the cost of Internet access introduce yet another obstacle for obtaining counseling? Does cybercounseling further alienate potential clients whom might have the greatest need for counseling? Even when given access to the Net, could a client competently engage cybercounseling without possibly having ever had a computer experience? Webcounseling seems to exacerbate equity issues already confronting live counseling.

❖ **Credentialing**: How will certification and licensure laws apply to the Internet as state and national borders are crossed electronically? Will counselors be required to be credentialed in all states and countries where clients are located? Could cybercounseling actually be the impetus for a national credential recognized by all states? Will we need to move towards global credentialing? Who will monitor service complaints out-of-state or internationally?

❖ **High tech v. high touch**: How can counselors foster the development of trusting, caring, and genuine working relationships in cyberspace? Until video transmission over the Web makes telecounseling a reality, cybercounseling relies on a process devoid of non-verbal or extraverbal behavior. Even if we were able to conduct real-time counseling over the Net via video, can this medium help us to communicate so as to foster the counseling core conditions? Further, Lago (1996) poses a key question: "Do the existing theories of psychotherapy continue to apply, or do we need a new theory of e-mail therapy? (p. 289)"' He then takes Rogers' (1957) work on the necessary and sufficient conditions for therapeutic change as his starting-point and lists the computer-mediated therapist competencies as: the ability to establish contact, the ability to establish relationship, the ability to communicate accurately with minimal loss or distortion, the ability to demonstrate understanding and frame empathic responses, and the capacity and resources to provide appropriate and supportive information. This proposal begs the question as to whether such relationship conditions as outlined by Rogers can be successfully transmitted and received via contemporary computer-mediated telecommunications media.

Russell A. Sabella, Ph.D.

❖ **Impersonation**: A famous cartoon circulated over the Net depicts a dog sitting in front of a computer. The caption says, "The nice thing about the Internet is that nobody knows you're a dog." Experienced Internet users can relate to the humor in this cartoon because they know that there are many people who hide behind the Net's veil of anonymity to communicate messages they ordinarily would not communicate in real life. Messages that convey unpopular sentiments and would ordinarily be met with castigation. Others rely on anonymity provided by the Net to play out fantasies or practical jokes. Who is your cyberclient, really? Does your client depict himself/herself as an adult and is actually a minor? Has the client disguised their gender, race, or other personal distinctions that may threaten the validity or integrity of your efforts.

❖ **Ethics**: How do current ethical statements for counselors apply or adapt to situations encountered online? For the most part, counselors can make the leap into cyberspace and use current ethical guidelines to conduct themselves in an ethical fashion. However, problems exist. The future will inevitably see a change in what it means to be ethical as we learn the exact nature of counseling online.

❖ **Crisis Management**: Difficulties in responding to crisis situations may arise both as a result of client anonymity and because the therapist may be unfamiliar with the local community resources available in the client's geographic region. In addition, local laws requiring mental health professionals to breech confidentiality and report a client's danger to self or others, or suspected incidents of child, elder, or spousal abuse, vary from one geographic jurisdiction to another. When the client resides in a different legal jurisdiction from the therapist, it is currently unclear which laws, those covering the therapists geographic region or those covering the client's geographic region, are applicable. This issue becomes more complex when differing nationalities are involved (Childress, 1998).

The Ethical Web Counselor

In 1995, the National Board for Certified Counselors (NBCC) appointed a webcounseling task force to examine the practice of online counseling and to assess the possible existence of any regulatory issues NBCC might need to address. The task force established a listserv composed of more than 20 individuals who had specific knowledge, expertise, skills and opinions regarding the practice of what is herein referred to as webcounseling. Soon it became apparent that counseling had a diverse presence on the Internet, from websites that simply promoted a counselor's home or office practice, to sites that provided information about counseling and others which actually claimed to offer therapeutic interventions either as an adjunct to face-to-face counseling or as a stand alone service. Some sites were poorly constructed, poorly edited and poorly presented. Others were run by anonymous individuals, individuals with no credentials or fraudulent credentials, and some sites were operated by individuals with appropriate credentials and years of professional experience. However these credentials were all based on education and experience gained in face-to-face counseling, and the relevance of these credentials to the practice of webcounseling is unknown. No one knew if the lack of visual input made a difference in the outcome of the counseling process. No one knew about the legality of counseling across state or national boundaries. No one knew if there was any relevant research in any field of communication which could shed light on these questions (Bloom, 1997).

Next, the NBCC task force created a document entitled *Standards for the Ethical Practice of Webcounseling*. The relative newness of the use of the Internet for service and product delivery leaves authors of such standards at a loss when beginning to create ethical practices on the Internet. This document, like all codes of conduct, changes as information and circumstances not yet foreseen evolve. However, each version of this code of ethics is the current best standard of conduct passed by the NBCC Board of Directors (see http://www.nbcc.org/ Reprinted by Permission). As with any code, and especially with a code such as this, created for an evolving field of work, NBCC and CCE welcome comments and ideas for further discussion and inclusion.

NBCC Webcounseling Standards

The development of these webcounseling standards has been guided by the following principles:

- These standards are intended to address practices which are unique to webcounseling and WebCounselors.

- These standards are not to duplicate non-Internet-based standards adopted in other codes of ethics.

- Recognizing that significant new technology emerges continuously, these standards should be reviewed frequently.

- webcounseling ethics cases should be reviewed in light of delivery systems existing at the moment rather than at the time the standards were adopted.

- WebCounselors who are not National Certified Counselors may indicate at their website their adherence to these standards, but may not publish these standards in their entirety without written permission of the National Board for Certified Counselors.

- The Practice of webcounseling shall be defined as "the practice of professional counseling and information delivery that occurs when client(s) and counselor are in separate or remote locations and utilize electronic means to communicate over the Internet."

In addition to following the NBCC Code of Ethics pertaining to the practice of professional counseling, Webcounselors shall:

1. Review pertinent legal and ethical codes for possible violations emanating from the practice of Web Counseling and supervision. Liability insurance policies should also be reviewed to determine if the practice of webcounseling is a covered activity. Local, state, provincial and national statutes as well as the codes of professional membership organizations, professional certifying bodies and state or provincial licensing boards need to be reviewed. Also, as no definitive answers are known to questions pertaining to whether webcounseling takes place in the WebCounselor's location or the WebClient's location, WebCounselors should consider carefully local customs regarding age of consent and child abuse reporting.

2. Inform WebClients of encryption methods being used to help insure the security of client/counselor/supervisor communications. Encryption methods should be used whenever possible. If encryption is not made available to clients, clients must be informed of the potential hazards of unsecured communication on the Internet. Hazards may include authorized or unauthorized monitoring of transmissions and/or records of webcounseling sessions.

Russell A. Sabella, Ph.D.

3. Inform clients if, how and how long session data are being preserved. Session data may include WebCounselor/WebClient e-mail, test results, audio/video session recordings, session notes, and counselor/supervisor communications. The likelihood of electronic sessions being preserved is greater because of the ease and decreased costs involved in recording. Thus, its potential use in supervision, research and legal proceedings increases.

4. In situations where it is difficult to verify the identity of WebCounselor or WebClient, take steps to address impostor concerns, such as by using code words, numbers or graphics.

5. When parent/guardian consent is required to provide Webcounseling to minors, verify the identity of the consenting person.

6. Follow appropriate procedures regarding the release of information for sharing WebClient information with other electronic sources. Because of the relative ease with which e-mail messages can be forwarded to formal and casual referral sources, WebCounselors must work to insure the confidentiality of the Webcounseling relationship.

7. Carefully consider the extent of self disclosure presented to the WebClient and provide rationale for WebCounselor's level of disclosure. WebCounselors may wish to ensure that, minimally, the WebClient has the same data available about his/her service provider as would be available if the counseling were to take place face to face (i.e., possibly ethnicity, gender, etc.). Compelling reasons for limiting disclosure should be presented. WebCounselors will remember to protect themselves from unscrupulous users of the Internet by limiting potentially harmful disclosure about self and family.

8. Provide links to websites of all appropriate certification bodies and licensure boards to facilitate consumer protection.

9. Contact NBCC/CEE or the WebClient's state or provincial licensing board to obtain the name of at least one Counselor-On-Call within the WebClient's geographical region. WebCounselors who have contacted an individual to determine his or her willingness to serve as a Counselor-On-Call (either in person, over the phone or via e-mail) should also ensure that the WebClient is provided with local crisis intervention hot line numbers, 911 and similar numbers in the event that the Counselor-On-Call is unavailable.

10. Discuss with their WebClients procedures for contacting the WebCounselor when he or she is off-line. This means explaining exactly how often e-mail messages are to be checked by the WebCounselor.

11. Mention at their websites those presenting problems they believe to be inappropriate for Webcounseling. While no conclusive research has been conducted to date, those topics might include: sexual abuse as a primary issue, violent relationships, eating disorders, and psychiatric disorders that involve distortions of reality.

12. Explain to clients the possibility of technology failure. The WebCounselor gives instructions to WebClients about calling if problems arise, discusses the appropriateness of the client calling collect when the call might be originating from around the world, mentions differences in time zones, talks about dealing with response delays in sending and receiving e-mail messages

13. Explain to clients how to cope with potential misunderstandings arising from the lack of visual cues from WebCounselor or WebClient. For example, suggesting the other person simply say, "Because I couldn't see your face or hear your tone of voice in your e-mail message, I'm not sure how to interpret that last message."

If the Internet really does herald a new age of user-friendly computer-mediated communication for the masses, will the world of counseling and psychotherapy be left behind? E-mail, originally developed to help desk-bound students and workers in commercial organizations, was modeled on the office memorandum. If computer communications are to mediate properly and effectively in therapeutic relationships, we need to strive continually to identify the salient interpersonal processes unique to therapeutic relationships, not borrow second-hand technology designed for business organizations by computer scientists. There needs to be collaboration between therapists, social scientists and computer scientists who together would identify therapy-salient processes, model them in terms of psycho-social communications theories, and finally design them into therapy-dedicated, computer-mediated communications systems. If we fail in this endeavor, we could find therapists in ten years' time still using technologies designed for corporate business communications or computer-banking as the means by which they conduct therapy with their clients at a distance (Sanders & Rosenfield, 1998).

In summary, the Internet, like any tool, is either helpful or harmful depending on the user's purpose, capability, and actions. Focusing on parts that are helpful and avoiding those which are not can be a difficult task because of the vastness and morphological nature of the Net. Issues of psychological health and overall well-being while using the Net for commendable ventures is enhanced by knowledge and skills which promote robust discovery.

CHAPTER SIX

Counseling MegaLinks

This chapter provides you with a categorized list of over 700 counseling related websites. These are sites which I have visited and found helpful over the years. By no means is the list exhaustive of the possibilities – only some good starting places. They are included to save you time in finding the most essential resources for your work. However, I encourage you to pay particular attention to the section which includes search engines and directories for seeking other related counseling resources. Note that my original list of sites was more comprehensive although was reduced by about 10% after checking their validity. That is, even the best of sites have been known, for whatever reason, to be deleted from the web. I anticipate that, although the listed sites are current at the time of publication, there may be several which will be deleted in the time you read this.

Many times a broken or unresponsive link may be caused by a server that is temporarily unresponsive or "down." In this instance, you might try back later. In other instances, individual documents may have been moved within a web site rather than deleted, perhaps during the remodeling of the site. This is probable if the web address goes beyond the root address. For example, if you are looking for the June 1999 issue of the *SchoolCounselor.com* newsletter at *www.schoolcounselor.com/newsletter/june1999* and it returns an error, you should go to the root directory (*www.schoolcounselor.com*) and look for apparent links to the newsletter section. Remember that the root directory usually encompasses three parts separated by dots or periods: the *www* and the domain name which includes both the word describing the site (*schoolcounselor*) and the extension (*com*). To get to the root directory, go to the end of the address in the location box of your browser and dele the address up to the root directory or domain. Then, press Enter on your keyboard. If you still cannot find the link you want, you might then look for a search tool that allows you to locate the resource. In this example, once

you find the site's search tool, enter the word "June" which should generate a set of search results that points you to the new location of this resource. Often, the resource you are looking for has been archived deep into the site. When none of these methods work, and if you deem the resource valuable enough, you could try finding the document in a web search engine such as *www.hotbot.com* in case the site has changed it's name entirely.

Lastly, I've included boxes next to each resource for your convenience as a way to check off the sites you have frequented. Once you visit a site you find especially beneficial, you may also want to bookmark it in your own browser for easy reference.

AUDIO & VIDEO

❏ **CNN Audioselect**
http://cnn.com/audioselect/help.html

❏ **Corey Deitz & Jay Hamilton RealAudio Archive**
http://www.radioearth.com/corjay.htm

❏ **DiscJockey.Com Internet Radio Station Network: The Net's Best Music in Real Audio**
http://discjockey.com/
Amazing selection, live too! Submit your requests.

❏ **Mike's Radio World Live Dance Music Radio**
http://ds.dial.pipex.com/town/place/abn39/ra8.htm
A guide to radio stations broadcasting in Real Audio.

❏ **Scott's RealAudio Links//**
uts.cc.utexas.edu/~semley/rlaudio.html
Links to sites that provide RealAudio streaming.

CAREER

❏ **Academic Employment Network**
http://www.academploy.com/

If you are looking for a teaching job or other academic position, a national employment search is but a click away!

❏ **America's Job Bank**
http://www.ajb.dni.us/

America's Talent Bank is a nationwide electronic resume system. To market their qualifications, job seekers enter resumes into this national network, which is then searched by employers for workers who meet their needs. Supported by the Department of Labor, America's Talent Bank (ATB) is a product of state employment service agencies and is provided as an additional service to the public.

❏ **Career and Educational PoWWWer**
http://www.coe.utk.edu/~PoWWWer/home.html

This site is for high school students, their parents, and professionals who work with high school students. It is a site for those who wish to use the vast resources that are available on the World Wide Web (WWW) for career and educational planning purposes.

❏ **Career Links**
http://www.tompetersgroup.com/p5.html
Articles and resources from Tom Peters.

❏ **Career INFO**
http://home.earthlink.net/~nfosource/

Links to career planning resources, educational planning resources, and books related to careers/college. Lots of free stuff too.

❏ **CareerLab—200 FREE Cover Letters**
http://www.careerlab.com/letters/default.htm

❏ **CareerMosaic**
http://www.careermosaic.com/

A HUGE site of helpful links, resources, databases, and links.

❏ **CareerPath.com**
http://www.careerpath.com/res/owa/home.display_rblogin?

Large number of job listings. Registration is free and only takes a minute.

❏ **CareerWeb**
http://www.cweb.com/

Many helpful articles, resources, online tests, and more for the job seeker.

❏ **Colleges and Universities in the United States**
http://www.clas.ufl.edu/CLAS/american-universities.html

As home pages are found for American Universities granting bachelor or advanced degrees, they are added here, one page per university.

❏ **Cornell Youth and Work Program**
http://www.human.cornell.edu/youthwork/

The Cornell Youth and Work Program fosters the transition of youth to adulthood through research and development on school-to-work opportunities.

❏ **DICE**
http://www.dice.com/

Job search engine for full-time, permanent & contract computer consulting and programming employment opportunities. Also available are quite a few career related tools.

❏ **Graduate School Guide Online**
http://www.schoolguides.com/
Comprehensive and easy to use.

❏ **Higheredjobs Online**
http://www.higheredjobs.com/

With the simple vision that if it provided a free place on the Internet where candidates and institutions could agree to meet, its founders believed the costly and complicated recruiting process could be reduced to a few simple clicks of a mouse.

❏ **HireEd.net**
http://www.hireed.net/home.cfm

HireEd.net is an online job bank and resume posting service sponsored by the Association for Supervision and Curriculum Development (ASCD).

❏ **In The Long Run**
http://www.asd.k12.ak.us/Schools/West/Future.html

West High School's Planning for the Future page. A nice list of career related sites.

❏ **Job Shadowing Resources**
http://www.jobshadow.org/

Groundhog Job Shadow Day is an initiative to engage students in the world of work. This site will help you get involved.

❏ **Knock'Em Dead: The ultimate job-seekers handbook**
http://www.knockemdead.com/

Basic job-hunting resources. The cover letter section features a cover letter questionnaire and checklist, as well as several useful samples.

❏ **Minorities' Job Bank**
http://www.minorities-jb.com/

Highly resourceful. Includes villages, a job bank, and links.

❏ **Take a Career Aptitude Test Online**
http://www.netguide.com/Snapshot/Archive?guide=Career&id=1310

From the site: "There are, of course, sites that charge you money for their services, as well as sites that offer free tests. This often is a case of "you get what you pay for," but some free tests can be enlightening too."

❏ **Occupational Outlook Handbook**
http://www.bls.gov/ocohome.htm

You can perform a keyword search on the Handbook, use the Index to the Handbook, or select from an occupational cluster ... and much more!

❏ **Peterson's Education Center**
http://www.petersons.com/

Within these thousands of pages of easy-to-use, organized content, you will find a wealth of information on elementary and secondary schools, colleges and universities, professional degree programs, study abroad and distance learning opportunities, executive management programs, financial aid, internships, summer programs, career guidance, and more.

❏ **Pima/Santa Cruz Equity/School to Work Resources**
http://www.geocities.com/Athens/Delphi/7786/index.html

Lots of resourceful material with links to materials, helpful internet addresses, workshops, organizations, additional equity support programs, pima/santa cruz counties school to work/equity team, resource people in our area, training opportunities, definition of equity, and implementation strategies.

❏ **School-to-Work Web Sites**
http://ncrve.berkeley.edu/NetGain/NETGain15.html

❏ **School-to-Work: Program Resources**
http://7-12educators.miningco.com/msub4.htm

❏ **Thayer Academy: College Counseling**
http://www.thayer.org/college/index.html

Useful links involving the entire college search and student success process.

❏ **The Bridges Initiatives Inc.**
http://www.bridges.com/

The latest tool for career exploration among K-12 children and the adults who want them to succeed.

❑ **The Five O'Clock Club**
http://www.fiveoclockclub.com/

❑ **The Florida School-to-Work Information Navigator**
http://www.flstw.fsu.edu/

A true clearinghouse for the whole country.

❑ **Monster Board**
http://www.monster.com/

A must see, first stop for career development.

❑ **The Princeton Review Guide to Your Career**
http://www.review.com/career/find/car_search_show.cfm?id=75

Read about a Day in the Life of a Guidance Counselor.

❑ **Washington Post's What Color is Your Parachute?**
http://www.washingtonpost.com/parachute

The Net Guide to aid job hunters and career changers who want to use the Internet as part of their job search.

❑ **Welcome to Career Transitions**
http://www.flinthills.com/~atway/transitions/

TRANSITIONS will give you more information to help you make informed decisions, easier problem solving, and open new options and worlds to you.

❑ **Welcome to Your Future**
http://www.angelfire.com/nj/hsstudentresourcepgs/index.html

Bidded as the high schoolers resource page, this site has many useful links to career and college exploration—quite comprehensive.

❑ **Which Traits Predict Job Performance?**
http://www.apa.org/monitor/jul95/personal.html

Full text article from the American Psychological Association.

❑ **Work Zone**
http://www.workzone.net/

Many fine and useful articles about career and job finding.

Russell A. Sabella, Ph.D.

CHILDREN

❏ **Adventures From The Book Of Virtues**
http://www.pbs.org/adventures/
From the Public Broadcasting System (PBS).

❏ **Arthur: The World's Most Famous Aardvark**
http://www.pbs.org/wgbh/arthur/
Fun grahics, games, puzzles, coloring, and more... from PBS.

❏ **BJ's homework helper page**
http://tristate.pgh.net/~pinch13/pinchright.htm
B.J. Pinchbeck's Homework Helper is produced by B.J., an 11 year old, and his Dad. Quite extensive!

❏ **Children's Literature Web Guide**
http://www.acs.ucalgary.ca/~dkbrown/
The Children's Literature Web Guide is an attempt to gather together and categorize the growing number of Internet resources related to books for Children and Young Adults. Much of the information that you can find through these pages is provided by others: fans, schools, libraries, and commercial enterprises involved in the book world.

❏ **CTW Family Workshop—Home of Sesame Street**
http://www.ctw.org/index/0

❏ **Cyber-Seuss**
http://www.afn.org/~afn15301/drseuss.html

❏ **Disney.com—The Web Site for Families**
http://www.disney.com/index.html

❏ **Focus Adolescent Services**
http://members.tripod.com/FocusStretch/Main.html
Description of services for programs, resources, and support for teen substance abusers.

❏ **Lucie Walters .. Adolessons Online**
http://www.lucie.com/
Lucie Walters, a Los Angeles newspaper columnist, offers advice to teens on subjects such as sexuality, depression, alcohol, pregnancy, romance, eating disorders and parents. Site contains an archive of past columns.

❏ **The KIDS Report**
http://scout.cs.wisc.edu/scout/KIDS/index.html
The KIDS Report is a biweekly publication produced by K-12 students as a resource to other K-12 students. It is an ongoing, cooperative effort of 12 classrooms from around the United States. Teachers assist and provide support, however students select and annotate all resources included in every issue of the KIDS Report. The publication is supported by the Internet Scout Project.

❏ **Welcome to Straight Talk About School**
http://www.balancenet.org/
Designed for teens, this site aims to provide advice and answers to frequently asked questions. It offers chat rooms for teens, new interactive monthly themes, and resources for parents and teachers.

COLLEGES

❏ **College and University Rankings—Online Sites and Controversy**
http://www.library.uiuc.edu/edx/rankings.htm

The purpose of this page is to draw together and provide context to various college ranking services.

❏ **College Is Possible: American Council on Education**
http://www.collegeispossible.org/

America's colleges and universities have prepared this site to guide you to the books, websites, and other resources that admissions and financial aid professionals consider most helpful.

❏ **CollegeEdge**
http://collegeedge.com/

This site is for high school/secondary school, International and transfer students who want to find the right college or university and inform the right college about themselves. Plus, information and guidance on scholarships, careers, majors, financial aid and more.

❏ **CollegeNET**
http://www.collegenet.com/

Take virtual tours of college campuses.

❏ **Colleges and Universities**
http://www.mit.edu/people/cdemello/univ-full.html

Quite the list!

❏ **FinAid: The Financial Aid Information Page**
http://www.finaid.org/

This page provides a free, comprehensive, independent, and objective guide to student financial aid. It was created by Mark Kantrowitz, author of The Prentice Hall Guide to Scholarships and Fellowships for Math and Science Students.

❏ **Preparing Your Child For College: 1996-97 Edition**
http://www.ed.gov/pubs/Prepare/

This resource book is designed to assist parents help their children, with the help of teachers and counselors—plan ahead to ensure they are prepared academically for the rigors of college and to save now and plan financially for the costs of a college education.

❏ **Princeton Review Counselor-O-Matic**
http://www.review.com/time/counselorOmatic/index.html

The Counselor-O-Matic starts by guiding you through a review of your course selection, grades, test scores, and extracurricular record. Using the information you provide, Counselor-O-Matic calculates an admissions rating for you that gives you an estimate of what your chances of admission are at most colleges. In fact, the process is very similar to the approach used by many colleges to evaluate applications.

❏ **ScholarAid**
http://www.scholaraid.com/

ScholarAid.com is a free, online scholarship directory with a database of over 500,000 national, state and local level sources of student financial aid.

❏ **StudentAffairs.com**
http://www.studentaffairs.com/index.html

Your guide to the Internet for college student affairs.

❏ **Students—Financial Aid Services—Intro**
http://www.collegeboard.org/finaid/fastud/html/intro.html

Chock filled with helpful resources. A financial aid calculator too!

❏ **U.S. Two-Year Colleges**
http://cset.sp.utoledo.edu/twoyrcol.html

One of the most complete list available: Over 1,000 U.S. two-year campus links.

Russell A. Sabella, Ph.D.

COUNSELING THEORY

❏ **AATBS Home Page**
http://www.aatbs.com/Home.HTM
Official site of the Association for Advanced Training in the Behavioral Sciences (AATBS).

❏ **Art Therapy**
http://www.vickyb.demon.co.uk/
This page may answer some questions you may have about Art Therapy, what it is and who may be able to benefit from it.

❏ **Art therapy links**
http://www.uofl.edu/sahs/et/otherurl.htm

❏ **Basics of Cognitive Therapy (MindStreet)**
http://mindstreet.com/mindstreet/cbt.html

❏ **Behavior Analysis, Inc.**
http://www.behavioranalysis.com/
This site is dedicated to providing useful and current information for practitioners and consumers of behavior analysis.

❏ **Behavior Home Page**
http://www.state.ky.us/agencies/behave/homepage.html

❏ **Behavioral Reinforcement Slide Show**
http://www.psyc.memphis.edu/pages/specials/behcomm/4Ch2Premack/sld001.htm

❏ **Bill O'Hanlon's PossibilityLand**
http://brieftherapy.com/
Access to information on psychotherapy, Brief Therapy, Solution-Oriented Brief Therapy, Solution-Focused Therapy, therapeutic hypnosis, and of course, Possibility Therapy.

❏ **C. G. Jung, Analytical Psychology, and Culture**
http://www.cgjung.com/cgjung/

❏ **Center For Creative Play Home Page**
http://trfn.clpgh.org/orgs/tccp/

The Center is a toy and technology lending library with over 1000 toys, a fully equipped computer lab, a child-friendly play area, and a parent resource center. The Center was started by parents and continues to run on parent voices.

❏ **Classical Adlerian Psychology Home Page—Alfred Adler Institute of San Francisco**
http://ourworld.compuserve.com/homepages/hstein/
Readings, demonstrations, and more.

❏ **Creative Arts Therapy Links**
http://www.mmbmusic.com/cat_links.html

❏ **Cross-Cultural Communication**
http://www.nwrel.org/cnorse/booklets/ccc/

❏ **Fran's CTRT Home Page (Control Theory)**
http://www.geocities.com/Athens/7449/index.html

❏ **Games Kids Play**
http://www.corpcomm.net/~gnieboer/gamehome.htm
The purpose of this page is two-fold: One, to let users remember some of those odd games we used to play and bring a smile to your face. Two, to try to catalog a fascinating piece of oral tradition, and make sure none of these games are ever lost forever. This site also include an indexed list of over 250 games.

❏ **Gestalt Therapy: An Introduction**
http://www.gestalt.org/yontef.htm

❏ **Institute for Reality Therapy in Ireland**
http://indigo.ie/~irti/irti.htm

❏ **Kid Power Play Therapy, Counseling, and Training**
http://www.snowcrest.net/kidpower/

The Kid Power web site is dedicated to empowering people with resources and information concerning play therapy, children, parenting, and adult counseling.

❏ **Mister Rogers' Neighborhood**
http://www.pbs.org/rogers/

Useful for teaching play counseling.

❏ **Person-Centered International**
http://www.negia.net/~1234/pci.htm

❏ **Psychology Tutorials and Demonstrations**
http://psych.hanover.edu/Krantz/tutor.html

❏ **psychotherapy-center.com**
http://www.psychotherapy-center.com/
A link to free articles.

❏ **Puppet Picks**
http://fox.nstn.ca/~puppets/picks.html
A puppet resource center.

❏ **Rational Home Page**
http://www.voyager.co.nz/~rational/
About the New Zealand Center for REBT.

❏ **Re-evaluation Counseling**
http://www.rc.org/
Re-evaluation Counseling is a process whereby people of all ages and of all backgrounds can learn how to exchange effective help with each other in order to free themselves from the effects of past distress experiences.

❏ **Reality Therapy**
http://www.kathycurtissco.com/dr.htm#Quotes

❏ **Sandplay Therapists of America**
http://www.sandplayusa.org/

Sandplay Therapists of America (STA) is a nonprofit organization established to train, support, and promote professional development in sandplay therapy in the tradition of Dora Kalff as based on the theories of C.G. Jung.

❏ **Solution Focused Therapy**
http://rdz.stjohns.edu/%7Esft/

❏ **The Case of Felix Ungar**
http://www.primenet.com/~dannell/andy/psych/cases/felixindex.html
Explore Felix from the viewpoint of various counseling approaches.

❏ **The National Association Of Cognitive-Behavioral Therapists (NACBT)**
http://www.nacbt.org/

COUNSELOR EDUCATION

❑ **Academic Info: Psychology**
http://www.academicinfo.net/psych.html

This site contains an annotated directory of Web sites devoted to the study of psychology.

❑ **ACES Technology Interest Network**
http://www.fortunecity.com/skyscraper/laser/214/

ACES Technology Interest Network is a group of counselor educators interested in the use of technology in the fields of counselor education and counseling.

❑ **Andy's Psychology Pages**
http://www.primenet.com/~dannell/andy/psych/psych.html

Andy says, "This page is the gateway to my psychology pages. In these pages I will try to entertain and inform. A number of these pages are research papers, notes and research materials I used while in graduate school."

❑ **Arkansas-Little Rock: College of Education Online**
http://www.ualr.edu/~coedept/

A page dedicated to the most useful information gateway and guide to the best resources available on the Internet for teachers.

❑ **Ask the Dream Doctor**
http://www.dreamdoctor.com/

Dream analysis sorted by category and a daily tip for healthy sleep habits are featured.

❑ **British Journal of Guidance and Counselling**
http://www.carfax.co.uk/bjg-ad.htm

❑ **Child Development Abstracts Online Edition**
http://www.journals.uchicago.edu/CDAB/journal/

The articles are selected from a diverse set of journals representing different disciplines.

❑ **Clincal Psychology Resources**
http://www.psychologie.uni-bonn.de/kap/links_20.htm

❑ **Counselor Education Resource Center - University of Louisville**
http://garcon.education.louisville.edu/~rasabe01/

This site is intended to assist counselor educators by providing information about course curriculum, pedagogical activities, and reference materials. The CERC also provides links to other World Wide Web sites that may be of interest in this regard.

❑ **Crisis, Grief, and Healing: Men and Women**
http://www.webhealing.com/

According to the author, "This page is meant to be a place men and women can browse to understand and honor the many different paths to heal strong emotions." The site provides many useful links to grief and healing infromational resources.

❑ **Dr Magoo's Office**
http://tuweb.ucis.dal.ca/~drmagoo/index.htm

A collection of case studies.

❑ **Education Policy Analysis Archives**
http://olam.ed.asu.edu/epaa/

❏ **Effective Presentations**
http://www.kumc.edu/SAH/OTEd/jradel/
effective.html

    Tutorials intended to aid in developing an effective oral presentation, designing effective visual aids for presentations, and creating an effective poster presentation.

❏ **Electronic Journals and Periodicals in Psychology and Related Fields**
http://psych.hanover.edu/Krantz/
journal.html

❏ **Erikson Tutorial Home Page**
http://snycorva.cortland.edu/
%7EANDERSMD/ERIK/

❏ **Ethics Updates Home Page**
http://ethics.acusd.edu/index.html

    Ethics Updates is designed primarily to be used by ethics instructors and their students. It is intended to provide updates on current literature, both popular and professional, that relates to ethics.

❏ **Exhibits Collection—Personality**
http://www.learner.org/exhibits/personality/

    A well done exhibit about personality.

❏ **Fenichel's Current Topics in Psychology**
http://www.tiac.net/biz/drmike/
Current.shtml

    As described by the author, this site provides useful general references for both professionals and the general public. It is not intended as a substitute for individualized professional evaluation or treatment. There are many good resources here, including information, support groups, and clinical treatment providers.

❏ **Goals 2000: Reforming Education to Improve Student Achievement**
http://www.ed.gov/pubs/G2KReforming/

    Document available also in PDF for download.

❏ **International Journal of Educational Technology (IJET)**
http://lrs.ed.uiuc.edu/ijet/

    IJET is published online biannually each year (beginning in 1998). The journal is of interest to academics, students, practitioners, and educational leaders who wish to keep abreast of scholarship, theory-building and empirical research in areas where educational instruction is offered through computer-based technologies. The scope of IJET includes research areas where education is offered through computer-based means such as CD-ROM, DVD, or the Internet.

❏ **Journal of Adult Development and Aging**
http://www.uncg.edu/ced/jada/
jadamen2.htm

    Official Publication of the Association for Adult Development and Aging, a division of the American Counseling Association.

❏ **Journal of Technology Education**
http://borg.lib.vt.edu/ejournals/JTE/jte-v7n1/miscellany.jte-v7n1.html

    The Journal of Technology Education provides a forum for scholarly discussion on topics relating to technology education. Manuscripts should focus on technology education research, philosophy, theory, or practice. In addition, the Journal publishes book reviews, editorials, guest articles, comprehensive literature reviews, and reactions to previously published articles. Past issues are available both in HTML and PDF formats.

❏ **Mental Health Net—PsychJournalSearch**
http://www.cmhc.com/journals/

    Database of links to over 1400 psychology journals.

❏ **National Program for Transforming School Counseling**
http://www.edtrust.org/brouch.html

    Summary of work being undertaken by the Education Trust for the school counseling initiative.

❏ **Online Dictionary of Mental Health**
http://www.shef.ac.uk/~psysc/psycho-therapy/

❏ **Online Psych: Mind Games**
http://www.onlinepsych.com/public/Mind_Games/

Mind Games is the place in Online Psych for fun and informative tests and quizzes. Each test takes only a few minutes and your score is given immediately.

❏ **OXAMWEB**
http://www.psychiatry.ox.ac.uk/oxamweb/frames.html

Another self-help page with lots of information.

❏ **Personality and IQ Tests**
http://www.davideck.com/online-tests.html

❏ **PrePracExp—University of Florida**
http://www.coe.ufl.edu/faculty/myrick/preprac/theproject.html

An example of displaying on the web, description and photos, of a classroom experience.

❏ **Psychology of Cyberspace—Computer and Cyberspace Addiction**
http://cybertowers.com//selfhelp/articles/internet/cybaddict.html

A link from the Self-Help and Psychology Magazine website, this paper begins, "A heated debate is rising among psychologists. With the explosion of excitement about the internet, some people seem to be a bit too excited. Some people spend way too much time there. Is this yet ANOTHER type of addiction that has invaded the human psyche?"

❏ **Psychotherapy, Education, and the Movies**
http://www.hesley.com/

This web site depicts popular movies that are placed at the service of therapy and education, a process described in the book, Rent Two Films and Let's Talk in the Morning. Through highlighting new movies, video releases, and classics, this site hopes to help clinicians, teachers and consultants harness the motivating power of films.

❏ **Raymond Perry, Jr., Ph.D., University of Wisconsin Oshkosh**
http://www.coehs.uwosh.edu/faculty/perry/

A compendium of useful links.

❏ **SALMON: Study and Learning Materials On-line**
http://salmon.psy.plym.ac.uk/year1/bbb.htm

Award winning site covering psychological topics such as Biological Basis of Behavior, Physiological Psychology, Perception, Psychological Research Techniques, and lots more.

❏ **School Counsellors Position Paper**
http://www.nswppa.org.au/counsel.html

From the NSW Primary Principals' Association.

❏ **Smoother Sailing—Information & Research**
http://www.des-moines.k12.ia.us/Other/Counseling/IR.html

Twenty-five counselors submitted case studies describing the problems, interventions and outcomes of a typical student with whom they had worked during the 1993-94 school year. The format of the case study requested that counselors provide information in the following areas: statement of the problem, data collection, interventions, and results. The report summarizes the case studies submitted by the 25 responding counselors.

❑ **Test Junkie**
http://www.queendom.com/
test_col.html#career

More fun and funny online tests.

❑ **The American School Board Journal**
http://www.asbj.com/

The award-winning, editorially independent education magazine published by the National School Boards Association.

❑ **The Company Therapist**
http://www.thetherapist.com/

A fictional site composed of therapist notes, actions, etc. Useful for learning via case studies.

❑ **The Institute for Psychohistory**
http://www.psychohistory.com/

This website contains extensive material reproduced from The Journal of Psychohistory and from the book in process by Lloyd deMause, "Childhood and History." In addition, it contains links to the Institute branches, the International Psychohistorical Association and PSYCHOHISTORY, a discussion list and chat room, with archives.

❑ **The Rewards & Trials of Guidance Counseling**
http://www.umm.maine.edu/BEX/students/TammyBernier/tb310.html

A paper by Tammy Bernier.

❑ **The Specialized Scholarly Monograph in Crisis**
http://www.arl.org/scomm/epub/papers/index.html

This site represents the first time that three organizations—the American Council of Learned Societies, the Association of American University Presses, and the Association of Research Libraries—have formally joined together to address in concert a whole raft of issues surrounding the publication of specialized scholarship.

❑ **The World Lecture Hall**
http://www.utexas.edu/world/lecture/

The World Lecture Hall (WLH) contains links to pages created by faculty worldwide who are using the Web to deliver class materials.

❑ **The World-Wide Web Virtual Library: Electronic Journals**
http://www.edoc.com/ejournal/webzine.html

This is the WWW Virtual Library Electronic Journals Catalog. Entries in this catalog are added and maintained through WILMA (Web Information-List Maintenance Agent).

❑ **Theory**
http://www.hwi.com/tygger/edpsych/default.html

Informative site which includes information and slide presentations about developmental, cognitive, information processing, and behavioral theories.

❑ **Third Annual TCC Online Conference**
http://leahi.kcc.hawaii.edu/org/tcon98/

A virtual conference (the Third Annual Teaching in Community Colleges Conference, Online Instruction: Trends & Issues II) with posted papers.

❑ **Web Site for Counselor Educators and Supervisors**
http://www.nevada.edu/~ces/

This web page is intended to serve as a repository of Internet resources helpful to Counselor Educators. A non-exhaustive list of resource links is provided, organized by thematic categories.

❑ **Welcome to the Resource Station— Education Articles**
http://www.classroom.com/resource/articles/

Especially for information about the Internet.

❑ **World-Wide Graduate School Directory**
http://www.gradschools.com/welcome.html

DIVERSITY AND MULTICULTURALISM

❏ **America's Stirfry**
http://www.americas-stirfry.com/

America's Stir-fry offers a broad variety of educational products, including over 75 popular children's book and video titles published in many of the languages of the world, Including English, Japanese, Chinese, Vietnamese, Korean, Spanish and Hawaiian.

❏ **Beyond Prejudice**
http://www.eburg.com/beyond.prejudice/

Beyond Prejudice is an extensive and flexible multimedia program that teaches participants how to identify and alter prejudicial behavior. This unique approach provides the guidance and the structure for taking positive action against the prejudices that divide us.

❏ **Cartes Virtuelles SOURD-PRISE !! E-Cards**
http://www.cvm.qc.ca/dcb/carte/index.htm

Send an electronic greeting card with pictures related to deafness, deaf, sign language, etc.

❏ **Combating Racism & Intolerance**
http://www.ecri.coe.fr/

❏ **Diversity Database, University of Maryland, College Park**
http://www.inform.umd.edu:8080/EdRes/Topic/Diversity/

A comprehensive index of multicultural and cultural diversity resources.

❏ **Diversity OnLine Home Page**
http://www.geocities.com/WestHollywood/Village/2428/

A monthly newspaper published by The Community Center, a non-profit GLBT service organization in Boise, Idaho.

❏ **Intercultural E-Mail Classroom Connections (IECC)**
http://www.stolaf.edu/network/iecc/

The IECC mailing lists are provided by St. Olaf College as a free service to help teachers and classes link with partners in other countries and cultures for e-mail classroom pen-pal and project exchanges.

❏ **JustCause**
http://www.webcom.com/~justcaus/

Works to discourage racism, prejudice and homophobia through the use of media campaigns that promote tolerance and diversity.

❏ **Minority On-Line Information Service (MOLIS)**
http://web.fie.com/web/mol/

❏ **Myth of the Melting Pot: America's Racial and Ethnic Divides**
http://www.washingtonpost.com/wp-srv/national/longterm/meltingpot/melt0222.htm

A three part series.

❏ **National Association of Gender Diversity Training**
http://www.primenet.com/~gender/

Dedicated to assisting individuals and businesses in creating a workplace culture of understanding, respect, and harmony between men and women.

❏ **National MultiCultural Institute (NMCI)**
http://www.nmci.org/

(NMCI) was founded in 1983 in response to our nation's growing need for new services, knowledge, and skills in diversity. Since then, they have had over 16,000 participants attending conferences and workshops.

❏ **National Society of Black Engineers Online**
http://www.nsbe.org/

❏ **Race Relations in America and President Clinton's One America Initiative**
http://www.policy.com/issuewk/98/0713/071398b.html

❏ **STANDARDS: The International Journal of Multicultural Studies**
http://stripe.colorado.edu/~standard/
This resource is free!

❏ **Two Faces of the Nation (PBS)**
http://www.pbs.org/wgbh/pages/frontline/shows/race/main.html
Frontline discussion of race relations in America.

❏ **Voice of the Shuttle: Minority Studies Page**
http://humanitas.ucsb.edu/shuttle/minority.html

EDUCATION

❏ **Best Practices in Education**
http://www.bestpraceduc.org/
A not-for-profit organization dedicated to working with American teachers to find effective educational practices from other countries to adapt and apply in United States schools.

❏ **Council for Basic Education**
http://www.c-b-e.org/
Many articles, kits, and publications.

❏ **Cynthia Good's Home Page**
http://www.fallriver.mec.edu/goodhomepg.html
A major resource for College and Career Planning intended for students, teachers, and parents.

❏ **Early Childhood Educators & Family Web Corner**
http://www.nauticom.net/www/cokids/
Index to all things Early Childhood!

❏ **ED Initiatives**
http://www.ed.gov/pubs/EDInitiatives/
A biweekly look at progress on the Secretary of Education'ss priorities.

❏ **ED's Oasis: Teacher Support for Classroom Internet Use**
http://www.edsoasis.org/
ED's Oasis' primary purpose is to make the Internet easier and more rewarding to use with students. ED's Oasis provides links to what educators around the country recommend as the most engaging student-centered web sites, and examples demonstrating effective classroom Internet use from successful teachers.

❏ **Education Central**
http://www.parentsoup.com/edcentral/

Part of the ParentSoup site, Education Central is set up to help parents with students of all ages find information and useful resources for school issues. The site includes a hot topic and information and resources categorized by grade levels. Users can also find discussion areas, a vocabulary list of "buzz words," and the homeroom section, which initiates discussions on current issues. The "Supplies" area of the site has tools and materials for parents and students such as school search sites and a college cost calculator.

❏ **Education Review- A Journal of Book Reviews**
http://www.ed.asu.edu/edrev/

Education Review (ER) publishes review articles of recently published books in education. ER contains sixteen departments covering the range of educational scholarship, and is intended to promote wider understanding of the latest and best research in the field.

❏ **Education World**
http://www.education-world.com/

Highly resourceful site that includes lesson plans, news, educational site ratings, and much more.

❏ **EDUFAX-Educational Resources for Consultants/Parents/Students.**
http://www.tiac.net/users/edufax/links.html

This site is chock full of information including newsletters and links to colleges and universities.

❏ **EdWeb**
http://edweb.gsn.org/

The purpose of this hyperbook is to explore the worlds of educational reform and information technology. With EdWeb, you can hunt down on-line educational resources around the world, learn about trends in education policy and information infrastructure development, examine success stories of computers in the classroom, and much, much more. EdWeb is a dynamic work-in-progress, and numerous changes and additions occur on a regular basis.

❏ **Evalutech**
http://www.sret.sreb.org/

A searchable database of curriculum related instructional materials specifically designed for K-12 students.

❏ **Filamentality 2**
http://www.kn.pacbell.com/wired/fil/

According to the site, Filamentality is a fill-in-the-blank interactive Web site that guides you through picking a topic, searching the Web, gathering good Internet sites, and turning Web resources into activities appropriate for learners. So it helps you combine the Filaments of the Web with a learner's mentality (get it?).

❏ **Indiana Department of Education**
http://ideanet.doe.state.in.us/

Highly informative for all educators.

❏ **Kathy Schrock's Guide for Educators**
http://www.capecod.net/schrockguide/

A classified list of sites on the Internet found to be useful for enhancing curriculum and teacher professional growth.

❏ **LETSNet Home Page**
http://commtechlab.msu.edu/sites/letsnet/

This website is dedicated to helping teachers experience the potential value of the Web in the classroom by providing actual examples of real teachers who are using the Internet today.

❏ **Meridian- Middle School Computer Technologies Journal**
http://www.ncsu.edu/meridian/

Full-text articles and resourceful links.

❏ **National Archives: The Digital Classroom**
http://www.nara.gov/education/classrm.html

Primary sources, activities, and training for educators and students.

❏ **National Foundation for the Improvement of Education**
http://www.nfie.org/

❏ **Online Innovation Institute**
http://oii.org/

The Online Innovation Institute (OII) is a results driven organization, which offers professional development workshops to help students and teachers improve classroom achievment.

❏ **Project Appleseed**
http://members.aol.com/pledgenow/appleseed/index.html

Information about the National Campaign for Public School Improvement, the Parental Involvement Pledge, National Parental Involvement Day, Public School Volunteer Week and Organized Parental Involvement.

❏ **Rethinking Schools Online**
http://www.rethinkingschools.org/

Chock full of information related to school choice, educational reform, social justice, and equity issues.

❏ **Teacher Magazine**
http://www.teachermagazine.org/

❏ **Teachnet.com**
http://www.teachnet.com/

Teachnet includes a free e-mail newsletter and and over 1,000 regular users on their Postings mailing list.

❏ **The Children's Book Council**
http://www.cbcbooks.org/

This guide is intended for the use of teachers and librarians, who authors, illustrators, parents, and booksellers. Some pages may only be accessed by members.

❏ **U.S. Department of Education Topics Search**
http://www.ed.gov/topicsaz/

To further assist you in finding education topics and information relevant to your needs.

❏ **U.S. Government Documents Ready Reference Collection**
http://www.columbia.edu/cu/libraries/indiv/dsc/readyref.html

❏ **Youth Resources**
http://www.uscharterschools.org/

This site, developed as a joint project by the U.S. Department of Education, California State University's Charter Schools Project, and the Policy Support and Studies Program at WestEd, was created to promote the sharing of information and innovations by the people running local charter schools. The site gives detailed information on state charter school policies, charter schools profiles, and information related to starting and running a charter school.

FAMILIES & PARENTING

❏ **Handouts for Parents**
http://henson.austin.apple.com/edres/
parents/parentmenu.shtml

Wonderful topics brought to us by Apple computers.

❏ **ParenTalk Newsletter**
http://www.tnpc.com/parentalk/
index.html

This online newsletter from the National Parenting Center includes articles from physicians and psychologists that deal with subjects from pregnancy to adolescence. Site search engine, forums and membership information are also listed.

❏ **Children Now**
http://www.dnai.com/%7Echildren/

Children Now uses research and mass communications to make the well being of children a top priority across the nation.

❏ **Disney's Family Page**
http://family.disney.com/

Lots of activities and fun things to do.

❏ **Facts For Families**
http://www.aacap.org/web/aacap/
factsFam/

According to the site, the American Academy of Child & Adolescent Psychiatry (AACAP) developed Facts for Families to provide concise and up-to-date information on issues that affect children, teenagers, and their families. The AACAP provides this important information as a public service and the Facts for Families may be duplicated and distributed free of charge as long as the American Academy of Child & Adolescent Psychiatry is properly credited and no profit is gained from their use.

❏ **Kidtools Home Page**
http://www.kidtools.com/

Information and product reviews on educational products for kids. Learn about the latest information on educational books, toys, software, audio and video products.

❏ **National Family Partnership**
http://www.nfp.org/

At its foundation, National Family Partnership is a network of parents who care about their kids and want to keep them safe from drugs. These parents, from different geographic areas, occupations and lifestyles, are united in one understanding: that prevention-keeping kids from ever using drugs-is far better than salvaging the health and well-being of kids abused by drugs.

❏ **National Parent Information Network**
http://npin.org/

The purpose of NPIN is to provide information to parents and those who work with parents and to foster the exchange of parenting materials. Materials included full text on NPIN have been reviewed for reliability and usefulness. Publications, brochures, and other materials that are merely listed on NPIN may not have been reviewed and are included for informational purposes only.

❏ **Parent Information**
http://www.users.fast.net/~wfeigley/
parent.html

Many resources in Spanish!

❏ **Parents for Improved Education—Fairfax County Public Schools**
http://www.geocities.com/CapitolHill/
9155/

The authors of the site explain: "We are parents of students being educated in Fairfax County Public Schools (Virginia) who have become increasingly concerned that despite the high ranking of standardized test scores, our children are not being properly educated in the core subjects." One link to a parent whom does not agree with the role of school counselors (http://www.geocities.com/CapitolHill/9155/counsel.html).

❏ **Parents Guide to the Internet**
http://www.ed.gov/pubs/parents/internet/
Viewable and downloadable!

❏ **Parents, Educators, and Publishers (PEP)**
http://www.microweb.com/pepsite/

An informational resource for parents, educators, and children's software publishers. The content of this site has been developed in response to the interests and needs of these three audiences.

❏ **Stepfamily Network**
http://www.stepfamily.net/

Educating stepparents, parents, family professionals, and stepchildren.

❏ **Teen Hoopla—An Internet Guide for Teens**
http://www.ala.org/teenhoopla/main.html

❏ **The Children's Partnership**
http://www.childrenspartnership.org/

A national, nonpartisan organization that provides timely information to leaders and the public about the needs of Americas 70 million children—and promotes ways to engage all Americans to benefit children.

❏ **The F.U.N. Place—Families United on the Net**
http://www.thefunplace.com/

Packed with articles, games, chatrooms, resources—truly fun for the whole family.

❏ **The Future of Children**
http://www.futureofchildren.org/

The primary purpose of The Future of Children is to disseminate timely information on major issues related to children's well-being, with special emphasis on providing objective analysis and evaluation, translating existing knowledge into effective programs and polices, and promoting constructive institutional change.

❏ **The You Can Handle Them All Web Site**
http://www.disciplinehelp.com/

Excellent site which contains a great deal of information and resources about discipline and behavior management.

❏ **Welcome to ParentTime!**
http://www.parenttime.com

GOVERNMENT RESOURCES

❏ **Bureau of Justice Statistics**
http://www.ojp.usdoj.gov/bjs/dtdata.htm

❏ **Earthlaw—E-Mail The House of Representatives!**
http://www.earthlaw.org/Activist/houseadd.htm

Site to facilitate contacting Congress and the Senate.

❏ **Government Technology—State and Local Govt Links**
http://govt-tech.govtech.net/onlineservices/connections/states.shtm

Links to U.S. States and Local Governments.

❏ **GPO Gate**
http://www.gpo.ucop.edu/search/default.html

Search United States government documents. Quite comprehensive and easy to use.

❏ **Institute for Intergovernmental Research (IIR)**
http://www.iir.com/

A research organization specializing in law enforcement, juvenile justice, and criminal justice issues.

❏ **Office of Justice Programs**
http://www.ojp.usdoj.gov/

Dedicated to comprehensive approaches, OJP's mission is to provide federal leadership in developing the nation's capacity to prevent and control crime, administer justice and assist crime victims.

❏ **Office of Juvenile Justice and Delinquency Prevention**
http://www.ncjrs.org/ojjhome.htm
OJJDP provides Federal leadership, through a comprehensive, coordinated approach, to prevent and control juvenile crime and improve the juvenile justice system.

❏ **Project EASI: Easy Access for Students and Institutions**
http://easi.ed.gov/
A collaborative effort among a diverse group of government, business and education leaders to reengineer the country's postsecondary financial aid delivery system.

❏ **21st Century Community Learning Centers**
http://www.ed.gov/offices/OERI/21stCCLC/
Yearly grants about after-school, weekend and summer programs for youth.

❏ **AERA Grants Program**
http://aera.ucsb.edu/
Online information and applications for various grants.

improving the infrastructure for conducting large-scale policy and practice-related educational research

❏ **Eschoolnews Technology Grants**
http://www.eschoolnews.com/grants/main.html
Come here to find the most up-to-date listings of K-12 technology grants and funding opportunities and awards.

❏ **Guide to U.S. Department of Education Programs and Resources**
http://web99.ed.gov/GTEP/Program2.nsf
Multiple ways to search.

❏ **GrantsWeb**
http://web.fie.com/cws/sra/resource.htm

❏ **InfoEd International**
http://www.infoed.org/default.stm
A complete suite of products for research administration and technology management.

❏ **Internet Prospector**
http://w3.uwyo.edu/~prospect/

❏ **NonProfit Gateway**
http://www.nonprofit.gov/
This site is designed as a central starting point to help non-profit organizations access online Federal information and services.

❏ **National Science Foundation**
http://www.nsf.gov/start.htm
The NSF funds research and education in science and engineering, through grants, contracts, and cooperative agreements. The Foundation accounts for about 20 percent of federal support to academic institutions for basic research.

❏ **NIH-Guide to Grants and Contracts Database**
http://www.med.nyu.edu/nih-guide.html

The NIH-Guide is distributed weekly to via E-mail to sites that require information about NIH's activities. For a number of years now, NYU has supported software to allow the so-called E-Guide to be stored and viewed. This software is currently being upgraded to provide access to the E-Guide database via the WWW.

❏ **SPIN**
http://spin.infoed.org/spinwww/spin2.htm

❏ **Technology Grants**
http://www.globalclassroom.org/grants.html

❏ **Technology Innovation Challenge Grant Projects**
http://www.ed.gov/Technology/challenge/grants1.html

Links to schools receiving the grant.

❏ **What Should I Know About ED Grants?**
http://www.ed.gov/pubs/KnowAbtGrants/

This booklet provides a non-technical summary of the Department of Education's discretionary grants process and the laws and regulations that govern it.

HUMOR AND INSPIRATION

❏ **E-greetings: Express yourself in every color!**
http://www.egreetings.com/e-products/m_main/cgi/homepage

❏ **Wonderful WWW Page of Homeschooling Humor**
http://users.aol.com/WERHSFAM/humor.html

❏ **Chicken Soup for the Soul**
http://www.chickensoup.com/

The official Chicken Soup for the Soul website, this one contains helpful links to submit your story, contact speakers, and highlights soup stories. Through this site, you may also subscribe to a listserv and have delivered via e-mail a daily dose of chicken soup for the soul.

❏ **The Positive Press: Good News Every Day**
http://www.positivepress.com/

The positive press site contains links to daily news stories of human strength, kindness, ingenuity, and perseverance. Sections include general, health, business, and "light." Also included is a positive saying of the day, a positive talk chatroom, and links to other inspirational information.

Positive News
Daily news stories of human strength, kindness, ingenuity and perseverance. Sections include General, Health, Business and Light.

Positive Saying of the Day
A new inspirational thought every day. See today's quote or browse the sayings archives.

Site Map

Positive Talk
Interact with other positive people! Participate in the community through the interactive bulletin board, read others' comments, or send in your own!

Positive.Net
Enjoy Essays written from a positive perspective, as well as Books and Stories that are sure to inspire.

INTERNET AND TECHNOLOGY TRAINING

❑ **Syllabus Press**
http://www.syllabus.com/about.html

Syllabus Press, based in San Jose, Calif., produces information products that cover technology use in the high school, college, and university curriculum. Syllabus Press' primary products are Syllabus magazine, the annual Syllabus conference, and regional Syllabus workshops.

❑ **Beginners' Central**
http://northernwebs.com/bc/

This site is dedicated to helping people learn to use that information in a coherent manner. Beginners' Central is based on a chapter by chapter structure. You may skip to any chapter you're interested in, or if you wish, you can start at the beginning and work your way forward.

❑ **Bibliography for Educator's Introduction to the Internet**
http://www.monroe.lib.in.us/~lchampel/netedbib.html

❑ **Bibliography on Evaluating Internet Resources**
http://refserver.lib.vt.edu/libinst/critTHINK.HTM

According to the author, Nicole Auer, this bibliography has grown with the increasing number of documents which address the problems and issues related to teaching and using critical thinking skills to evaluate Internet resources.

❑ **Blue Web'n Applications**
http://www.kn.pacbell.com/cgi-bin/listApps.pl?Education&(Counseling)

Blue Web'n is a searchable database of outstanding Internet learning sites categorized by subject area, audience, and type (lessons, activities, projects, resources, references, & tools). Blue Web'n does not attempt to catalog all educational sites, but only the most useful sites—especially online activities targeted at learners. The address cited here will take you directly to the counseling subject area.

❑ **Bob Cozby's Computer Links**
http://cust2.iamerica.net/coz/COMPUTER.HTM

Highly resourceful, including links to many search engines, history of the Net, HTML tools/utilities, Plug-ins and filters, computer companies, jobs, operating systems, and more.

❑ **BUILDER**
http://www.builder.com/Authoring/Html/

Tips and tricks about Web development.

❑ **Creating A Homepage**
http://members.aol.com/teachemath/create.htm

Helpful place for beginning web authors.

❑ **Crimes Against Children Facilitated by the Internet**
http://www.fbi.gov/archives/congress/children.htm

Interesting reading, this is the Statement of Stephen R. Wiley, Chief, Violent Crime and Major Offenders Section, Federal Bureau of Investigation, before the House Judiciary Committee Subcommittee on Crime. Washington, D. C., November 7, 1997

❑ **Data Fellows Anti-Virus HOAX warnings page**
http://www.datafellows.com/news/hoax/

This page is considered the industry standard information source for new virus hoaxes and false alerts.

❑ **Disney's Internet Guide**
http://www.disney.com/dig/today/

Disney's Internet Guide (DIG) is designed to enhance the online experience of both kids and families, Dig is yet another component of Disney.com's vast array of specialty features. Stay tuned as we continue to introduce new categories and activities to Dig's exciting offerings.

❑ **E-Mail, Listservs, Tips on Penpals Slideshow**
http://siec.k12.in.us/~west/slides/penpal/sld001.htm

❏ **Educational Technology for Schools**
http://fromnowon.org/

An educational technology journal with full-text articles.

❏ **ERIC-EECE Electronic Discussion Groups**
http://ericeece.org/listserv.html

❏ **ESD Training Materials**
http://www.yamhillesd.k12.or.us/ESDPage/handouts/handouts.html

An extensive collection of training hand-outs, many of which are available on-line. These handouts have been developed over the last several years and are primarily for Macintosh applications, but handouts for Windows will soon be available.

❏ **Evaluating Web Resources**
http://www.science.widener.edu/~withers/webeval.htm

❏ **Finding Information on the Internet—A Tutorial**
http://www.lib.berkeley.edu/TeachingLib/Guides/Internet/FindInfo.html

Brought to us by the library folks at the University of California, Berkeley, this is a most excellent free resource.

❏ **Frank Condron's World O'Windows**
http://www.conitech.com/windows/index.asp

Frank Condron's World O'Windows is a collection of useful news, resources, and tips about Microsoft's current and future versions of Windows, including Windows 95, Windows 98, and Windows NT.

❏ **Gulf Coast Community College—Netscape Basics**
http://www.gc.cc.fl.us/t4t/nettutor/index.htm

This tutorial provides an overview of the basic design and functions of the Netscape browser. The tutorial offers both a straight-forward, linear presentation of each Netscape's basic functions and more in-depth descriptions of the inner workings of Netscape and the World Wide Web.

❏ **GVU's 8th WWW Survey Results**
http://www.gvu.gatech.edu/user_surveys/survey-1997-10/

This is the main document for the Graphic, Visualization, & Usability Center's (GVU) 8th WWW User Survey. GVU runs the Surveys as public service and as such, all results are available online (subject to certain terms and conditions).

❏ **Index to Web Guides**
http://www.monroe.lib.in.us/~lchampel/

List of Internet related topics with instruction and handouts from Lisa Champelli.

❏ **Institute for the Transfer of Technology to Education**
http://www.nsba.org/itte/

A program of the National School Boards Association which works actively with school districts across North America that are exploring creative ways to teach and learn with technology.

❏ **Integrating the Internet**
http://seamonkey.ed.asu.edu/~hixson/index/index5.html

Use this page to find primary resources, projects, a weekly newsletter, units of study, and a tutorial to help you plan projects and class homepages.

❏ **International Society for Technology in Education**
http://www.iste.org/

The International Society for Technology in Education (ISTE) is the largest teacher-based, nonprofit organization in the field of educational technology. Its mission is to help K-12 classroom teachers and administrators share effective methods for enhancing student learning through the use of new classroom technologies.

❏ **Internet 101: The Internet Guide for Teachers and Parents**

http://www.horizon.nmsu.edu/101/

Also for counselors, this site helps educators deal with the Internet in their classrooms, and to helping parents guide their children as they explore the world wide web. Gathered here are many resources, helpful hints, and valuable explanations that can help ease your transition to online education, including straight talk about dealing with Internet pornography and copyright issues.

❏ **Internet Search Advantage**

http://www.cobb.com/isa/

Articles and tips on searching the WWW.

❏ **Internet World: The Voice of E-Business and Internet Technology**

http://www.internetworld.com/

A great place to start for learning about the Internet and Net related events/information.

❏ **Interpersonal Computing and Technology Journal**

http://www.helsinki.fi/science/optek/

A scholarly, peer-reviewed journal, published four times a year. The journal's focus is on computer-mediated communication, and the pedagogical issues surrounding the use of computers and technology in educational settings.

❏ **Life on the Internet Young, Smart and On Line**

http://www.pbs.org/internet/stories/ng/index.html

❏ **Life on the Internet: Exploring the Internet**

http://www.screen.com/start/guide/default.html

Comprehensive! Inside each section, you'll find links to the latest version of Internet software, guides for additional background, resource lists, and search tools—thousands and thousands of destinations.

❏ **NEA Teaching, Learning & Technology Technology Briefs**

http://www.nea.org/cet/BRIEFS/briefs.html

Information about current and emerging education technology and related topics.

❏ **Netiquette Home Page**

http://www.albion.com/netiquette/index.html

❏ **PBS Kids : T E C H K N O W**

http://www.pbs.org/kids/techknow/

Kids can take a WebLicence exam which demonstrates safe navigation skills.

❏ **PC Webopaedia home page**

http://www.pcwebopaedia.com/

Online encyclopedia and search engine dedicated to computer technology.

❏ **ReviewBooth**

http://www.reviewbooth.com/

This Web site provides easy access to computer hardware and software reviews and evaluations.

❏ **Schools in Cyberspace**

http://homepages.strath.ac.uk/~cjbs17/Cyberspace/index.html

A collection of pages with links, hints and tips to help schools get the most of the Internet as a resource to support learning and teaching.

❏ **Search Tips and Tricks**

http://www.imaginarylandscape.com/helpweb/www/seek.html

❏ **Searching for Information on the Internet**

http://www.netskills.ac.uk/resources/searching/search1/search1.html

❑ **Take a Walk on the Wired Side**
http://www.lib.utexas.edu/Exhibits/wired/case1.html

The authors of this site want us to know that, "Although we do not have to whole-heartedly embrace all new technologies, we should recognize the need to objectively assess the merits and failings of these resources to succeed in our information society—a society which demands that we learn skills necessary to locate reliable resources, efficiently search for answers, and carefully evaluate the answers we find."

❑ **Tech Tips for Teachers**
http://www.essdack.org./tips/index.html

A collage of topics and tips including electronic portfolios.

❑ **Technology @ Your Fingertips**
http://nces.ed.gov/pubs98/tech/index2.htm

Describes a process for getting the best possible technology solution for your organization. In this downloadable book you will find the steps you should take to identify your technology needs, consider your options, acquire the technology, and implement a technology solution that will serve you today and provide a foundation for your organization's technology in the future.

❑ **Technology Connections**
http://www.mcrel.org/connect/tech/index.html

These pages provide online resources available to help educators, administrators, and parents answer common questions and solve problems related to the implementation and use of technology in education. New topics are added periodically.

❑ **Technology for Teachers—Basic Computing Concepts**
http://www.gc.cc.fl.us/t4t/concepts/index.htm

❑ **The HTML Goodies Home Page**
http://www.htmlgoodies.com/

HTML Goodies has won extensive industry recognition and more than 75 awards for its quality and comprehensive coverage. This site contains hundreds of unique tutorials for HTML, XML, SGML and DHTML as well as one of the Web's most comprehensive repositories for JavaScript and other scripting languages.

❑ **Toward Internet Literacy**
http://www.cbriansmith.com/

❑ **Using and Understanding the Internet**
http://www.pbs.org/uti/

More than 300 links to quickly get you on your way, organized by topics, in the Beginners Guide to the Internet. After exploring the Guide and learning about Net applications, you can qualify for their "seasoned user certificate" by testing your knowledge in their Understanding & Using The Internet Quiz.

❑ **Using the Internet, for Teachers, Schools, Students; an Introduction**
http://www.geocities.com/Athens/4610/index.htm

❑ **Web Site Garage—One Stop Shop for Servicing Your Web Site**
http://www.websitegarage.com/

Plug in a URL and have this site review the effectiveness of the site and make recommendations for a "tune-up."

❑ **WebReference.com**
http://www.webreference.com/index2.html

❑ **Welcome to Webteacher**
http://www.webteacher.org/winexp/welcome.html

E-mail, video conferencing, chat rooms, Web page design, Internet safety, and curriculum searches. This site a self-paced Internet Tutorial that puts both basic and in-depth information about the World Wide Web at your fingertips.

K-12 SCHOOLS: GUIDANCE & COUNSELING

❑ **Adams Middle School Counseling Department**
http://www.wcresa.k12.mi.us/wayne-westland/frconten.htm

Links to class scheduling, peer mediation, conflict resolution, individual and group counseling, classroom support, referral to outside agencies, make-up homework, career guidance, attendance monitoring, and new student orientation.

❑ **Anacortes HS Guidance and Counseling Services**
http://www.cnw.com/~deets/guidance.htm

❑ **Cave Spring Junior High School-Roanoke, Virginia**
http://www.rcs.k12.va.us/csjh/

❑ **Clinton High School Guidance Department's Webpage**
http://www.cusd15.k12.il.us/hs/Guidance/cchsguiddept.htm

Students and parents will find this resource helpful in accessing the latest college and career planning information. This site serves students and their families by furnishing helpful information on a variety of topics.

❑ **Collingswood High School Guidance Department**
http://collingswood.k12.nj.us/high/guidance/

Links including college information, career exploration, financial aid, homework help, Internet introduction, college & career research, guidance newsletter, and college links.

❑ **Farley Elementary School**
http://fly.hiwaay.net/~swaim/counsel.htm

Farley Elementary School

Judy Swaim says, "Our school provides individual, small group, and large group counseling and guidance. Each class at Farley attends guidance classes once every two weeks. We discuss many different topics including study skills, getting along with each other, and careers. Be sure to check out my list of guidance materials to find examples of materials and lessson plans and my homepage to find interesting links to other sites. These links are a presentation on Using Technology in Counseling and Conflict Resolution."

❑ **Northeastern Clinton Central School District**
http://www.slic.com/nccs/home.html
Has both a career and college center.

❑ **Urbana High School Guidance and Counseling**
http://www.cmi.k12.il.us/~furrersa/guid_couns.html

Links include Guidance Information, Testing (ACT, SAT, AP, etc.), College and University Information, Jobs for Grads, Financial Aid and Scholarships, Options Other Than College For the Student Athlete, Career Information, Wellness, ADD, LD, and Grief.

❑ **Arrowhead Guidance Department**
http://www.methacton.k12.pa.us/arrowhead/default.htm
Lots of valuable resources and fun photos!

❑ **Batesville Primary School**
http://www.venus.net/~batepri2/counseling/counseling.html

❑ **Benjamin Franklin School Counselor**
http://www.bcsd.stier.org/bfranklin/counselor/Index.htm

❏ **Bill McCane's Counseling Corner**
http://www.indep.k12.mo.us/WC/
bmccane.html

❏ **Blanchet High School Guidance and Counseling**
http://www.blanchet.k12.wa.us/counsgui/
overview.html

❏ **Block Island School Homepage**
http://www.bi.k12.ri.us/
Links include study skills, financial aid information, kids stuff, college/work, peer/ mentor resources, teachers, parents, and social/environmental responsibility. This site is searchable.

❏ **Bob Turba's CyberGuidance Office**
http://www.geocities.com/Athens/9893/
This site calls itself a virtual high school guidance office created by Bob Turba, Chairman of Guidance Services at Stanton College Preparatory School located in Duval County, Jacksonville, Florida. The site contains links to information about college, scholarship, financial aid, career, homework, and tutoring.

❏ **Bow High School Guidance Information**
http://www.bow.k12.nh.us/bhs/Guidance/
Default.htm

❏ **Bryan High School Guidance/Counseling**
http://www.ops.org/bryansr/Guidance/
guid.htm

❏ **Burnt Chimney Elementary School Guidance**
http://www.frco.k12.va.us/burntchimney/
guidance.htm

❏ **Center Point-Urbana High School Counseling Office**
http://www.cen-pt-urb.k12.ia.us/paul.htm

❏ **College Resource Center**
http://www.district125.k12.il.us/crc/
The CRC contains a wide variety of informational resources such as college pamphlets, videos, catalogs, and reference

books that will assist and guide one through the college selection process.

❏ **Community High School Guidance & Counseling**
http://communityhigh.org/counseling/
resources.html

❏ **Davis Counseling Home Page**
http://www.esd105.wednet.edu/DavisHS/
counseling/index.html

❏ **Fairfax High School Guidance Dept.**
http://www.fcps.k12.va.us/FairfaxHS/
guidance.htm

❏ **Galloway Township Public Schools**
http://www.gtps.k12.nj.us/special/
guideflyer.html

❏ **Hollywood Elementary School Counseling Page**
http://198.76.225.3/hes/counseling.htm

❏ **Jim Thorpe Area Senior High School Guidance Department**
http://www.jtasd.k12.pa.us/highschool/
guidance/jtasdguidance.html
Excellent resource—links to information for parents, courses, college, financial aid & scholarships, career, standardized testing, and special education.

❏ **Mark Veronica's School Counseling Resource Center**
http://www.acsu.buffalo.edu/~veronica/
guidance.html

❏ **Millard South Counseling Center**
http://www.esu3.k12.ne.us/districts/
millard/south/guid/msguid.html

❏ **Monacan High School Guidance Department**
http://www.chesterfield.k12.va.us/Schools/
Monacan_HS/guid/guidpg.htm

❏ **Mount Carmel High School—Guidance and Counseling Department**
http://www.mchs.org/infoguide.html

❏ **Northern Burlington Guidance Department**
http://www.nburlington.com/nbc-web/guidance/guidance.htm

❏ **Patuxent High School Guidance Department**
http://calvertnet.k12.md.us/schools/phs/phsguidance.html

❏ **Prospect Heights Middle School Guidance & Counseling**
http://www.gemlink.com/~phms1/general_info/guidance.html

❏ **Sabino's Counseling Department**
http://www.azstarnet.com/~sabino/reed.html

❏ **South Salem High School Guidance and Counseling Deptartment**
http://www.viser.net/~sshs/counsel.htm

❏ **Spring Branch Independent School District's Guidance Services**
http://www.spring-branch.isd.tenet.edu/instruc/guidance/INDEX.HTM

❏ **Springfield High School Counseling Center**
http://www.springfield.k12.vt.us/schools/shs/guidance/

❏ **St. Gertrude Guidance and Counseling**
http://www.saintgertrude.org/schoolinfo/guidance.htm

❏ **Stonewall Jackson Senior High School Guidance**
http://www.pwcs.edu/sjhs/guidance.htm

❏ **The Virtual Guidance Counselor**
http://home.ican.net/~aweiler/guidance/guidpage.htm

❏ **Topping Elementary**
http://www.nwmissouri.edu/~0202615/INDEX.HTML

❏ **Urbana High School Guidance and Counseling**
http://www.cmi.k12.il.us/~furrersa/

❏ **Valencia High School Guidance & Counseling Department**
http://www.hart.k12.ca.us/valencia/about/guidance.htm

❏ **Vandercook Lake High School Counselors Page**
http://scnc.vandy.k12.mi.us/counsel.htm

❏ **West Springfield High School Career Center**
http://www.wshs.fcps.k12.va.us/career/career.htm

❏ **Westmeade Elementary School Counseling Program**
http://personalweb.edge.net/~westmead/sc.html

❏ **Windsor H.S. Guidance**
http://www.windsor.k12.mo.us/hsguide

MENTAL HEALTH

❏ **Behavior OnLine: The Mental Health and Behavioral Science Meeting Place**
http://www.behavior.net/index.html

According to the site, Behavior OnLine aspires to be the premier World Wide Web gathering place for mental health professionals and applied behavioral scientists—a place where professionals of every discipline can feel at home.

❏ **Computers in Mental Health**
http://www.ex.ac.uk/cimh/

The site aims to encourage the development of useful computing applications in the field of mental health. There is an associated discussion list which is open to professionals with an interest in computing and mental health.

❏ **Counseling E-zine**
http://www.gate.net/~rational/ezine0198.html

Counseling E-zine is about the newest developments in the field of mental health, including counseling, psychotherapy, marriage and family therapy, social work, and psychiatry. The e-zine is disseminated quarterly and includes e-mail from users, current news items, professional chat activities, articles, and links.

❏ **Counseling Resources on the Net**
http://www.csun.edu/%7Ehfedp001/links.html

Highly resourceful site with many links brought to us by the department of Educational Psychology and Counseling, California State University at Northridge.

❏ **CyberPsychologist—Rob Sarmiento, PhD**
http://www.cyberpsych.com/althome.html
An example of online counseling.

❏ **Internet Mental Health**
http://www.mentalhealth.com/

The goal of this site is to, "... improve understanding, diagnosis, and treatment of mental illness throughout the world." Internet Mental Health is a free encyclopedia of mental health information. Contains many links and a search engine!

❏ **Mental Health InfoSource**
http://www.mhsource.com/

This is an interactive megasite which includes many links, resources, opportunities to ask questions, and earn CEU's.

❏ **Mental Health Licensure Resources**
http://www.tarleton.edu/%7Ecounseling/coresour/lllpc.htm

This page was created to provide up-to-date licensure information and resources for individuals practicing in mental health fields. The site contains information on how to contact licensing boards, preparation for exams, current issues, and state board rules, regulations, and application procedures.

❏ **Mental Health Net**
http://www.cmhc.com/

Mental Health Net is an award-winning guide to mental health, psychology, and psychiatry online. The site currently indexes over 7,500 refereed resources and is home to over 9,000 regular members.

❏ **Mental Health Net—PsychNews International**
http://www.cmhc.com/pni/

An electronic publication distributed on a monthly basis (except for combined August-September and December-January issues) devoted to issues in psychology, psychiatry and the social sciences. FREE.

❏ **Prep Test NCE Licensure Exam Links**
http://www.licensure.com/trlinks/links.html
A most excellent site for reviewing, especially for certification/licensure examinations.

❑ **Psych Central: Dr. John GROHOL's Mental Health Page**
http://www.grohol.com/

The site titled Psych Central: Dr. John Grohol's Mental Health Page, is boasted as a personalized one-stop index for psychology, support, and mental health issues, resources, and people on the Internet. This site has been reviewed by The Wall Street Journal, Newsweek, U.S. News & World Report, the Washington Post, USA Today, The Village Voice, Business Week and dozens of other publications!

❑ **School Activities**
http://www.ag.uiuc.edu/~disaster/csndactx.html

❑ **Self Improvement Online**
http://www.selfgrowth.com/

Billed as the definitive web guide to personal growth, self improvement, self-help and personal power. This site is designed to be an organized directory referencing information in other Web Sites on the World Wide Web.

❑ **Tarleton Student Counseling Center Self-Help**
http://www.tarleton.edu/~counseling/

Has both self-help information, links, and counseling resources.

❑ **Tests**
http://www.psychtests.com/tests_frm.html

❑ **College News Online**
http://www.collegenews.com/

A free campus newswire and student service dedicated to meeting the Internet needs of students, graduates and others interested in higher education.

❑ **eSchoolNews.com**
http://www.eschoolnews.org/

K-12 school technology newspaper including info about technology funding opportunities and plenty of news. One of my favorites.

❑ **HealthScout: Watching the Medical World for News About You**
http://www.healthscout.com/

❑ **Internet Research News**
http://www.coppersky.com/ongir/news/
Also available via e-mail, free.

❑ **Government Resources on the Web**
http://www.lib.umich.edu/libhome/Documents.center/whatsnew.html

❑ **Business Week Online**
http://www.businessweek.com/
Lots of information and resources.

❑ **CNN Interactive**
http://www.cnn.com/

❑ **Education Week on the Web**
http://www.edweek.org/
Archived full-text articles, products and services, magazines, daily news, and special reports.

❑ **Mercury Center**
http://www.mercurycenter.com/

❏ **NewsDirectory: Newspapers and Media**
http://www.ecola.com/
Magazines and television too.

❏ **Pilot Online—Hampton Roads, Virginia**
http://www.pilotonline.com/

❏ **Recovery Network News**
http://www.recoverynetwork.com/news/
The Recovery Network conducts a weekly media sweep and provides information about prevention and recovery and substance use. The site boasts digests and the latest news from over 1,400 sources. At this time, Recovery Network News contains approximately one week's worth of article digests from such sources as the Wall Street Journal, USA Today, the Washington Post, Reuters, the New York Times, and Investors Business Daily, among other sources. The news can be downloaded as a Microsoft Word file, and interested readers can also subscribe to a weekly e-mail version.

❏ **San Francisco Chronicle on The Gate**
http://www.sfgate.com/cgi-bin/chronicle/
list-sections.cgi

❏ **The Chronicle of Higher Education**
http://chronicle.com/

❏ **The Nando Times**
http://www.nando.net/

❏ **USA TODAY**
http://www.usatoday.com/

❏ **USA TODAY Latest news (Education)**
http://www.usatoday.com/educate/
body.htm
An online gateway to the world of education by the folks at USA Today.

CYBERCOUNSELING

❏ **Body, Mind & Spirit—What's your EQ?**
http://www.utne.com/cgi-bin/eq
Online instrument for learning about your EQ.

❏ **Counseling Without Walls—Phone Counseling Help**
http://www.counselingwithoutwalls.com/
Counseling Without Walls (CWW) is a professional, privately-owned company that delivers telephone counseling services 24 hours a day, 7 days a week.

❏ **CyberCouch.com**
http://www.cybercouch.com/
Some helpful articles and links.

❏ **Metanoia Guide To Internet Mental Health Services**
http://www.metanoia.org/imhs/intro.htm
This site is a comprehensive, independent consumer guide to the psychotherapists and counselors who provide services over the Internet; compiled by consumers, for consumers.

❏ **Online psychotherapy and counseling—CyberAnalysis Clinic**
http://www.cyberanalysis.com/
Another example of an online therapist.

❏ **SELF-Therapy Training Program**
http://www.execpc.com/~tonyz/

❏ **Therapy Online**
http://www.therapyonline.ca/

❏ **The On-Line Books Page**
http://www.cs.cmu.edu/books.html
The On-Line Books Page is a directory of books that can be freely read right on the Internet. It includes: An index of thousands of on-line books on the Internet Pointers to significant directories and archives of on-line texts Special exhibits and more!

ORGANIZATIONS

- **American Association for Marriage and Family Therapy**
  http://www.aamft.org/

- **Advocates for Youth**
  http://www.advocatesforyouth.org/

- **Association for Multicultural Counseling and Development**
  http://edap.bgsu.edu/AMCD/

- **American Association of Pastoral Counselors**
  http://www.metanoia.org/aapc/

- **American Association of School Administrators**
  http://www.aasa.org/

- **American College Personnel Association**
  http://www.acpa.nche.edu/

- **American Council For Drug Educatoin**
  http://www.acde.org/

- **American Counseling Association**
  http://www.counseling.org/

- **American Dance Therapy Association Home Page**
  http://www.adta.org/

- **American Hospice Foundation**
  http://www.americanhospice.org/header.htm

- **American Psychological Association**
  http://www.apa.org/

- **American School Counselor Association**
  http://www.schoolcounselor.org/

- **American School Health Association**
  http://www.ashaweb.org/profile/

- **American Vocational Association**
  http://www.avaonline.org/

- **APsa: The American Psychoanalytic Association**
  http://www.apsa.org/

- **Association for Counselor Education and Supervision**
  http://www.siu.edu/~epse1/aces/

- **Association for Death Education and Counseling**
  http://www.adec.org/

- **Association for Specialists in Groupwork**
  http://blues.fd1.uc.edu/~wilson/asgw/

- **Association for Supervision and Curriculum Development**
  http://www.ascd.org/

- **Australian School Counsellors**
  http://www.acr.net.au/counsellors/

- **Benton Foundation**
  http://www.benton.org/

  The Benton Foundation works to realize the social benefits made possible by the public interest use of communications. Bridging the worlds of philanthropy, public policy, and community action, Benton seeks to shape the emerging communications environment and to demonstrate the value of communications for solving social problems. Through demonstration projects, media production and publishing, research, conferences, and grantmaking, Benton probes relationships between the public, corporate, and nonprofit sectors to address the critical questions for democracy in the information age.

❏ **Council for Accreditation of Counseling and Related Educational Programs**
http://www.counseling.org/CACREP/main.htm

The Council for Accreditation of Counseling and Related Educational Programs (CACREP) was formed in 1981. This site contains access to a Directory of CACREP accredited programs, a student's guide to accreditation, the 2001 standards revision process, and the CACREP Board of Directors.

❏ **Canadian Guidance and Counselling Association**
http://www.geocities.com/Athens/5628/

❏ **Chi Sigma Iota**
http://www.csi-net.org/

❏ **Children and Adults with Attention Deficit Disorder**
http://www.chadd.org/

Through its professional advisory board, and other leaders in the field of ADHD, CH.A.D.D. brings you accurate, current information on medical, scientific, educational and advocacy issues.

❏ **College Parents of America**
http://www.collegeparents.org/

❏ **Creative Partnerships for Prevention**
http://www.cpprev.org/contents.htm

According to the site, the goal of this national initiative is to provide current information, ideas, and resources on how to use the arts and humanities to enhance drug and violence prevention programming, foster resiliency in youth, and implement collaborations within communities to strengthen prevention programs for youth. The materials developed for this initiative have been designed with the guidance of educators, prevention specialists, youth workers, and professionals from cultural institutions (arts and humanities organizations, museums, libraries, etc.). This site includes demonstrations, profiles of existing programs, a "community center", and links to other resources.

❏ **Florida School Counselors Association**
http://webcoast.com/schools/FSCA/

❏ **Health Action Information Network**
http://www.hain.org/

The Health Action Information Network (HAIN) is a non-profit non-government organization established in 1985 based in Quezon City, the Philippines. It is involved in health education and research and mainly works with community-based organizations involved in health and development.

❏ **International Association of Marriage and Family Counselors**
http://familycounselors.org/

❏ **Kids Can Make A Difference**
http://www.kids.maine.org/

Kids Can Make a difference (KIDS), an educational program for middle- and high school students, focuses on the root causes of hunger and poverty, the people most affected, solutions, and how students can help. The major goal is to stimulate the students to take some definite follow-up actions as they begin to realize that one person can make a difference.

❏ **National Association of Alcoholism and Drug Abuse Counselors**
http://www.naadac.org/

❏ **National Association of Secondary School Principals**
http://www.nassp.org/

❏ **National Association of Social Workers**
http://www.nau.edu/~sociology/socialwork/naswi.html

❏ **National Middle School Association**
http://www.nmsa.org/

❏ **National Association for College Admission Counseling**
http://www.nacac.com/index.html

❏ **National Association for Self-Esteem**
http://www.self-esteem-nase.org/

The purpose of the NASE is to fully integrate self-esteem into the fabric of American society so that every individual, no matter what their age or background, experiences personal worth and happiness. This site is highly resourceful by providing useful links, contacts, educational programming information, and a whole lot more.

❏ **National Association of Elementary School Principals**
http://www.naesp.org/

❏ **National Board for Certified Counselors**
http://www.nbcc.org/index.htm

❏ **National Career Development Association**
http://ncda.org/

❏ **National Center for Injury Prevention and Control**
http://www.cdc.gov/ncipc/ncipchm.htm

As the lead federal agency for injury prevention, NCIPC works closely with other federal agencies; national, state, and local organizations; state and local health departments; and research institutions. This site contains updates, reports, and grant information.

❏ **National Clearinghouse for Alcohol and Drug Information**
http://www.health.org/

The National Clearinghouse for Alcohol and Drug Information (NCADI) is the information service of the Center for Substance Abuse Prevention of the Substance Abuse and Mental Health Services Administration in the U.S. Department of Health & Human Services. NCADI is the world's largest resource for current information and materials concerning substance abuse.

❏ **National Committee to Prevent Child Abuse**
http://www.childabuse.org/

Chock full of information, resources, statistics, chapter contact information, and advocacy tips—this site is a must see.

❏ **National Crime Prevention Council On-Line Resource Center**
http://www.ncpc.org/

The National Crime Prevention Council (NCPC) is a private, nonprofit, tax-exempt organization whose mission is to prevent crime and build safer, more caring communities. The site contains useful information about crime prevention, community building, comprehensive planning, and even fun stuff for kids.

❏ **National Depressive and Manic-Depressive Association**
http://www.ndmda.org/

❏ **National Educational Service**
http://www.nes.org/

❏ **National Employment Counseling Association**
http://www.geocities.com/Athens/Acropolis/6491/

❏ **National Families in Action**
http://www.emory.edu/NFIA/

National Families in Action is a national drug education, prevention, and policy center based in Atlanta, Georgia. The organization was founded in 1977. Its mission is to help families and communities prevent drug abuse among children by promoting policies based on science.

❏ **National Homeschool Association**
http://www.n-h-a.org/

❏ **National Institute of Mental Health**
http://www.nimh.nih.gov/home.htm

❏ **National Institute on Early Childhood Development and Education**
http://www.ed.gov/offices/OERI/ECI/

The organization sponsors comprehensive and challenging research in order to help ensure that America's young children are successful in school and beyond—and to enhance their quality of life and that of their families.

❏ **National Opportunity NOCs**
http://www.opportunitynocs.org/

This site is a database of national not-for-profit organizations which can be useful to work with in the school setting.

❏ **National PTA**
http://www.pta.org/index.stm

❏ **National Victim Center**
http://www.nvc.org/

❏ **North Central Association for Counselor Education and Supervision**
http://www.uc.edu/~yagergg/ncaces/NCACES.HTM

❏ **North Carolina Peer Helper Association**
http://members.aol.com/ncpha/

North Carolina Peer Helper Association

"Teaching People To Help Each Other"

❏ **Organization Concerned about Rural Education**
http://www.ruralschools.org/

❏ **Ohio Counseling Association**
http://www.ohiocounselingassoc.com/onlinenews.html

❏ **Ontario School Counsellors' Association**
http://ouacinfo.ouac.on.ca/osca/index.htm

❏ **Points of Light Foundation**
http://www.pointsoflight.org/

The Foundation's mission is to engage more people more effectively in volunteer community service to help solve serious social problems. This site should be your starting place for volunteering and similar activities.

❏ **School Counsellor's Association of New-foundland**
http://www.stemnet.nf.ca/Organizations/SCAN/

❏ **Tennessee Counseling Association**
http://edge.net/~tca/

❏ **The Council of Chief State School Officers**
http://www.ccsso.org/

The Council of Chief State School Officers (CCSSO) is a nationwide, nonprofit organization composed of the public officials who head departments of elementary and secondary education in the states, the District of Columbia, the Department of Defense Education Activity, and five extra-state jurisdictions. CCSSO seeks its members' consensus on major educational issues and expresses their view to civic and professional organizations, federal agencies, Congress, and the public. Through its structure of standing and special committees, the Council responds to a broad range of concerns about education and provides leadership on major education issues.

❏ **The National Center for Charitable Statistics at The Urban Institute**
http://nccs.urban.org/

The National Center for Charitable Statistics (NCCS) is the national repository of data on the nonprofit sector in the United States. Its mission is to develop and disseminate high quality data on nonprofit organizations and their activities. Links to documents, state profiles, resources on nonprofits and philanthropy, factsheets, and more.

❏ **The National Self-Help Clearinghouse**
http://www.selfhelpweb.org/

❏ **The National Education Association**
http://www.nea.org/

❏ **Welcome to Six Seconds- Resources Emotional Intelligence**
http://www.6seconds.org/home.shtml

A nonprofit organization to support EQ for individuals, families, schools & communities. The group provides training and materials that transform current research into effective practice.

❏ **Wisconsin School Counselor Association**
http://www.planethelp.com/wsca/

Information about membership and counseling reltated links.

❏ **YWCA of the USA**
http://www.ywca.org/

PEER HELPER PROGRAMS

❏ **Advocates for Youth—Peer Education**
http://www.advocatesforyouth.org/peer.htm

Resources about peer education focus on peer-led sexual health programs. Peer mediation, peer counseling, peer mentoring, peer helping, and peer tutoring are all different.

❏ **CALIFORNIA ASSOCIATION OF PEER PROGRAMS**
http://www.pomona.k12.ca.us/~capp/

The California Association of Peer Programs is dedicated to the initiation, enhancement, and promotion of youth service through quality peer programs.

❏ **Conflict and Peace Studies**
http://www.synapse.net/~acdi20/links/conflict.htm

Tons of resources!

❏ **Conflict Mangement**
http://www.coe.ufl.edu/faculty/myrick/conflictmanagement/conflictmanagement.html

Authored by Dr. Robert D. Myrick of the University of Florida, this site provides a virtual guidance unit about conflict resolution. Includes information, activities, and quotes.

❏ **Conflict Resolution/Peer Mediation**
http://www.coe.ufl.edu/CRPM/CRPMhome.html

A research project from the University of Florida.

❑ **Emergency Support Network**
http://www.tunnecliffe.com.au/
articles.html

Articles on this site are largely about peer helping issues taken from the Emergency Support Newsletter. With acknowledgement, you are free to reproduce these for other publications.

❑ **Fujifilm Photopals**
http://www.scholastic.com/photopals/

❑ **GreatKids Profiles**
http://www.greatkids.com/profiles.html

These are the kids who far exceed all of our expectations. Read their stories and submit your own.

❑ **Health Education/Peer Counseling**
http://healthcenter.ucdavis.edu/
healthed.html

This Health Education Program at the Cowell Student Health Center promotes wellness and disease/injury prevention through confidential peer counseling services, small- or large-group education, and a variety of publications. Trained peer counselors, workshop seminars, and printed materials (pamphlets and resource library) are available.

❑ **Healthy Oakland Teens**
http://www.caps.ucsf.edu/hotindex.html

Read about the Healthy Oakland Teens Project (HOT) which began in the fall of 1992 at an urban, ethnically diverse junior high school. The project's goal is to reduce adolescents' risk for HIV infection by using peer role models to advocate for responsible decision making, healthy values and norms, and improved communication skills. You can view and download their entire curriculum.

❑ **Israeli Schools Looking for Keypals**
http://ietn.snunit.k12.il/byschool.htm

If you want to have your students buddy-up with Israeli students, this site is a must.

❑ **Justice Information Center (NCJRS): Peer Justice and Youth Empowerment**
http://www.ncjrs.org/peerhome.htm

An implementation guide for teen court programs in PDF format.

❑ **Keypals**
http://www.collegebound.com/keypals/

The mission of KeyPals is to give K-12 students and their teachers this an "intriguing" opportunity to communicate.

❑ **National Mentoring Partnership**
http://www.mentoring.org/

This partnership advocates for the expansion of mentoring; a resource for mentors and mentoring initiatives nationwide.

❑ **National Service-Learning Cooperative Clearinghouse**
http://www.nicsl.coled.umn.edu/

❑ **Ontario Peer Helpers' Association**
http://ouacinfo.ouac.on.ca/osca/opha.htm

❑ **Orange Coast College Peer Helpers**
http://www.occ.cccd.edu/Peer/OCC4.HTM

❑ **Peer Assistance & Leadership**
http://nhs.nisd.com/whatis.html

A program at Nacogdoches High School, Texas.

❑ **Peer Center**
http://www.peercenter.org/

A community drop-in center for those individuals who endure the pain of mental illness.

❑ **Peer Helpers at Taylor Road Middle School**
http://trms.k12.ga.net/~abaggett/peer-hp.html

❑ **Peer Helpers of Ontario**
http://www.ncboard.edu.on.ca/peers/
index.htm

❏ **Peer Helping**
http://www.sentex.net/~casaa/peer-helping/index.html

Brought to us from the Canadian Association of Student Activity Advisors, this site has many articles and tutoring tips.

❏ **Peer Mediation Association of Maine**
http://www.kynd.com/~lundin/pmam/

❏ **Peer Ministry for Campus Ministry Partner Congregations**
http://www.elca.org/dhes/lcm/peermin.html

❏ **Peer Players**
http://www.peerplayers.com/

The Peer Players of Austin Community College in Austin, Texas, is a student organization which teaches and promotes peer education through theater. Check out their pictures and scripts.

❏ **Peer Resources**
http://www.peer.ca/

Their mission is to provide high quality training, superior educational resources, and practical consultation to persons who wish to establish or strengthen peer helping, peer support, peer mediation, peer referral, peer education, peer coaching, and mentor programs in schools, universities, communities, and corporations.

❏ **Placer County Peer Court**
http://silentvoices.org/peercourt/index.html

Placer Peer Court is a partnership that challenges the entire community to take an active role in solving juvenile crime.

❏ **Sweet Briar College Academic Resource Center Peer Mentoring**
http://www.arc.sbc.edu/mentoring.html

Also a link to peer tutoring and other helpful resources.

❏ **The PALS Peer Mentoring Program**
http://www.calstatela.edu/academic/pals/

PALS, the Partnership for Academic Learning and Success program is a Peer Mentoring program designed specifically to help targeted first-time Freshmen meet educational, financial and other challenges associated with beginning college life. The PALS Program offers a unique support system geared toward helping you to start college on the right feet and to enjoy your experience at Cal State L.A.

❏ **The Peer Power Centre**
http://www.peerpower.on.ca/index.html

The goal of the Peer Power Centre is to empower youth with the knowledge, skills, and access to resources they need, to better help themselves and their peers. This site contains useful info and especially resources for your peer program.

❏ **The Peer Support Foundation**
http://www.peersupport.com.au/

An educational organisation committed to improving the quality of life for Victorian school students through peer group influence. Their intention is to help students resist peer pressure to behave anti-socially, adjust easily to a new grade or school, contribute to the spirit of community, and promote responsibility, self-confidence and leadership qualities. This site may help facilitatie ideas in structuring your own program.

❏ **The People for Peace Conflict Resolution Center**
http://members.aol.com/pforpeace/cr/index.htm

❏ **The Well Woman Peer Education Program**
http://www.barnard.columbia.edu/health/well_woman/peered.htm

❏ **Welcome to Teen Court**
http://tqd.advanced.org/2640/

This web site is provided for communities interested in beginning a Teen Court and also for existing Teen Courts to communicate and share resources with one another.

❏ **Welcome to U of G's Peer Helper Homepage**
http://www.uoguelph.ca/csrc/peerhelp/

❏ **Yes You Can!**
http://www.ed.gov/pubs/YesYouCan/

The publication, Yes, You Can: A Guide for Establishing Mentoring Programs to Prepare Youth for College. Also availabe for PDF download.

❏ **YLGB Peer Support Project**
http://www.peer-support.demon.co.uk/

This peer support project provides peer support services for young lesbians, gays & bisexuals in Greater Manchester.

❏ **A Web of On-line Dictionaries**
http://www.bucknell.edu/%7Erbeard/diction.html

Linked to more than 500 dictionaries of over 140 different languages.

❏ **Acronym Finder**
http://www.mtnds.com/af/

Look up 65,000 acronyms/abbreviations & their meanings. A searchable database containing common acronyms and abbreviations about all subjects, with a focus on computers, technology, telecommunications, and the military.

❏ **Address Directory—Politicians Of The World**
http://www.trytel.com/~aberdeen/

❏ **Al's Lots O' Links Psychology Info**
http://www.capecod.net/~aroberti/links/psych.htm

Useful and abundant links to counseling and psychology.

❏ **AlphaSearch**
http://www.calvin.edu/Lib_Resources/as/

According to the site, The primary purpose of AlphaSearch is to access the finest Internet "gateway" sites. The authors of these "gateway" sites have spent significant time gathering into one place all relevant sites related to a discipline, subject, or idea.

❏ **Cable in the Classroom Online**
http://www.ciconline.com/

Cable in the Classroom is a $420 million public service effort supported by 38 national cable networks and over 8,500 local cable companies. These networks and local cable companies act as a partner in learning with teachers and parents by providing a free cable connection and over 540 hours per month of commercial-free educational programming to schools across the country.

Russell A. Sabella, Ph.D.

❏ **Consumer World**
http://www.consumerworld.org/

CONSUMER WORLD®

Consumer World is a public service site which has gathered over 1700 of the most useful consumer resources on the Internet, and categorized them here for easy access.

❏ **Corbis Experience The Place for Pictures on the Internet**
http://pix.corbis.com/postcard/
Send an electronic postcard with one of millions of photos.

❏ **Counseling, Parenting, & Education the Rendezvous**
http://www.ida.net/users/marie/rendez~1.htm
This site is a unified effort by professional counselors who have had years of experience as researchers, administrators, and counselors. The information found in these pages is free. You will also find links to some excellent sites which provide related information. Most importantly, you will find links to pages which are regularly updated and which are related to various counseling subjects.

❏ **Education Journal Annotations**
http://www.soemadison.wisc.edu/IMC/journals/anno_AB.html
This annotated list of current education journals, developed and maintained by the staffs of the University of Wisconsin-Madison Instructional Materials Center (IMC) and the Kansas State University Libraries (KSU), is designed to provide descriptive annotations and Internet links for selected journals in education with an emphasis on titles supportive of K-12 education and teacher education.

❏ **Federal Resources for Educational Excellence**
http://www.ed.gov/free/
Federal Resources for Educational Excellence (FREE) makes hundreds of Internet-based education resources supported by agencies across the U.S. Federal government easier to find.

❏ **JCTP Website**
http://www.apa.org/science/jctpweb.html
The Joint Committee on Testing Practices (JCTP) was established in 1985 by the American Educational Research Association (AERA), the American Psychological Association (APA), and the National Council on Measurement in Education (NCME). The American Counseling Association (ACA) and the American Speech-Language-Hearing Association (ASHA) joined JCTP in 1987. The National Association of School Psychologists (NASP) has since joined JCTP, which now consists of ACA, AERA, APA, ASHA, NASP, and NCME. Each association appoints two representatives to JCTP, preferably including one who is closely associated with test development and publishing. Staff support for the JCTP is provided by APA's Science Directorate. This site contains many valuable full-text documents, events, links, and project descriptions.

❏ **K12OPPS Mailing List Archive**
http://archives.gsn.org/k12opps/

K12OPPS List

This site is designed to help you find individuals connect with classroom teachers around the world; find interesting and productive global collaborative learning projects; and build, advertise, and conduct your own original collaborative projects.

❏ **Learn2**
http://www.learn2.com/index.html

Dubbed as the ability utility, this site can help you leanr the things that "make life easier and/or more interesting: everything from the essentials of life to the esoteric, from practical to just plain fun.

❏ **Legal Information Institute**
http://supct.law.cornell.edu/supct/

The Legal Information Institute offers Supreme Court opinions under the auspices of Project Hermes, the court's electronic-dissemination project. This archive contains (or will soon contain) all opinions of the court issued since May of 1990. In addition, our collection of over 580 of the most important historical decisions of the Court is available on CD-ROM and (with reduced functionality) over the Net.

❏ **Microsoft in K-12 Education**
http://www.microsoft.com/education/k12/

❏ **MLA Style**
http://www.mla.org/main_stl.htm

The only MLA documentation style are the only ones available on the Internet that are authorized by the Modern Language Association of America.

❏ **My Hero**
http://myhero.com/home.asp

An interactive educational website, visitors may read about great figures like Rosa Parks, Martin Luther King, Jr., Mark Twain, and others, including many local heroes. They suggest their own heroes and write short biographies about them. Children honor inspiring parents, parents honor brave children. From peacemakers such as Nelson Mandela to scientific visionaries like Albert Einstein, the My Hero web page has allowed thousands of children and their parents a chance to tell the world about the people who they most respect and admire. In honoring others, visitors, especially children, begin to realize their own power and potential.

❏ **National Study of School Evaluation Useful Links**
http://www.nsse.org/useful.html

❏ **Practitioner Developed Educational-Counseling Resources**
http://www.worldviewpub.com/

The source for educator and counselor-developed, ready-to-use video-driven conflict resolution, social skills and discipline training programs for preteens, teenagers and parents.

❏ **SuperKids Educational Software Review**
http://www.superkids.com/

SuperKids reviews and rates educational software based on a carefully developed set of criteria. Reviews are written by teams that include educators, parents, and children from across the United States.

❏ **Talbot's Student Planning**
http://www2.environs.com:443/talbot/

A selection of colleges, schools, and other assists for after high school.

❏ **The Counseling Zone**
http://www.gate.net/~rational/indexchat.html

Transcripts of counseling related Internet chats.

❏ **The State of the World's Children 1999**
http://www.unicef.org/sowc99/

Also available in PDF.

❏ **The Virtual Reference Desk**
http://www.vrd.org/

A Project of the ERIC Clearinghouse on Information & Technology and the National Library of Education with support from the Office of Science and Technology Policy.

❏ **Vocabulary**
http://www.vocabulary.com/

Participate in free vocabulary puzzles to enhance vocabulary mastery.

❏ **KidsCampaigns!**
http://www.kidscampaigns.org/home.html
    Learn more about this nationwide campaign. Includes a great link to children's mental health.

❏ **Oxford Text Archive**
http://firth.natcorp.ox.ac.uk/ota/public/index.shtml
    Recently appointed as a Service Provider for the UK-based Arts and Humanities Data Service, the Oxford Text Archive forms part of a national network of centres dedicated to the dissemination of quality, scholarly electronic resources, and to the support of UK-based academics involved with the creation of such materials.

❏ **WLH—Psychology**
http://www.utexas.edu/world/lecture/psy/
    The Psychology part of the World Lecture Hall which contains pages created by faculty worldwide who are using the Web to deliver class materials. See also distance education courses offered by The University of Texas System.

❏ **Zines on the Net**
http://fromnowon.org/zines.html
    This is a partial listing of the hundreds of Zines (electronic magazines) which can be found on the Internet.

RESEARCH & WRITING

❏ **APlus Research & Writing for High School and College Students**
http://www.ipl.org/teen/aplus/

    Includes a guide to researching and writing a paper, help for finding information in cyberspace and in your library, and links to online resources for research and writing.

❏ **Bill Trochim's Center for Social Research Methods**
http://trochim.human.cornell.edu/index.html
    According to the author, this website is for people involved in applied social research and evaluation. In addition to his own work, you'll find lots of links to other locations on the Web that deal in applied social research methods. You'll also find comprehensive course resource centers for this instructor's courses at Cornell, previously published and unpublished papers, detailed examples of current research projects, useful tools for researchers (like a guide to selecting a statistical analysis), an extensive online textbook, a bulletin board for discussions, and more.

❏ **BUBL Information Service Home Page**
http://bubl.ac.uk/
    Billed as a national information service for the higher education community, this site aims to provide a pathway to guide librarians, information professionals, academics and researchers through the maze of resources on the Internet by offering a structured and user-friendly gateway, mainly in the form of the BUBL subject tree.

❏ **Encyclopedia.com from Electric Library**
http://www.encyclopedia.com/

This site conveniently places an extraordinary amount of information at your fingertips. More than 17,000 articles from The Concise Columbia Electronic Encyclopedia, Third Edition have been assembled to provide free, quick and useful information on almost any topic.

❏ **ERIC Clearinghouse on Elementary and Early Childhood Education**
http://ericps.ed.uiuc.edu/ericeece.html

The Educational Resources Information Center (ERIC) is a national information system designed to provide users with ready access to an extensive body of education-related literature. Established in 1966, ERIC is supported by the U.S. Department of Education, Office of Educational Research and Improvement (OERI), and is administered by the National Library of Education.

❏ **ERIC Clearinghouse on Assessment and Evaluation**
http://ericae.net/main.htm

Contains a search engine, test locator, assessment FAQ's, bookstore, and a full-text library.

❏ **Guide to U.S. Department of Education Programs and Resources**
http://web99.ed.gov/GTEP/Program2.nsf

❏ **Library and Database Search Services**
http://www.oberon-res.com/librarys.htm

❏ **Library of Congress**
http://www.loc.gov/

The **LIBRARY** *of* **CONGRESS**

SEARCH THE CATALOG | SEARCH OUR WEB SITE | WEB SITE MAP

 USING the LIBRARY *Catalogs, Collections & Research Services*

 **THOMAS** *Congress At Work* **BICENTENNIAL 1800-2000** *Libraries • Creativity • Liberty*

COPYRIGHT OFFICE *Forms & Information*

 **AMERICAN MEMORY** *America's Story in Words, Sounds & Pictures* **TODAY in HISTORY**

 EXHIBITIONS *An On-Line Gallery* **FREUD**

THE LIBRARY TODAY *News, Events & More*

 **HELP & FAQs** *General Information*

❏ **Library Research Guides—UC Berkeley Libraries**
http://library.berkeley.edu/TeachingLib/Guides/

Including many services to individuals outside of the institution, this page is a collection of all of the Research Guides created by the UCB libraries.

❏ **Locus of Control Scale**
http://www.cl.uh.edu/edu/orgbeh/orgpub/survey/locus.html

This questionnaire is similar, but not identical, to the original locus of control scale. When you have finished the survey, you may have the computer score it for you.

❏ **National Center for Education Statistics**
http://www.ed.gov/NCES/

The Purpose of the Center is to collect and report "...statistics and information showing the condition and progress of education in the United States and other nations in order to promote and accelerate the improvement of American education."

❏ **National Education Goals**
http://www.negp.gov/webpg720.htm

This page provides electronic access to a variety of publications issued by the National Education Goals Panel.

❏ **No Sweat.com**
http://www.homeworkheaven.com/
Help for homework!

❏ **How to Put Questionnaires on the Internet**
http://salmon.psy.plym.ac.uk/mscprm/forms.htm

❏ **The Internet Public Library Education Reference**
http://www.ipl.org/ref/RR/static/edu0000.html

Information about schooling and instruction and the provision of knowledge or training in a particular area or for a particular purpose.

❏ **The Internet Writing Journal**
http://www.writerswrite.com/journal/

Known as the a one-stop resource for professional writers.

❏ **The Psychology of Cyberspace**
http://www1.rider.edu/~suler/psycyber/
psycyber.html

According to the owner, the purpose of this web site or "online hypertext book" is to explore the psychological dimensions of the environments created by computers and online networks. It is intended as an evolving conceptual framework for understanding the various psychological components of cyberspace and how people react to and behave within it.

❏ **UMich Documents Center**
http://www.lib.umich.edu/libhome/
Documents.center/

The Documents Center is a central reference and referral point for government information, whether local, state, federal, foreign or international. Its web pages are a reference and instructional tool for government, political science, statistical data, and news.

❏ **White House Conference**
http://www.exnet.iastate.edu/Pages/
families/nncc/wh/whconf.html

Children, Youth, and Families at risk initiative update. Site includes links to information about the latest research in brain development, child development resouces, and suggested discussion topics.

❏ **American Association of Colleges for Teacher Education: Education Policy Resource and Information Clearinghouse**
http://www.edpolicy.org/

This clearinghouse is designed to help people access information on education policy at the national, regional, or state level. To access information, click on the region or state in which you are interested.

❏ **ACSES, the Universe's Smartest Bookfinder**
http://www.acses.com/

Checks out price, availability, shipping times and shipping costs of any book at over 25 online stores. Really works.

❏ **Adolescence Directory**
http://education.indiana.edu/cas/adol/
adol.html

An electronic guide to information on adolescent issues. It is a service of the Center for Adolescent Studies at Indiana University. Educators, counselors, parents, researchers, health practitioners, and teens can use ADOL to find Web resources for a wide variety of topics.

❏ **AnyWho**
http://www.tollfree.att.net/tf.html

In addition to information published in white pages telephone directories, AnyWho also lists e-mail addresses, home page URLs, FAX numbers, and toll-free numbers supplied by individuals.

❏ **Apple Learning Interchange**
http://henson.austin.apple.com/edres/
curric.shtml

Resources for integrating technology into the classroom, complete with curriculum and lesson plans.

❏ **Best Information on the Net**
http://www.sau.edu/CWIS/Internet/Wild/
Neatnew/index.htm

Chosen by librarians at O'Keefe Library, St. Ambrose University.

❏ **BrainPlay.com: Smart Choices for Growing Kids.**
http://www.brainplay.com/

Many reviews for children's software and opportunity to purchase online.

❏ **ChildLine UK Web Site**
http://www.childline.org.uk/

ChildLine is the UK's free national helpline for children and young people in trouble or danger. A host of factsheets on many topics!

❏ **Chuck Eby's Counseling Resources**
http://www.cybercomm.net/~chuck/guide.html

❏ **CLN WWW**
http://www.cln.org/cln.html

This page is designed to help K-12 teachers integrate technology into their classrooms. The site boasts over over 220 menu pages with more than 3,900 annotated links to educational WWW sites, as well as over 100 WWW resources of our own—all organized within an intuitive structure.

❏ **Coolsig**
http://www.coolsig.com/

Want a new e-mail signature file? Something fun? You've come to the right place. Coolsig is now the biggest signature collection on the Internet!

❏ **Counseling and Guidance**
http://www.fau.edu/library/guidance.htm

The links page from the Florida Atlantic University Libraries.

❏ **Counseling and Guidance Resources**
http://www.fontana.k12.ca.us/district/edservices/burton/counsel.html

❏ **Counseling and Guidance Resources from Carrie's Crazy Quilt**
http://www.mtjeff.com/~bodenst/counsel.html

❏ **Counseling for Children**
http://www.montgomery-al.com/cfc/

❏ **Counseling Grads Center**
http://www.delphi.com/counselinggrads/

This forum is intended for use by Counseling Graduate Students as a vehicle for the exchange of ideas, as a source of information, and as a place where questions and concerns of counseling students regarding course work, research, employment opportunities, and counseling as a profession can be shared.

❏ **Counseling Internet Resources**
http://voled.doded.mil/dantes/refpubs/inet-res.htm

From the Department of Defense Voluntary Education Program.

❏ **CounselorNet**
http://www.plattsburgh.edu/projects/cnet/

CounselorNet is a World Wide Web site at the State University of New York at Plattsburgh which indexes materials useful for counselors in schools, agencies, and colleges.

❏ **EdPub On-Line Ordering System**
http://www.ed.gov/pubs/edpubs.html

This system is intended to help you identify and order U.S. Department of Education products. You can use searching options to identify the specific products you are seeking. During the initial stage of this system, individuals will be able to only request 1 product per order. After a few weeks, you will be able to order up to 5 different products per order.

❏ **Electronic Catalog of NCES Products and On-Line Library**
http://nces.ed.gov/pubsearch/index.html

Find information about publications and data products that the National Center for Education Statistics has released. In most cases you may also browse the content of the publication or download files that you can work with on your own computer.

❏ **Electronic School**
http://www.electronic-school.com/

Electronic School chronicles technological change in the classroom, interprets education issues in a digital world, and offers readers— some 80,000 school board members, school administrators, school technology specialists, and other educators—practical advice on a broad range of topics pertinent to the implementation of technology in elementary and secondary schools throughout North America.

❏ **FindingStone Counseling, Consulting, Education & Training**
http://www.findingstone.com/

Some online tests, lots of info, and useful links.

❏ **First Step Communications: EdSightings**
http://www.firststep.com.au/education/edsightings.html

This site a free e-mail service to help identify and inform users of useful educational Web sites.

❏ **Free Art Ideas For Kids, Parents, and Teachers**
http://members.tripod.com/~artworkinparis/index-3.html

This site should be useful for ideas and activities when conducting play counseling with children or making art a part of other guidance and counseling interventions.

❏ **Guidance & Counseling Curriculum Guide**
http://www.graceland.edu/~jackg/curr_guide/guide_co.htm

Well created document divided by guidance & counseling goals by grade level.

❏ **Guidance Sites**
http://www.cesa9.k12.wi.us/guidance.htm

❏ **Guidance, Sociology, & Psychology on the Net**
http://www.li.net/~ndonohue/guide.html

❏ **Guides for Citing Online/Web Sources**
http://www.nouveaux.com/guides.htm

❏ **High School Survival Kit**
http://cuip.uchicago.edu/www4teach/98/teams/peerpals/home.htm

Includes communication, note taking, time management, homework, reading strategies, testing, peer relations, and teacher resources.

❏ **Homeschooling Resource Catalogs**
http://www.home-ed-press.com/HSRSC/hsrsc_03cts.html

❏ **How Do You Feel Today?**
http://www.howdoyoufeeltoday.com/

❏ **Icon Collections—Images for Your Web Page**
http://www.monroe.lib.in.us/~lchampel/imgarch.html

You can find collections of images on the WWW that you can use to decorate your own Web page. Generally, the images in these archives are in the "public domain," which means they don't have any copyright restrictions on them. Or, the creators of the images have given their permission for others to use the images for free.

❏ **In and Out of the Classroom with Microsoft PowerPoint 97**
http://www.microsoft.com/education/curric/ppt97/

On online guidebook for using MS Powerpoint.

❏ **International Counselor Network (ICN)**
http://edge.net/~ruste/icn.html

According to the author and listowner, Ellen Rust, The International Counselor Network (ICN) was started in order to cut down on the isolation felt by many counselors who do not have enough time or opportunity to connect with their colleagues in person. The network has grown to over 1000 members since it began in February, 1993. Members are from several countries and all U.S. states and include counselors, counselor educators, graduate students, and others interested in counseling issues. ICN members collaborate by sharing ideas, resources, and discussions about mental health issues. They share articles or papers they have written and ask for comments or reactions. Those who are more familiar with the Internet guide newcomers to useful WWW sites, other mailing lists, and counseling resources. Instructions for subscribing are included.

❏ **Kelly Bear**
http://www.kellybear.com/frames.htm

The Kelly Bear materials were created to provide easy-to-use resources that would strengthen communication and positive relationships between adults (parents, grandparents, teachers, counselors) and children ages 3-9. They help children understand their feelings, become socially competent, learn to be responsible, and develop healthy living habits.

❏ **Kim's Korner for Teacher Talk**
http://www.angelfire.com/ks/teachme/icebreakers.html

A description of icebreakers and energizers you can incorporate in your work.

❏ **Learn CPR**
http://www.learncpr.org/index.html

LEARN CPR
you can do it!

An extensive guide and informational resouce for CPR training (to supplement the real thing).

❏ **LifeMatters: Well-Being & Health Forums, Courses, and Products**
http://www.lifematters.com/

LifeMatters is a synthesis of our professional experience as counselors and educators and personal life experiences. Our contribution is promoting the point of view that taking charge of one's health and well-being; physically, mentally, emotionally and spiritually, is a possibility for everyone.

❏ **ListBot**
http://www.listbot.com/
Start your own free e-mail list!

❏ **Lorrie's Links: A Collection of Guidance and Counseling Resources**
http://vm.nmu.edu/LOBURHAN/http/home.html

❏ **Microsoft's Homepage**
http://www.microsoft.com/ie40.htm
Tons of free and valuble resources!

❏ **National Education Telecommunications Network**
http://www.netn.net/20111.htm

❏ **New Middle School Teacher Guide**
http://www.middleweb.com/1stDResources.html

Includes sections and resources about the first days of school, new teachers, books for new and restless teachers, and general resources.

❏ **Northwest Education Magazine**
http://www.nwrel.org/nwedu/

The site offers valuable information about programs and services such as training & technical assistance; research & development for educational improvement; and education & community services.

❏ **Online Psych**
http://www.onlinepsych.com/index.html/

Many mental health forums and links to articles, games, issues, and databases.

❏ **Online Writing Center**
http://www.colostate.edu/Depts/WritingCenter/

The Online Writing Center at Colorado State University is an ongoing project created by the Center for Research on Writing and Communication Technologies. A highly resourceful site with many useful links.

❏ **Outta Ray's Head English Lesson Plans**
http://www3.sympatico.ca/ray.saitz/

A collection of lesson plans with handouts by Ray Saitz and many contributors.

❏ **PBS TeacherSource**
http://www.pbs.org/teachersource/

PBS TeacherSource makes it easy to locate and use the best television and Web resources available, as well as keep you on top of important community services provided by your PBS station.

❏ **PDFzone.COM**
http://www.pdfzone.com/

Your online hub to all things Acrobat & PDF.

❏ **PedagoNet**
http://www.pedagonet.com/

An innovative search engine, PedagoNet facilitates the exchange of learning resources. Books, chat room, discussion forum, jobs, clipart, webpage creation, postcards, valuable links and free information are available.

❏ **Prevention Yellow Pages**
http://www.tyc.state.tx.us/prevention/40001ref.html

A worldwide directory of programs, research, references and resources dedicated to the prevention of youth problems and the promotion of nurturing children.

❏ **Promising Practices in School Counselling**
http://ednet.edc.gov.ab.ca/sct/PPSchool.html

❏ **PsychNews International: Resources**
http://userpage.fu-berlin.de/~expert/RESOURCES/resources.html

A HUGE list of counseling and psychology related sources (sites, listservs, and more).

❏ **PubList.com**
http://www.publist.com/

PubList.com is the most comprehensive directory of information about more than 150,000 publications and more than 8000 newspapers around the world. It's easy to use. And it's free. I did a search using the term "counseling" and received an impressive list of 31 journals ranging from Abstracts of Research in Pastoral Care and Counseling to the Senior Counseling Letter. This database provides ISBN numbers, circultation, publication periods, and much more!

❏ **Resiliency In Action (RAI)**
http://www.resiliency.com/

The purpose of RAI is to spread the news of resiliency through sharing research and facilitating the practical application and evaluation of the resiliency paradigm. The site also contains an opportunity to subscribe to a newsletter ($30 for individuals), sample articles, calendar of events, and a speaker list.

❑ **Ripple Effects**
http://www.rippleeffects.com/

Ripple Effects, Inc. is a San Francisco-based company that provides software tools to help with the social-emotional elements that affect productivity, academic achievement and everyday happiness.

❑ **S.C.O.R.E. CyberGuides**
http://www.sdcoe.k12.ca.us/score/cyberguide.html

According to the site, CyberGuides are supplementary, web-based units of instruction centered on core works of literature. They are designed for the classroom with one online computer. Each CyberGuide contains a student and teacher edition, objectives, a task and a process by which it may be completed, teacher-selected web sites and a rubric. CyberGuides aligned with California's Academic Content Standards as indicated in the Teacher Guides.

❑ **Safe Kids**
http://www.safekids.com/

Tips, advice and suggestions to make your family's online experience fun and productive!

❑ **Sample Lesson Plan**
http://udel.edu/~kenlev/lessonplan.htm

A sample classroom guidance lesson plan written by Ken Levering about being a good student. Includes an online pretest and related links.

❑ **School Counseling Resources**
http://www.indep.k12.mo.us/WC/wmccane.html

❑ **School Counseling Resources**
http://www.libraries.wright.edu/libnet/subj/cou/cpmeta/sc.html

❑ **Scout Report**
http://wwwscout.cs.wisc.edu/scout/report/

Surf Smarter.

Published every Friday both on the web and by e-mail, it provides a fast, convenient way to stay informed of valuable resources on the Internet.

❑ **Smoother Sailing—Charting the Course**
http://www.des-moines.k12.ia.us/Other/Counseling/SmootherSailing.html

From the site: Smoother Sailing, Des Moines' unique elementary counseling program, helps children cope with the "rough seas" of growing up. Praised nationally as a model of excellence among elementary couseling programs, Smoother Sailing affects the lives of more than 15,000 children in the 42 elementary schools of the Des Moines Public School District.

❑ **Stuart's Internet Links for Counselling Rescources**
http://members.theglobe.com/Stuart44/counsel/frame_p1.htm

❑ **Student Leader Magazine Online**
http://www.studentleader.com/

This leadership magazine for college and college-bound students is a great resource for any who want to develop leadership skills. Each issue has stimulating articles that include leadership tips from students at schools all across the USA.

❑ **Study Guides for Testing, Reading, Writing, and Classroom Participation**
http://www.iss.stthomas.edu/studyguides/

❏ **Symantec AntiVirus Research Center**
http://www.sarc.com/

THE place to go for virus and antivirus information.

❏ **T.H.E. Journal**
http://www.thejournal.com/Theinfo/media/over.htm

T.H.E. JOURNAL provides educators with a nationwide forum in which they can share their successful experiences in employing technology to improve learning and its administration. Each issue is equivalent to attending an educational technology seminar in the convenience of a subscriber's own home or office.

❏ **Technology in School Counseling**
http://cbweb1.collegeboard.org/cblist/html/techsch.html

This is the place for online exchanges among school counselors and counselor educators relating to the use of technology in school counseling.

❏ **Test Anxiety Scale**
http://www.learningskills.com/test.html

A printable test online.

❏ **The Ethics Connection**
http://www.scu.edu/Ethics/homepage.shtml

From the opening homepage, the user is presented with opportunities to interact: links to other sections of the site, areas of dialogue and practicing ethics, and the latest news and publications in the field of ethics and the site itself. A powerful, site-specific internal search engine enables users to pinpoint the data which they might need among hundreds of constantly refined libraries of ethical information and decision-making tools.

❏ **The George Lucas Educational Foundation**
http://www.glef.org/learnlive/download/download.html

Free online copy of the book Learn & Live in PDF format.

❏ **Web Resources for Counselors**
http://www.clark.net/pub/carolr/WebRsc.html

Another web portal for school counselors.

❏ **Webtime Stories**
http://www.kn.pacbell.com/wired/webtime/

An annotated collection of web sites for people who love children's literature.

❏ **YDRF-TeamYouth**
http://www.teamyouth.com/

YDRF stands for the Youth Development and Research Fund. This site targets at-risk youth, especially in prisons, group homes, juvenile institutions, schools, programs and street corners. According to the organization, their message is about staying alive, free and developing options beyond the streets.

❏ **You Can Make the Peace**
http://children.state.mn.us/mnpeace/mnpeace.htm

This site highlights the Minnesota State-wide Violence Prevention Multi-Media Campaign and includes information about the campaign, ads, things people can do, and other resources.

SEARCH ENGINES AND DIRECTORIES

❏ **100hot**
http://www.100hot.com/
A tracking of the 100 most frequented websites in various areas from business to health and fitness.

❏ **Academic Info**
http://www.academicinfo.net/
Academic Info is a subject directory of Internet resources tailored to a college and university audience. Each subject guide is an annotated listing of the best general Internet sites in the field, as well as a gateway to specialized and advanced research tools. On each page you may find links to online publications, language and study aids, reference materials, databases, archives, virtual libraries, tutorials or other educational materials.

❏ **Alexa**
http://www.alexa.com/
Alexa is a free advertising-supported Web navigation service. It works with your browser and accompanies you as you surf, providing useful information about the sites you are viewing and suggesting related sites.

❏ **All-in-One Search Page**
http://www.albany.net/allinone/
Over 400 of the Internet's best search engines, databases, indexes, and directories in a single site. A good starting place for research.

❏ **Alta Vista Main Page**
http://www.altavista.digital.com/
Recent successes in translation have made it possible for words, phrases, and even entire web sites to be translated into many different languages. Innovations like this have made our search service, the number one choice for millions of Internet users. Many utilities and other kinds of search capabilities are also available at this site.

❏ **American Alumni Directory**
http://www.aad.net/
Fully interactive, the American Alumni Directory features Alumni Registration and a Message Board. This resource is completely free and provides a way to contact class-mates, stay in touch with friends and keep up with reunions.

❏ **American School Directory**
http://www.asd.com/
The American School Directory is the Internet guide to all 106,000 K-12 schools, providing information and communication for teachers, students, parents, local communities and families planning a move.

❏ **Anzwers**
http://www.anzwers.com.au/cgi-bin/print_search.pl
Explore over 21,000 subjects.

❏ **APA PsychCrawler Search Engine**
http://www.psychcrawler.com/
PsychCrawler is a product of the American Psychological Association created to provide quick access to quality content in the field of psychology. This search engine currently indexes five organizational sites that have "substantial authoritative content in the area of psychology." PsychCrawler searches the Websites of the APA, the National Institute of Mental Health, the Substance Abuse and Mental Health Services Administration, the US Department of Health and Human Services, the Center for Mental Health Services, and the APA Help Center.

❏ **Ask Jeeves for Kids!**
http://www.ajkids.com/

Fun for adults too!

❏ **AT&T Toll-Free Internet Directory**
http://www.anywho.com

There are more than 150,000 businesses and organizations listed here and ALL of them offer toll-free numbers for your convenience.

❏ **Beaucoup Search Engines**
http://www.beaucoup.com/engines.html

Beaucoup reports to have more than 1,200 listings of engines, directories and indices (800+ on the first page alone) across the world. Truly one to check out!

❏ **collegeBOT**
http://www.collegebot.com/

Featuring unique web pages of Universities, Colleges, K-12 and other Education Resources.

❏ **Debriefing**
http://www.debriefing.com/

An effective metasearch engine.

❏ **Deja News Research Service, Inc**
http://www.dejanews.com/

With more than 50,000 discussion forums—each its own community—Deja News is the place on the Web to meet people with the same interests, debate popular issues and expand your knowledge.

❏ **DevSearch—The Web Developer's Search Engine**
http://devsearch.com/

This search engine is a expansive index of 23 Web sites that contain detailed information for the HTML developer.

❏ **Direct Hit**
http://www.directhit.com/

By analyzing the activity of millions of previous Internet searchers, Direct Hit determines the most popular and relevant sites for your search request.

❏ **Dogpile**
http://www.dogpile.com/

Results are a bit much to get through although worth exploring.

❏ **Education World**
http://db.education-world.com/perl/ browse

Chock full of resources including lesson plans, educational site reviews, administrative issues, financial planning, and much more.

❏ **Electric Library Personal Edition**
http://www.elibrary.com/

Whether for work, school, or home, you'll have immediate and unlimited access to hundreds of full-text magazines and newspapers, along with newswires, books, transcripts and thousands of pictures and maps! Some cost for this service.

❏ **E-mail Discussion Groups and Lists**
http://www.webcom.com/impulse/ list.html

This page is intended as a one-stop information resource about e-mail discussion groups or "lists."

❏ **ERIC Digests**
http://www.ed.gov/databases/ ERIC_Digests/

❏ **Excite NetSearch**
http://www.excite.com/

❏ **Galaxy Search Engines Guidance and Counseling (Education)**
http://galaxy.tradewave.com/galaxy/ Social-Sciences/Education/Guidance-and- Counseling.html

❏ **Google!**
http://www.google.com/

One of the newest kids on the block known for its page ranking feature.

❏ **GoTo.com—Search Made Simple.**
http://www.goto.com/

GoTo.com, the new, simpler search engine which provides users with the fastest and easiest way to find the most relevant web sites on any topic.

❏ **GOVBOT—Government search engine**
http://eden.cs.umass.edu/Govbot/

The GovBot Web site is an index of more than 840,000 U.S. government and military Web sites. This search engine indexes only sites with .gov and .mil domain name suffixes so you wont get back any non-government Web pages.

❏ **Graduate School Directories—Educational and School Counseling**
http://www.gradschools.com/listings/menus/edu_counsel_menu.html

❏ **HotBot**
http://www.hotbot.com/

❏ **InfoSeek**
http://www.infoseek.com/

❏ **KidsClick!**
http://sunsite.berkeley.edu/KidsClick!/

KidsClick! was created by a group of librarians at the Ramapo Catskill Library System, as a logical step in addressing concerns about the role of public libraries in guiding their young users to valuable and age appropriate web sites.

❏ **Liszt**
http://www.liszt.com/

Find one or more of over 90,000 mailing lists.

❏ **LookSmart**
http://www.looksmart.com/

❏ **Lycos Pictures and Sounds**
http://www.lycos.com/picturethis/

A special search feature that lets you search for only sound files. This search engine allows you to use radio buttons to search for sound-related sites. You can also access the sound search engine via a dropdown box from Lycos main page.

❏ **Lycos: Your Personal Internet Guide**
http://www.lycos.com/

Currently the second most visited hub on the Internet, with more than 40 percent reach.

❏ **Magellan**
http://www.mckinley.com/

❏ **MapQuest!**
http://www.mapquest.com/

❏ **Mental Health Metasearch**
http://www.shef.ac.uk/~psysc/psychotherapy/metasearch.html

The InterPsych Mental Health Search Engine provides the facility to search this site and over one hundred other major sources of mental health information, including many organizations which do not have search engines on their own web sites.

❏ **MetaCrawler**
http://www.metacrawler.com/

Great for searching multiple engines at once.

❏ **My Virtual Reference Desk**
http://www.refdesk.com/myency.html

❏ **New Riders' Official World Wide Web Yellow Pages**
http://www.mcp.com/newriders/wwwyp/index.html

Billed as the authoritative encycolopedia of computing by Macmillan Computer Publishing, this site is not only a search engine but chock full of other resources such as directories and downloads.

❏ **NewsEdge NewsPage**
http://www.newspage.com/

The place to go for tracking news about industries and companies.

❏ **Northern Light Search**
http://www.northernlight.com/

❏ **Open Text**
http://www.opentext.com/

❏ **Pete Garriga's Beyond ...The Black Stump**
http://home.mira.net/~lions/index.html

Interesting directory of links.

❏ **ProFusion**
http://www.profusion.com/

For sophisticated researchers who know what they want.

❏ **Project Vote Smart—A Voter's Self-Defense System**
http://www.vote-smart.org/

Find the performance of over 13,000 political leaders.

❏ **Reference.COM Search**
http://www.reference.com/

Reference.COM makes it easy to find, browse, search, and participate in more than 150,000 newsgroups, mailing lists, and web forums.

❏ **ROGET'S Search Form**
http://humanities.uchicago.edu/forms_unrest/ROGET.html

❏ **SavvySearch**
http://www.savvysearch.com/

❏ **Library of Congress Finding Aids**
http://lcweb2.loc.gov/faid/

❏ **SEARCH.COM**
http://search.com/

❏ **Snap**
http://www.snap.com/

❏ **StudyWEB**
http://www.studyweb.com/index2.htm

❏ **Switchboard Home Page**
http://www.switchboard.com/

Anyone with a Web browser can look up the names, phone number and street addresses of friends, colleagues and businesses, typically in less than a second.

❏ **The Argus Clearinghouse**
http://www.clearinghouse.net/

A selection of topical guides.

❏ **The List—The Definitive ISP Buyer's Guide**
http://thelist.internet.com/

Find Internet Service Providers virtually anywhere.

❏ **The Ultimate White Pages**
http://www.theultimates.com/white/

This site is designed to be fast and simple. Just type your search criteria into the first search engine (Yahoo). Type in all the items you know. The items will be automatically copied to the other forms by a Javascript applet. Then hit Search on the first search engine you want to query. A new browser window opens with the search results. Then switch back to the original window and hit submit on the next one. You can search as many as you want until you are satisfied with the results.

❏ **Tile.Net**
http://www.tile.net/

❏ **TKM's Education Web Search**
http://alpha.tkm.mb.ca/education/
index.html

Highly specific to educational sites.

❏ **Who's Who in Mental Health on the Web**
http://idealist.com/wwmhw/

A database of over a thousand mental health professionals around the world and their practice and networking interests.

❏ **WhoWhere?!**
http://www.whowhere.lycos.com/

WhoWhere offers a variety of services that makes searching for people and businesses on the Internet a quick and easy process.

❏ **WWWomen.com! The Premier Search Directory for Women Online!**
http://www.wwwomen.com/

❏ **Yahoo**
http://www.yahoo.com/

A premier search engine uniquely categorized by humans.

❏ **Yahooligans!**
http://www.yahooligans.com/
Kids only version of Yahoo.

❏ **Zip Code Lookup and Address Information**
http://www.usps.gov/ncsc/
Your letter carrier will love you.

❏ **Citation Bibliographic and Research Note Data**
http://www.oberon-res.com/

Citation is a bibliographic database system which installs on the Tools menu of MSWord 6.0c, 7, and now 97, as well as WordPerfect for Windows 6.0a, 6.1, 7, and 8—so it is always available to you as you are writing. The program reports to support over 1000 publishing styles for footnotes/ endnotes, numbered references, and bibliographies, and provide you with one of the most powerful and easy to use custom report writers available. A free demonstration copy is available for download.

❏ **Cog & Psy Sci: Software**
http://matia.stanford.edu/cogsci/
software.html

Brought to us from the good people at Stanford's psychology department.

❏ **Computers In Mental Health**
http://www.ex.ac.uk/cimh/software.htm

These pages list software items applicable to mental health. Using a frame- capable browser, topics can be selected from the list of keywords on the left to give links to descriptions of specific products.

❏ **Educast: The Education News Service for Teachers & Administrators**
http://www.educast.com/

Unlike conventional screen savers, Educast displays valuable news and information, and connects you to first-rate Internet sites with the click of a mouse.

❏ **ELIZA**
http://www-ai.ijs.si/eliza/eliza.html

ELIZA—a friend you could never have before. Use the original attempt at virtual counseling.

❑ **FerretSoft**
http://www.ferretsoft.com/netferret/
index.html
Excellent web search software, one of which is free (WebFerret) and highly useful.

❑ **File Mine—Dig Our Downloads of Shareware, Games and Commercial Demos**
http://www.filemine.com/

❑ **Jumbo!**
http://www.jumbo.com/

❑ **Microsoft Chat Home**
http://microsoft.com/windows/ie/chat/
Explore links to information about Microsoft Chat 2.5 and Microsoft V-Chat 2.0. You'll find out about their features, how to use them to chat with others on the Internet, and how to author your own customized chat site.

❑ **PC Educational**
http://www.sharewarejunkies.com/
winedu.htm

❑ **Shareware Psychological Consultation**
http://www.netpsych.com/share/

❑ **SHAREWARE.COM**
http://www.shareware.com/

❑ **The Freebie Zone's**
http://www.wizardry-design.com/
souvenir.shtml

❑ **ThinkWave: Education Software for Teachers**
http://www.thinkwave.com/
A free gradebook program.

❑ **TUCOWS**
http://www.tucows.com/
TUCOWS is your place on the Web to access the latest and greatest Windows 95/98, Windows NT, Windows 3.1 and Macintosh Internet Software, performance rated and checked for viruses.

❑ **WinSite**
http://www.winsite.com/
Billed as the planet's largest software archive for Windows shareware and trialware on the Internet.

❑ **WinThemes.com**
http://www.winthemes.com/v4/
Default.asp?P=Main
A Windows enhancement site.

❑ **ZDNet Software Library**
http://www.zdnet.com/swlib/

SPECIAL EDUCATION

❏ **ADDHELP—Attention Deficit Disorder**
http://www.addhelp.com/home.html

❏ **Deaf World Web**
http://dww.deafworldweb.org/

❏ **Gifted Children Monthly**
http://www.gifted-children.com/

❏ **Hoagies' Gifted Education Page**
http://www.ocsc.com/hoagies/gift.htm
A comprehensive resource guide for education of gifted children. It's full of great information, with links to the most complete, easiest to use, resources on nearly every aspect of gifted education available on the Internet, plus lots of annotations and first hand information provided by parents facing the same challenges that you are facing.

❏ **National Center to Improve Practice in Special Education**
http://www.edc.org/FSC/NCIP/ncipnet_top.html
NCIPnet houses a series of facilitated discussion conferences focusing on technology and special education. NCIPnet enables you to communicate with other members of NCIPnet—technology coordinators, staff developers, teachers, specialists, clinicians, administrators, university faculty, parents, advocates, and consumers—who share a common desire to improve the use of technology with students who have disabilities.

❏ **National Clearinghouse for Professions in Special Education**
http://www.cec.sped.org/ncpse.htm
As the only national information center of its type, the Clearinghouse gathers, develops, and disseminates information on recruitment, preservice preparation, employment opportunities, and attrition and retention issues.

❏ **National Information Center for Children and Youth with Disabilities**
http://www.nichcy.org/

❏ **Our-Kids Website**
http://rdz.stjohns.edu/lists/our-kids/
Our-Kids is a support group for parents, caregivers and others who are working with children with physical and/or mental disabilities and delays. According to the site, the Our-Kids list consist of over 700 people representing children of varying diagnoses (e.g., indefinite developmental delays and sensory integration problems, cerebral palsy, or rare genetic disorders). The site's mission is to provide information and support for Our-Kids and their caregivers.

❏ **Special Education Resources on the Internet**
http://www.hood.edu/seri/serihome.html
Special Education Resources on the Internet (SERI) is a collection of Internet accessible information resources of interest to those involved in the fields related to Special Education. This collection exists in order to make on-line Special Education resources more easily and readily available in one location.

❏ **Special Education World Congress 2000**
http://cid.unomaha.edu/~wwwsped/wc/2000.html
Papers, programs, and professional contacts.

❏ **Special Education, Learning Disabilities Resources, Services, Professionals**
http://www.iser.com/
ISER helps parents find local special education professionals to help with learning disabilities and attention deficit disorder assessment, therapy, advocacy, and other special needs.

Internet Special Education Resources
A nationwide directory of professionals who serve the learning disabilities and special education communities

Russell A. Sabella, Ph.D.

❏ **The Federal Resource Center for Special Education**
http://www.dssc.org/frc/

❏ **The Individuals with Disabilities Education Act Amendments of 1997**
http://www.ed.gov/offices/OSERS/IDEA/

❏ **The LD OnLine Home Page**
http://www.ldonline.org/

As described by the site, an interactive guide to learning disabilities for parents, teachers, and children.

❏ **UVa Special Education Web Site**
http://curry.edschool.virginia.edu/go/specialed/

Special Education Resources from the Curry School of Education at the University of Virginia.

SPECIAL TOPICS

❏ **11 Ways to Keep Your New Year's Resolution to Quit Smoking**
http://www.quitsmoking.com/tips.htm

❏ **A Place for Us...Oppositional Defiant Disorder Support Group**
http://www.conductdisorders.com/

❏ **ADHD Special Needs Resources for Misunderstood Kids...Outside the Box!**
http://home.att.net/~shagberg/

Billed as a place for parents and teachers who recognize the special needs of misunderstood kids.

❏ **Concerned Counseling Eating Disorders Website-Anorexia, Bulimia, Compulsive Over**
http://www.concernedcounseling.com/eatingdisorders/eatingdisordersindex.html

❏ **Dr. Kimberly Young—The Center for Online Addiction**
http://netaddiction.com/

❏ **Lightning Strike Pet-Loss Support Page**
http://www.netwalk.com/~copydoc/frame_pet-loss.htm

❏ **Maine Project Against Bullying**
http://lincoln.midcoast.com/~wps/against/bullying.html

❏ **Men Bibliography**
http://online.anu.edu.au/~e900392/mensbiblio/MensBiblioMenu.html

❏ **Youth Suicide Prevention Programs (full text)**
http://aepo-xdv-www.epo.cdc.gov/wonder/prevguid/p0000024/entire.htm

❏ **Anxiety Disorders Education Program**
http://www.nimh.nih.gov/anxiety/

A national education campaign developed by the National Institute of Mental Health (NIMH) to increase awareness among the public and health care professionals that anxiety disorders are real medical illnesses that can be effectively diagnosed and treated.

❏ **Attention Deficit Hyperactivity Disorder**
http://www.med.virginia.edu/medicine/clinical/pediatrics/devbeh/adhdlin/

The Attention Deficit Hyperactivity Disorder (AD/HD) Clinical Support Module on the World Wide Web is designed to link basic science knowledge with clinical application in the diagnosis and treatment of this disorder.

❏ **Basics of Sleep Behavior**
http://bisleep.medsch.ucla.edu/sleepsyllabus/

❏ **Bipolar Disorder**
http://www.nimh.nih.gov/publicat/bipolar.htm

❏ **CDC National AIDS Clearinghouse**
http://www.cdcnac.org/

This site contains many publications and helpful links (e.g., informationa bout HIV/AIDS, STD, TB, databases, ordering procedures for free publications, a poster gallery, psa's for youth, and online tutorials, and more).

❏ **Children, Stress, and Natural Disasters**
http://www.ag.uiuc.edu/~disaster/teacher.html

❏ **Counseling and Supervision Via theWWW/Internet**
http://osu.orst.edu/instruct/coun510/ethics/coun.htm

The information presented is adapted from both the American Counseling Association (ACA), American Psychological Association (APA), and Oregon State University ethical standards of practice.

❏ **Dr. Ivan's Depression Central**
http://www.psycom.net/depression.central.html

This site is a clearing house for information on all types of depressive disorders and on the most effective treatments for individuals suffering from major depression, manic-depression (bipolar disorder), cyclothymia, dysthymia and other mood disorders.

❏ **Emotional Intelligence (EQ)**
http://eqi.org/

❏ **EQ—Tests of Emotional Intelligence**
http://library.advanced.org/11585/eq/test.htm

Although no validated paper-and-pencil tests of emotional intelligence exist, two "fun" versions of emotional intelligence tests have been developed.

❏ **Exploratorium**
http://www.exploratorium.edu/

The Exploratorium is a museum of science, art, and human perception with over 500 interactive "hands on" exhibits. Each year more than 600,000 visitors come to the Exploratorium, over 95,000 students and teachers come on field trips, and more than 2000 teachers attend professional development programs which focus on inquiry-based teaching and learning in the K-12 classroom.

❏ **Fast Food Facts—Interactive Food Finder**
http://www.olen.com/food/index.html

Includes nutritional information for more than 1,000 fast-food items.

❏ **FMF—911 For Women**
http://www.feminist.org/911/
1_supprt.html
   Created by the Feminist Majority Foundation, this site offers feminist and women related resources.

❏ **Get Your ANGRIES Out**
http://members.aol.com/AngriesOut/

   Lessons in conflict resolution designed for children, adults and families.

❏ **Girl Power!**
http://www.health.org/gpower/index.htm
   The national public education campaign sponsored by the Department of the Health and Human Services to help encourage and empower 9- to 14- year old girls to make the most of their lives.

❏ **GriefNet**
http://www.griefnet.org/
   Poetry, prose, quotes, thoughts and ideas and other resources that communicate the grief of separation by death. The site also allows visitors to post eulogies in memory of their loved ones.

❏ **Heather Solomon Memorial**
http://www.arctic.ca/LUS/
Heather_Solomon.html
   An example of how a school paid tribute to a teacher who lost a battle with cancer.

❏ **Helping Children cope with Disaster**
http://www.sarbc.org/ciskid1.html

❏ **HIV InSite**
http://hivinsite.ucsf.edu/
   This site provides a great deal of information about prevention, social issues, news, and medical info. Also available is a biweekly (free) newsletter and an interactive expert advice feature.

❏ **Information For Teachers And Child-Care Providers**
http://www.diabetes.org/ada/teacher.htm

❏ **It Takes All Kinds Discussions**
http://www.pbs.org/cgi-bin/pov/
learn_discuss/public/discuss.cgi

❏ **Jon's Homeschool Resource Page**
http://www.midnightbeach.com/hs/

❏ **Lisa Taylor Austin's Web Page on Gangs**
http://www.gangcolors.com/

❏ **National Center for Bilingual Education**
http://www.ncbe.gwu.edu/

❏ **Pat McClendon's Clinical Social Work Page**
http://www.ClinicalSocialWork.com/

❏ **Pet Loss**
http://www.primenet.com/~meggie/
petloss.htm

❏ **Positive Discipline**
http://www.empoweringpeople.com/
   Articles, a free newsletter, books, training, and site search engine.

❏ **Radiance: The Magazine For Large Women**
http://www.radiancemagazine.com/

An upbeat, positive magazine about body acceptance with a kids section.

❏ **Rape—Let's Stop It**
http://www.ocs.mq.edu.au/~korman/feminism/Rape/

❏ **RealAudio about Dealing with Death from NPR**
http://www.npr.org/programs/death/971103.death.html

Roundtable Discussion on End of Life Issues taped on Monday November 3rd on All Things Considered.

❏ **Resources and Information on Alcohol, Tobacco and Other Drugs**
http://www.arf.org/isd/info.html

❏ **School Psychology Resources Online— Sandra Steingart,Ph.D.**
http://www.bcpl.net/~sandyste/school_psych.html

This site contains information about learning disabilities, ADHD, gifted, autism, adolescence, parenting, psychological assessment, classroom management, special education, K-12, mental health, reading, research, and more. Users can reprint valuable handouts for parents and teachers.

❏ **Sexual Abuse By Teachers IS a Problem**
http://home.earthlink.net/~jaye/

The goal of this site is to increase the public's awareness of Educator Sexual Abuse by breaking silence in a strong, united voice.

❏ **Sexual Harassment Case Profiles**
http://www.inform.umd.edu/EdRes/Topic/WomensStudies/GenderIssues/SexualHarassment/

This is a high quality women's studies database.

❏ **Sexual Harassment in Schools**
http://www.de.psu.edu/harass/analysis/schools.htm

Information for this section came largely from the American Association of University Women's report, "Hostile Hallways: The AAUW Survey on Sexual Harassment in America's Schools, June 1993.

❏ **Sexual Harassment Websites**
http://www.de.psu.edu/harass/websites/websites.htm

❏ **Sexual Harrassment Guidance [OCR]**
http://www.ed.gov/legislation/FedRegister/announcements/1997-1/031397b.html

Office of Civil Rights document titled Sexual Harassment Guidance: Harassment of Students by School Employees, Other Students, or Third Parties.

❏ **Shape Up America!**
http://www.shapeup.org/

This website is designed to provide you with the latest information about safe weight management, healthy eating, and physical fitness.

❏ **State Laws and Regulations (Homeschooling)**
http://www.home-ed-press.com/HSRSC/hsrsc_lws.rgs.html

❏ **Suggestions for Teachers and School Counselors**
http://www.compassionatefriends.com/teachers.htm

Dealing with grief and bereavement.

❏ **Suicide Information & Education Center (SIEC)**
http://www.siec.ca/

This simple, but resourseful page is searchable and contains links to information resources, a library, Frequently Asked Questions (FAQ), training, and helpful crisis support.

❏ **The Body: AIDS Treatment News**
http://www.thebody.com/atn/atnpage.html

Information about "reports on experimental and standard treatments, especially those available now. The reporters interview physicians, scientists, other health professionals, and persons with AIDS or HIV; they also collect information from meetings and conferences, medical journals, and computer databases. Long-term survivors have usually tried many different treatments, and found combinations which work for them. AIDS Treatment News does not recommend particular therapies, but seeks to increase the options available." Past issues are available and searchable.

❏ **The WholeFamily Center—Kid-Teen Center**
http://www.wholefamily.com/index.shtml

Winner of many awards, this highly decorated site is dedicated to healthy living among parents, couples, and teens. Users may "hang out" in the teen center and join the on-line family drama, "talk" with teens from next door to around the world. The site also has on-line teen advisor; a "raising" your parents section, family workout room; evaluation center to identify the problems areas and strengths in your relationships with friends and family; reference center, chat rooms, free newsletter, and much more.

❏ **Trauma Info Pages**
http://www.efn.org/~dbaldwin/trauma.htm

The purpose of this site is to provide information about traumatic stress for clinicians and researchers in the field. New information is added once or twice a month.

❏ **US Department of Education Technology Initiatives**
http://www.ed.gov/Technology/

❏ **Violence in Schools Initiative**
http://europa.eu.int/en/comm/dg22/violence/home.html

This initiative aims at reinforcing European co-operation on issues related to safety at school and violence. Since this initiative is envisaged for an initial two year period, the extent of cooperation will be limited and will address in particular the exchange of information and experiences through participation in joint actions.

❏ **Virtual Presentation Assistant**
http://www.ukans.edu/cwis/units/coms2/vpa/vpa.htm

An online tutorial for improving your public speaking skills.

❏ **WEBster's Death, Dying and Grief Guide**
http://www.katsden.com/death/general.html

A site of "The best places to visit to learn about coping with grief, and grief counseling resources."

CHAPTER SEVEN

Internet Glossary

The prolifiration of computer and network technology has made a ubiquitous impact on our culture and way of life to the extent that those involved with technology might see themselves as part of a subculture. As with any culture, the technology subculture, or technoculture, uses distinctive terminology or language that must be learned to effectively conceptualize, communicate, and practice rituals and norms of the culture. Similar to a beginning counseling student who must first learn the language of various theoretical constructs to more successfully apply them, counseling students must also learn and understand the language of technology. "Geekspeak," as such a language is affectionately called, allows counselors to apply knowledge of technological processes towards developing requisite skills.

Geekspeak encompasses distinctive words, and especially acronyms, (e.g., FTP, FAQ, DNS, MPEG, HTML, URL, PPP, POP3, and ASCII to name a very few) which represent certain computer and network objects and procedures. Speaking fluent Geekspeak means that a counselor must also learn and understand the jargon of the technoculture. For instance, consider the following Geekspeak excerpts and their translations:

Geekspeak: Because the file is 22 megs and won't get past his firewall, I'll have to use the sneakernet.

Translation: Because a computer file is too large (22 megabytes) and will not travel past a recipient's security measures, the sender of the file will have to resort to transporting the data by carrying physical media such as diskettes from one computer to another, instead of transferring the data over a computer network.

Geekspeak: The counseling theories channel had a flame war after a newbie lurker posted without first reading the FAQ.

Translation: The user in this case is a chat room newcomer who is seen as someone who regularly reads the group's postings although either never or infrequently contributes. During an Internet chat discussion dedicated to counseling theories, he/she posted a question or request for information that has already been frequently addressed over the group's communication history. The information is considered common knowledge and disruptive to the group's current focus. If the user would have first consulted the group's frequently asked questions (FAQ) file as common Internet etiquette calls for, he/she would have been a more highly informed and constructive participant. Consequently, the post began an acrimonious dispute among members of the group.

So as to make this glossary useful and comprehensive, I augmented this list which the best and most laconic definitions from several sources which included Education World Internet Glossary (www.education-world.com), Squareonetech (www.Squareonetech.com), Microsoft (www.microsoft.com), Webopedia (www.webopedia.com) and (http://www.icactive.com/_internetglossary.html):

Acceptable Use Policy. A statement of the procedures, rights and responsibilities of a user of a technology solution and any disciplinary procedures that will be enforced for misuse of the technology.

Bandwidth. A measurement of a network's transmission speed, how much data a network can transfer in a given amount of time.

Baud rate. The number of transitions per second made by a modem.

Bitnet. An education and research network that makes up part of the Internet, mainly used for e-mail & listservs.

Bits per second (BPS). Measurement of the data transmission for a modem or network.

Bookmark. The process of saving a URL in your Web browser. Allows the user to return to a particular site or entry by making a record of it.

Bounced. When an e-mail message is returned to sender due to a failure to deliver, the message has been "bounced".

Browser. Software that lets you locate, view, and retrieve information on the World Wide Web using a graphical user interface or GUI.

BTW. Abbreviation for "By the Way" used in e-mail, newsgroup, and chat communication.

Bug. A glitch that keeps a software program from being able to perform all of its capabilities or that affects its ability to function.

Bulletin board system. A service dedicated to a specific topic where users post messages that are read by others. It is a computer or computers that offer dial-in communication which offers users the ability to send e-mail, use news-groups, and sometimes access the Internet. For example, see www.schoolcounselor.com/bbs

Byte. The amount of memory space needed to store one number, letter, or symbol in a computer.

CD-ROM (compact disc-read only memory). A round silver colored plastic disk that comes with massive amounts of information embedded and ready to be used. Unlike diskettes, CD-ROM disks can be read by any type of computer with a CD-ROM drive.

Chat. To communicate in real-time through the Internet. When you chat with someone, the typed words appear on a "shared" screen.

Client-server. Two computer systems linked by a network or modem connection where the client computer uses resources by sending requests to the server computer.

Compressed files. Most Internet files are reduced in size to make transfer easier and faster. Programs may be uncompressed by simply launching them or may require other software such as PKUNZIP (www.winzip.com) after they are transferred.

Connect time. The duration of time a computer is connected to a telecommunications service.

Database. A collection of information stored oftentimes in a computerized format. Examples: library catalogs, school records, search engines, and financial data.

Dial-up connection. Connecting to an Internet service provider through a modem and telephone line, typically a Point-to-Point Protocol (PPP) connection.

Disk. A round plastic magnetic device on which computer programs and data are saved. there are three main types of disks: hard disks (maintained inside the computer usually indicated by c:), diskettes (a.k.a. floppy disks usually indicated by a:), and compact disks (see CD-ROM, usually indicated by d: or e:).

DNS. Abbreviation for Domain Name System. A distributed client-server database system which links domain names with their numerical IP addresses.

Domain name. The name of a computer or server on the Internet in the form of a string of names or numbers, separated by periods.

Download. The transfer a file or files from a remote computer to the user's computer.

Electronic mail (E-mail). A letter or memo sent to a person or group electronically on the Internet; messages are stored on a computer until the receiver accesses the system and reads the message.

E-mail address. A user's electronic mailbox name or address, needed for linking the sender of e-mail and the recipient.

Ethical standards. Guidelines for the appropriate use of technology solutions and the maintenance of privacy of the contents of the system. These are generally specified in an Acceptable Use Policy, particularly where there is concern about the security of the system or the availability of objectionable materials obtained throughout the system. Counselors should also refer to their designated professional ethical documents (e.g., American School Counselor Association, www.schoolcounselor.org) for other ethical guidelines related to the use of technology.

FAQ. Abbreviation for Frequently Asked Questions. A document (often a hypertext document) containing common questions and answers for a particular website or topic. This list is especially prepared to help novice users to more quickly adapt to new standards of practice, especially in a chat room or listserv discussion.

File. Information stored on a magnetic media such as a disk which may contain a computer program, a document, or a collection of data.

Finger. Internet service that provides information about the users on a particular computer.

Freeware. Software that is available free of charge for personal use.

Flame. Personal verbal attacks on other Internet users, via e-mail, USENET, or mailing lists. Flame wars occur when a series of flames are sent back and forth between two or more people.

FTP. Short for "file transfer protocol." It's a system of rules for communicating over the Internet, and it allows you to transfer files to and download files from other computers. A browser such as Microsoft« Internet Explorer contains the tools you need to handle FTPs. So with Internet Explorer, you can download any file available on the Internet. Anonymous FTP allows you to connect to remote computers and to transfer publicly available computer files or programs.

Gateway. A computer system that connects two incompatible services such as a commercial online service and the Internet.

GIF. Graphical Interchange Format is a commonly used graphics file format for image files on the Internet.

Gopher. A play on the words "go for." A text menu-based browsing service on the Internet. The user selects an item on the menu and is led to either a file or another menu.

Hardware. Physical parts of a computer and its peripherals that you can touch (e.g., monitor, keyboard, hard disk, floppy drive).

Home page. The main page of hypertext-based information for an individual or organization on the World Wide Web (WWW).

HTML (Hypertext Markup Language). A programming language used to build Web sites. It contains standard codes, or tags, that determine how a Web page looks when your browser displays it. HTML tags also make possible the hyperlinks that connect information on the World Wide Web.

HTTP. Abbreviation for Hyper Text Transfer Protocol. Often this is the initial sequence of letters in a web address.

Interface. The connection between a computer and the person trying to use it. It can also be the connections required between computer systems so that communication and exchanges of data can take place.

Internaut. Slang for someone who is an experienced Internet user.

Internet address (a.k.a. IP address). An assigned series of numbers unique to each computer on the Internet which is used to identify it for data exchanges.

Intranet. Network internal to an organization that uses Internet protocols and browsers.

Internet. The worldwide, interconnected system of computer networks.

Internet Protocol (IP). A protocol that ensures data goes where it is supposed to go on the Internet.

Internet Relay Chat (IRC). An Internet service accessed through software programs that features real-time communication on channels devoted to specific topics.

ISP. Abbreviation for Internet Service Provider. A company that provides access to the Internet, such as a phone company or other commercial enterprises.

JAVA. An object-oriented programming language developed by Sun Microsystems to create applets, or programs that can be distributed as attachments to Web documents. An applet can be included in an HTML page, much as an image can be included. When you use a Java-capable browser to view a page containing a Java applet, the applet's code is transferred to your system and executed by the browser.

JPEG (Joint Photographic Experts Group). An image file format that is common to the Internet.

LAN. Abbreviation for Local Area Network. Used to connect computers over a short distance such as computers within the same organization, company, or office.

LISTSERV. An e-mail list server. A computer program that maintains lists of e-mail addresses in order that users can participate in an electronic discussion or conference. There are thousands of listserv on all imaginable topics.

Login/Logon. The process entering in information related to an account name and its password in order to access a time-sharing computer.

Logout/Logoff. A command that notifies the host computer that the user is ready to disconnect from the system.

Microsoft Internet Explorer. A graphical World Wide Web browser.

Modem. Acronym for modulator-demodulator. A modem is a device or program that enables a computer to transmit data over telephone lines. Modems may be internal or external to the computer case and are classified according to the speed (kps or kilobytes per second) with which they receive information (28.8kps, 36kps, 58.6kps).

Mosaic. A browser program developed by the National Center for Supercomputing Applications that provides the internet user with a point-and-click interface to WWW, Gopher, FTP, and other Internet services

Netiquette. The unwritten "rules" of etiquette used on the Internet.

Netscape. A graphical World Wide Web browser.

Network. A set of computers that all use the same protocol in order to exchange information among themselves.

Newbie. Slang for someone who is new to the Internet or a specific aspect of it.

Newsgroup. A discussion group that is related to one topic.

Password. Secret code of letters and numbers needed to gain access to a time-sharing computer or FTP system, or to protect Web pages.

Peripheral. A device that is attached to a computer, such as a monitor, keyboard, mouse, modem, printer, scanner, and speakers.

Posting. Can refer to a message or article that appears on a newsgroup or message board system, or the act of sending an electronic message to a newsgroup or message board.

PPP. Abbreviation for Point to Point Protocol. It is a protocol used for sending information via a modem which is connected to the Internet.

Protocol. The rules make possible the exchange of messages between users on the Internet, or within any given network.

Plug-in. A software component required by an Internet browser to expand its abilities. For example, LiveAudio is a Netscape plug-in that enables it to play audio.

Resolution. The clarity of the images produced on a monitor screen or printout.

Scripting. A programming shortcut that gives nontechnical users a way to create richer content on their computers and gives programmers a quick way to create simple applications. Scripting enables you to set and store variables, and work with data in your HTML code. Many Web sites now employ scripting to check the browser a user is running, validate input, work with applets or controls, and communicate to the user.

Search Engine. A tool or program which allows keyword searching for relevant sites or information on the Internet.

Shareware. Software distributed on the basis of an honor system. Most shareware is delivered free of charge, but the author usually requests that you pay a small fee if you like the program and use it regularly. By sending the small fee, you become registered with the producer so that you can receive service assistance and updates. You can copy shareware and pass it along to friends and colleagues, but they too are expected to pay a fee if they use the product.

SLIP. Stands for Serial Line Internet Protocol. Similar to PPP, this is another protocol that is used with a modem to establish an internet connection.

Smiley. A sideways happy face, made using text characters. It is generally used in e-mail to signify that the statement preceding it is a joke, or sarcasm, in an effort to prevent anyone from becoming offended. It is usually made with a colon, followed by a dash, and then a parentheses, e.g. :-) but there are endless variations.

Snail mail. Slang for regular, paper mail sent through the postal services (also surface mail).

Streaming Audio/Video. Media files on the Internet that play as they are being downloaded.

Suite. A collection of software programs (e.g., word processor, spreadsheet, presentation, database, and voice recognition) that are sold together and are supposed to work together efficiently and use similar commands.

TCP/IP. Short for Transmission Control Protocol/Internet Protocol. A group of protocols that specify how computers communicate over the Internet. All computers on the Internet need TCP/IP software.

Telnet. An Internet command that allows your computer to directly connect and interact with remote computers, often through a text-based 'terminal' environment. Often involves the need for passwords and access information.

Unix. A computer operating system developed by AT&T Bell Labs and used to develop the Internet. It is no longer the sole operating system used to run servers.

Upgrade. To install a higher version or release of software on a computer system, or too add memory or newer types of equipment to a computer system.

Upload. Transferring a file or files from the user's computer to a remote computer.

URL. Short for Uniform Resource Locator. A string of characters used to uniquely identify a page of information on the Web.

Usenet. A group of computers that exchange network news information.

Users. The people who use technology as a tool to do their jobs.

WAIS. Short for Wide Area Information Server. An Internet search service that locates documents containing a keyword or phrase.

WAN. Stands for Wide Area Network. A network of computers that covers a large geographical distance such as a state.

Whois. An Internet database that provides information on a person or an organization.

WWW. Stands for World Wide Web. A very popular Internet service that organizes information using a hypertext and hypermedia system of linking documents, FTP sites, gopher sites, WAIS, and telnet.

Other Terms That Have Circulated the Net And Have Become Part of the Net Culture Include:

404. Someone who's clueless. From the World Wide Web message "404, URL Not Found," meaning that the document you've tried to access can't be located. "Don't bother asking him...he's 404."

Alpha Geek. The most knowledgeable, technically proficient person in an office or work group. "Ask Russ, he's the alpha geek around here."

Cobweb Site. A World Wide Web Site that hasn't been updated for a long time. A dead web page.

Egosurfing. Scanning the net, databases, print media, or research papers looking for the mention of your name.

Elvis Year. The peak year of something's popularity. "Barney the dinosaur's Elvis year was 1993."

Keyboard Plaque. The disgusting buildup of dirt and crud found on computer keyboards. "Are there any other terminals I can use? This one has a bad case of keyboard plaque."

Tourists. People who are taking training classes just to get a vacation from their jobs. "We had about three serious students in the class; the rest were tourists."

World Wide Wait. The real meaning of WWW.

Russell A. Sabella, Ph.D.

References

ACCA (American Corporate Council Association). 1999. Available online: [http://www.acca.com]

Alternative Collegiate Computing Association (ACCA; 1999). Available online: [http://acca.nmsu.eduAVelcome.html].

American School Counselor Association. (1984). ASCA position statement: Ethical standards for school counselors. *The School Counselor, 32,* 84-87.

Arnold, A.M. (1998). Rape in cyberspace: Not just a fantasy. *Off Our Backs, 28(2),* 12-13.

Associated Press. (May 31, 1998). Study: Internet 'addicts' often show other disorders.

Basic Web Browsing, (1998). Available online: [http://www.micro soft. com/magazine/guides/internet/].

Begole, C., & Panepinto, J. (1995, September). The promise of PCs at school. *School PC: Supplement to Family PC Magazine, 8-9.*

Bevilacqua, A. (1997). Computers and the law. Available online: [http://wings.buffalo.edu/Complaw/CompLawPapers/bevilacq.html.

Bialo, E. R., & Sivin-Kachala, J. (1996). *The effectiveness of technology in schools: A summary of recent research.* Washington, DC: Software Publishers Association.

Bleuer, J. C., & Watz, G. R. (1983). *Counselors and computers.* Ann Arbor: ERIC/CAPS. The University of Michigan.

Bloom, J.W. (November, 1997). *NBCC WebCounseling Standards.* Alexandria, VA: Counseling Today. Available online: [http://www. counseling. org/ctonline/archives/ct I 197/webcounseling. htm].

Brent, E. E., & Anderson, R. E. (1990). *Computer applications in the social sciences.* Philadelphia: Temple University Press.

Cairo, P. C., & Kanner, M. S. (1984). Investigating the effects of computerized approaches to counselor training. *Counselor Education and Supervision, 24,* 212-221.

Casey, J. A., Bloom, J. W., & Moan, E. R. (1994). Use of technology in counselor supervision. In L. D. Borders (Ed.), *Counseling supervision.* Greensboro: University of North Carolina, ERIC Clearinghouse on Counseling and Student Services. (ERIC Document Reproduction Service No. ED 372 357)

CAST (Center for Applied Special Technology). (1996). The role of online communications in schools: A national study. Peabody, MA. Available online: [http://www. cast. org/ stsstudy. html] (version current at April 1998].

Chapman, W., & Katz, M. R. (1983). Career information systems in the secondary schools: A survey and assessment. *Vocational Guidance Quarterly, 32,* 165-177.

Childress, C. (1998). Potential risks and benefits of online psychotherapeutic interventions. Available online [http://www.ismho.org/issues/9801.htm].

Cohen, L. (1998). Conducting research on the Internet. Available online: [http://www.albany.edu/library/internet].

Computer units dethrone television as most desired household appliance, reports new survey. (January 8, 1998). Lexmark International, Inc. Available online: [http://www.merc.com].

Cooksey, B. (October 11, 1992). Strong skills key to workplace of future. Shreveport Times.

Courtois, M. P. (1995). Cool tools for searching the Web: A performance evaluation. *Online, 19(6)*, 1418, 20- 22, 24, 26-28, 30, 32.

D'Andrea, M. (1995). Using computer technology to promote multicultural awareness among elementary school-age students. *Elementary School Guidance & Counseling, 30(l)*, 45-55.

D'Souza, P. V. (1991). The use of electronic mail as an instructional aid: An exploratory study. *Journal of Computer-Based Instruction, 18(3)*, 106-110.

DeLoughry, T. J. (1995). Well-appointed Web pages. *Chronicle of Higher Education, 41(37)*, pA 19, 2 1.

Diederich, T. (1998) Web use among students continues to climb. Available online: [www.idg.com].

Dwyer, D. (April, 1994). Apple classrooms of tomorrow: What we've learned. *Educational Leadership, 51(7)*, 4-10.

Ekstrom, R., & Johnson, C. (Eds.). (1984). Computers in counseling and development: Introduction and over- view. *Journal of Counseling and Development, 63*, 132.

Evaluating Internet Information. (1998) Available online: [http://sol.slcc.edu/lr/navigator/discovery/eval.html].

Fargen, T. (1996). Surfing the Internet in gym class: Physical education E-mail KeyPals. *Teaching & Change, 3 (3)*, 272-28 1.

Fong, C., McCollum, P.S., & Pool, D. A. (1985). Computer-assisted rehabilitation services: A preliminary draft of the Texas casework model. *Rehabilitation Counseling Bulletin, 28*, 219-232.

Froehle, T. C. (1984). Computer-assisted feedback in counseling supervision. *Counselor Education and Supervision, 24*, 168-175.

Fulton, D. (August, 1998). E-rate: A resource guide for educators. ERIC Clearinghouse on Information & Technology, Available online: [http://ericir.syr.edu].

Gerler, E. (1995). Advancing elementary and middle school counseling through computer technology. *Elementary School Guidance & Counseling, 30(l)*, 8-15.

Gilster, P. (1997). Digital literacy. New York: Wiley.

Glover, B. L. (1995). DINOS (drinking is not our solution): Using computer programs in middle school drug education. *Elementary School Guidance & Counseling, 30(l)*, 55-62.

Grassian, E. (1998). Thinking critically about world wide web resources. UCLA College Library Available online: [http://www.library.ucla.edu/libraries/college/instruct/web/critical.htm].

Grohol, J.M. (1997). *The insider's guide to mental health resources online.* New York, NY: The Guilford Press.

Grumman, C. (June 26, 1996). HTTP: www.help logged on, tuned in and hooked on the Internet: There are those who just can't stop surfing. Chicago Tribune, pg. 1.

Guide to Network Resource Tools, (1993). Available on-line: [http://rs.intemic.net/nicsupport/fyi/fyi23.html##www].

Haring-Hidore, M. (1984). In pursuit of students who do not use computers for career guidance. *Journal of Counseling and Development, 63*, 139-140.

Harris, J. (1972). *Computer-assisted guidance systems.* Washington, DC: National Vocational Guidance Association.

Hart, J. (1993). Computer communications for advisors. *NACADA Journal, 13(2)*, 27-33.

Heinemann, R. (1995). Netiquette guide for keypals. Available online: [http://www.reedbooks.com.au/heinemann/global/kplnetqt.html]

Help. (1998) Internet Explorer 4.0 Online Help.

Herr, E. L. (1984). New technologies in guidance in an age of technology. *Educational and Vocational Guidance Bulletin, 41*, 24-4 1.

Hofstetter, F. T. (1998). *Internet literacy.* Boston, MASS: McGraw Hill.

Howell, J. L. (1992). Computer usage by Arizona public school counselors. Unpublished doctoral dissertation, Northern Arizona University, Flagstaff.

HP E-mail Mentor Program - Largest Telementoring Program HP E-mail Mentor Program - One on One Telementoring, (1997). Available online: [HTTP:// mentor.external.hp.com]

Hu, J. (July, 6, 1998). Political hackers hit 300 sites. Available online: [http:// www.cnetnews.com].

Hu, J. (August 12, 1998). Study: Net users watch less TV. Available online: [http:// www.cnetnews.com].

Indiana's fourth grade project: Model applications of technology. Second Year, 1989-90. (1990). Indiana State Department of Education. Indianapolis: Advanced Technology, Inc. Available online: [http:// www.buddynet.netd (version current at April 1998).

Internet parental control frequently asked questions (FAQ). (May 22, 1998). Voters telecommunications watch. Available online: [http:// www.vtw.org/parents/index.html].

Katz, M. R., & Shatkin, L. (1983). Characteristics of computer-assisted guidance. *The Counseling Psychologist, 11(4)*, 15-3 1.

Kehoe, C. (1997). Visualization and usability center's world wide web study. Available online: [http://www.gvu.gatech.edu/user-surveys/survey-1997-10d.

Kivlighan, D. M., Jr., Johnston, J. A., Hogan, R. S., & Mauer, E. (1994). Who benefits from computerized career counseling? *Journal of Counseling & Development, 72(3)*, 289-292.

Kulik, J.A. (1994). Meta-analytic studies of findings on computer-based instruction. In E.L. Baker and H.F. O'Neil, Jr. (Eds.), *Technology assessment in education and training*. Hillsdale, NJ: Lawrence Erlbaum.

Lago, C. (1996). Computer therapeutics. *Counseling, 7*, 287-289.

LaQuey, T. (1994). The Internet companion: A beginner's guide to global networking (2nd edition) Available online: [http://www.obs-us.com/obs/english/books/editinc/top.htm].

Lipton, B. (July 8, 1998). E-mail death threat spreads. Available online: [www.cnet news.com].

Magid, L. (1996). Yahooligans Rules for Online Safety. Available online: [http:// www.yahooligans.com]

McClure, C. R. (1996). Libraries in the global, national, and local networked information infrastructure. ERIC document #ED402955

McCormick, N. B., & McCormick, J. W. (1992). Computer friends and foes: Content of undergraduates' electronic mail. *Computers in Human Behavior, 8(4)*, 379-405.

McMurdo, G. (1995). How the Internet was indexed. *Journal of Information Science, 21*(6), 479-489.

McNamara, P. (October 7, 1998). Keeping an eye on e-mail. Available online: [http:// cnn.com/TECH/computing/9810/07/ eyemail.idg/index.html].

Mighty Media, Inc., (1997). Available on-line [HTTP://www.mightymedia.com/KeyPals.

Moore, R. L. (1990). Computer applications by Arkansas school counselors in conducting K-12 guidance and counseling programs. Unpublished doctoral dissertation, University of Arkansas, Fayetteville.

Mudore, C. (1988). Computers, ethics, and the school counselor. *Clearing House, 61(6)*, 283-284.

Myrick, R. D., & Sabella, R. A. (1995). Cyberspace: New place for counselor supervision. *Elementary School Guidance & Counseling, 30(l)*, 35-44.

Neukrug, E. S. (1991). Computer-assisted live supervision in counselor skills training. *Counselor Education and Supervision, 31(2)*, 132-138.

Norman, K. (1996). Introducing students to the World Wide Web. *Teaching Music, 3(5)*, 34-36.

Poling, D. J. (1994). E-Mail as an effective teaching supplement. *Educational Technology, 34(5),* 53-55.

President's Information Technology Advisory Committee Interim Report to the President (August, 1998). National Coordination Office for computing, Information, and Communications, 4201 Wilson Blvd., Suite 690, Arlington, VA 22230, 703-306-4722.

Pyle, K. R. (1984). Career counseling and computers: Where is the creativity? *Journal of Counseling and Development, 63,* 141-144.

Robson, D., & Robson, M. (1998). Intimacy and computer communication. *British Journal of Guidance & Counseling, 26(l),* p. 33-41.

Rogers, C.R., (1957). The necessary and sufficient conditions of therapeutic personality change. *Journal of Consulting Psychology, 21,* 95-103.

Rust, E. B. (1995). Applications of the International Counselor Network for elementary and middle school counseling. *Elementary School Guidance & Counseling, 30(l),* 16-25.

Sabella, R. (1996). School counselors and computers: Specific time saving tips. *Elementary School Guidance & Counseling, 31(2),* p. 83-96.

Sabella, R. A. (1998). World Wide Web resources for counseling children and adolescents with disabilities. *The Professional School Counselor.2(l),* 47-53.

Sabella, R.A. (1998). Practical technology applications for peer helper programs and training. *Peer Facilitator Quarterly, 15(2),* 4-13.

Sampson, J. P., Jr., & Krumboltz, J. D. (1991). Computer-assisted instruction: A missing link in counseling. *Journal of Counseling & Development, 69,* 395-397.

Sampson, J.P. (1986). Computer technology and counseling psychology: Regression toward the machine? *The Counseling Psychologist, 14(4),* 567-583.

Sampson, J.P., & Pyle, K. R. (1983). Ethical issues involved with the use of computer-assisted counseling, testing, and guidance systems. *The Personnel and Guidance Journal, 61,* 283-287.

Sampson, J. P., Jr. (1990). Computer-assisted testing and the goals of counseling psychology. *The Counseling Psychologist, 18,* 227-239.

Sampson, J.P., Kolodinsky, R.W., & Greeno, B.P. (1997). Counseling on the information highway: Future possibilities and potential problems. *Journal of Counseling and Development, 75(3),* 203-212.

Sanders, P., & Rosenfield, M. (1998). Counseling at a distance: Challenges and new initiatives. *British Journal of Guidance & Counseling, 26(l),* p. 5-10.

Scales, B. J., & Felt, E. C. (1995). Diversity on the World Wide Web: Using robots to search the Web. *Library Software Review, 14(3),* 132-136.

Schaefermeyer, M. J. (1988). Communicating by electronic mail. *American Behavioral Scientist, 32(2),* 112-123.

Schrock, K. (1998). Evaluation of world wide web Sites: An annotated bibliography. ERIC Clearinghouse on Information & Technology. Available online: [http://ericir.syr.edu/ithome].

Sellers, J. (1994). Answers to commonly asked primary and secondary school Internet user questions. Available online: [http://chs.cusd.claremont.edu/www/people/rmuir/rfc1578.html]

Sharf, R. S., & Lucas, M. (1993). An assessment of a computerized simulation of counseling skills. *Counselor Education and Supervision, 32,* 254-266.

Sherman, R.A. (1998). Richard's no-nonsense guide to the Internet for seniors. Phoenix, AZ: Double B Publishing.

Shulman, H. A., Sweeney, B., & Gerler, E. R. (1995). A computer-assisted approach to preventing alcohol abuse: Implications for the middle school. *Elementary School Guidance & Counseling, 30(l),* 63-77.

Russell A. Sabella, Ph.D.

Solid Ground (September, 1998). Weak links in your security chain. Available online: [www.firststep.com].

Sproull, L. S. (1986). Using electronic mail for data collection in organizational research. *Academy of Management Journal, 29(l),*159-169.

Stem, E. (1996). High-tech help on the Internet. *Psychology Today, 29(5).*

Suler, J. (1998). The psychology of cyberspace Available online: [http://www.tulsa.oklahoma.net/~jnichols/cyber.html].

Sullivan, D. (1998). Search engine watch. Available online: [http://searchenginewatch.com]

Symons, A. K. (1996). Intelligent life on the Web and how to find it. *School Library Journal, 42(3),* 106-109.

Tapscott, D. (1998). *Growing up digital: The rise of the Net generation.* New York, NY: McGraw-Hill.

The Web Tutorial. (1998). WebTeacher. Available online: [http://www.webteacher.org].

The Four Comers of the Internet: Search engine secrets. (August, 1997). Available online: [http://www.squareonetech.com/].

Thomas, L.G., & Knezek, D.G. (1998). Technology Literacy for the Nation and for Its Citizens. International Society for Technology in Education. Available online: [http://www.iste.org].

Using the Internet, for teachers, schools, students; an introduction, (1997). Available online [http://www.geocities.com/Athens/4610/].

Walton, M. (April 17, 1998). Survey: Black students less Web-connected than whites. Cable News Network. Available online: [www.cnn.com].

Walz, G. R. (1984). Role of the counselor with computers. *Journal of Counseling and Development, 63,* 135- 138.

Walz, G. R. (1996). Using the I-Way for career development. In R. Feller & G. Walz (Eds.), *Optimizing life transitions in turbulent times: Exploring work, learning and careers,* Greensboro: University of North Carolina, ERIC Clearinghouse on Counseling and Student Services. p. 415-427.

Webopedia. (1999). Electronic forms. Available online: [http://webopedia.internet.com/TERM/f/form.html].

WebReference. (1999). What makes a great website? Available online: [http://www.webreference.com/greatsite.html].

WebsiteJournal. (November 10,1998) Vol. 1(9). Available online: [http://www.WebSiteJournal.com].

Weinraub, M. (April 16, 1998). Online divide exists between blacks, whites - study. Reuters International. Available online: [http://www.reuters.com].

Willard, N. (1996). A legal and educational analysis of K- 12 internet acceptable use policies. Available online: [http://www.erehwon.com/kl2aup].

Young, K.S. (1998). Center for on-line addiction: Resources on the psychology of cyberspace. Available online: [http://netaddiction.com].

Yrchik, J. (March 25, 1994). The national information infrastructure: Requirements for education and training. National Coordinating Committee on Technology in Education and Training.

BIBLIOGRAPHY

The following are selected readings, many of which are online for your convenience, to further learn about information technology and related issues:

Abilock, D. (1996). Integrating e-mail into the curriculum. *Technology Connection, 3(5)*, 23-25.

Alexander, J., & Marsha, T. (1996). Teaching critical evaluation skills for world wide web resources. Available online: [http://www.science.widener.edu/~withers/webeval.htm].

Argus Associates, Inc. (1997). Clearinghouse: Information rating system. Available online: [http://www.clearinghouse.net/ratings.html]

Barry, D. (1997). *Dave Barry in Cyberspace*: New York, NY: Fawcett Book Group.

Cusumano, M.A., & Yoffie, D.B. (1998). *Competing on Internet time: Lessons from Netscape and its battle with Microsoft.* Mankato MN: Mankato MN: The Free Press.

Beck, S. (1997). The good, the bad, and the ugly: Or why it's a good idea to evaluate websources. New Mexico State University Libraries. Available online: [http://lib.nmsu.edu/staff/susabeck/eval.html].

Berkowitz, R.E. (1996). Helping with Homework: A parent's guide to information problem-solving. ERIC Document Reproduction Service No ED402950. Available online [http://ericae.net/db/digs/ED402950.htm].

Brandt, D.S. (1998). Evaluating information on the Internet. Available online [http://thorplus.lib.purdue.edu/~techman/evaluate.htm]

Brusca, F. & Canada, K. (1991). The technological gender gap: Evidence and recommendations for educators and computer-based instruction designers. *Educational Technology Research and Development, 39(2)*, 43-51.

Carmichael, J. (1991). In a different format: Connecting women, computers, and education using Gilligan's framework." Unpublished Masters thesis. Concordia University, Canada.

Ciolek, T. M. (Ed.). Information quality. Available online: [http://www.ciolek.com/WWWVL-InfoQuality.html).

Drake, L., Rudner, & Lawrence M. (1995). Internet Resources for Guidance Personnel. ERIC Document Reproduction Service No ED391988. Available online [http://ericae.net/db/digs/ED391988.htm].

Durndell, A. (1990). Why do female students tend to avoid computer studies? *Research in Science & Technological Education, 8(2),* 163-170.

Edwards, P. (1990). The army and the microworld: Computers and the politics of gender identity. *Signs, 16(1),* 102-127.

Eisenberg, M. B. & Spitzer, K. L. (1991). Information technology and services in schools. In M. E. Williams (Ed.), *Annual Review of Information Science and Technology: 26,* 243-285.

Engle, M. The seven steps of the research process. Available online: [http://www.library.cornell.edu/okuref/research/skill1.htm)

Erlich, R. (December 14, 1992). Sexual harassment an issue on the high-tech frontier. *MacWeek, 20-21.*

Ferrell, K. (October 9, 1997). Truth, lies, and the Internet. CINET. Features. Digital Life. Available online [http://www.cnet.com/Content/Features/Dlife/Truth/].

Fish, M.C., Gross, A.L., & Sanders, J.S. (1986). The effect of equity strategies on girls' computer usage in school. *Computers in Human Behavior. 2(2),* 127-134.

Grassian, E. (1995). Thinking critically about World Wide Web resources. Available online: [http://www.library.ucla.edu/libraries/college/instruct/critical.htm].

Harris, R. Evaluating Internet research sources. Available online: [http://www.sccu.edu/faculty/R_Harris/evalu8it.htm].

Hernon, P. (1995). Discussion forum: Disinformation and misinformation through the Internet: Findings of an exploratory study. *Government Information Quarterly, 12(2),* 133-139.

Hill, J. A. & Misic, M.M. (1996). Why you should establish a connection to the Internet. *TechTrends, 41(2),* 10-16.

Hockey, S. (1994). Evaluating electronic texts in the Humanities. *Library Trends, 42(4),* 676-693.

Jacobson, T., and Cohen, L. (1998). Evaluating Internet Sites. Available online [http://www.albany.edu/library/internet/evaluate.html].

Janicke, L. (1994). Resource selection and information evaluation. Available online: [http://alexia.lis.uiuc.edu/~janicke/Evaluate.html].

Kapoun, J. (1998). Teaching undergrads web evaluation. *College and Research Libraries News, 59(7),* 522-523.

Kent, P. (1998). *The complete idiot's guide to the Internet* (5th ed.). Carmel, IN: Que.

Kerka, S. (1996). Distance Learning, the Internet, and the World Wide Web. Available online: [http://ericae.net/db/digs/D395214.htm].

Kramer, P.E., & Lehman, S. (1990). Mismeasuring women: A critique of research on computer ability and avoidance. *Sign, 16(1),* 158-172.

Lawton, G. (December 14, 1992). The network is the medium. MacWeek, p. 20.

Martin, R. (1197). The Influence of Technology on the Helping Professions. ERIC Document Reproduction Service No ED412461.

McLachlan, K. (1998). Teacher's cyberguidel Available online: [http://www.cyberbee.com/guide1.html].

Miller, E. B. (1996). *The Internet resource directory for K-12 teachers and librarians.* Englewood, CO: Libraries Unlimited, Inc.

Ormondroyd, J., Engle, M., & Cosgrave, T. How to critically analyze information sources. Available online: [http://www.library.cornell.edu/okuref/research/skill26.htm].

Pfaffenberger, B. (1996). *Web search strategies.* New York: MIS:Press.

Richmond, B. (1997). Ten C's for evaluating Internet resources. Available online: [http://www.uwec.edu/Admin/Library/10cs.html].

Schrock, K. (Ed.). Kathy Schrock's Guide for educators: Critical evaluations surveys. Available online: [http://www.capecod.net/schrockguide/eval.htm].

Shoemaker, B. (1996). Cyberspace class: Rewards and punishments. ERIC Digest #ED40057. Available online: [http://ericae.net/db/digs/ED400574.htm].

Stevens, DT., &; Lundberg, D.J. (1998). The emergence of the Internet: Enhancing career counseling. *Journal of Career Development, 24(3),* 195-208.

Tennant, R. (1996). Internet basics: Update 1996. ERIC Clearinghouse on Information & Technology #392 466.

Tillman, H. N. (1996). Evaluating quality on the net. Available online: [http://www.tiac.net/users/hope/findqual.html].

Treloar, A. (1995). Scholarly publishing and the fluid World Wide Web. Available online: [http://www.csu.edu.au/special/conference/apwww95/papers95/atreloar/atreloar.html].

Uretsky, S. (1996). Bad medicine: Beware of useless or dangerous medical advice online. *Internet World, 7(2).* 54-55.

Russell A. Sabella, Ph.D.